D0908332

Street Gang Patterns and Policies

Recent Titles in
STUDIES IN CRIME AND PUBLIC POLICY
Michael Tonry and Norval Morris, General Editors

Can Gun Control Work?
James B. Jacobs

Penal Populism and Public Opinion: Lessons from Five Countries
Julian V. Roberts, Loretta J. Stalans, David Indermaur, and Mike Hough

Mafia Brotherhoods: Organized Crime, Italian Style
Letizia Paoli

When Prisoners Come Home: Parole and Prisoner Reentry
Joan Petersilia

The Contradictions of American Capital Punishment
Franklin E. Zimring

Thinking about Crime: Sense and Sensibility in American Penal Culture
Michael Tonry

Juvenile Justice in the Making
David S. Tanenhaus

Fallen Blue Knights: Controlling Police Corruption
Sanja Kutnjak Ivković

Changing the Guard: Developing Democratic Police Abroad
David H. Bayley

Street Gang Patterns and Policies
Malcolm W. Klein and Cheryl L. Maxson

Street Gang Patterns and Policies

MALCOLM W. KLEIN
CHERYL L. MAXSON

2006

Oxford University Press, Inc., publishes works that further
Oxford University's objective of excellence
in research, scholarship, and education.

Oxford New York
Auckland Cape Town Dar es Salaam Hong Kong Karachi
Kuala Lumpur Madrid Melbourne Mexico City Nairobi
New Delhi Shanghai Taipei Toronto

With offices in
Argentina Austria Brazil Chile Czech Republic France Greece
Guatemala Hungary Italy Japan Poland Portugal Singapore
South Korea Switzerland Thailand Turkey Ukraine Vietnam

Published by Oxford University Press, Inc.
198 Madison Avenue, New York, New York 10016

www.oup.com

Library of Congress Cataloging-in-Publication Data
Klein, Malcolm W.
Street gang patterns and policies / by Malcolm W. Klein and Cheryl L. Maxson.
p. cm. — (Studies in crime and public policy)
ISBN-13 978-0-19-516344-5
ISBN 0-19-516344-3
1. Gangs—United States. 2. Gangs—United States—Prevention.
3. Juvenile delinquency—United States—Prevention.
I. Maxson, Cheryl Lee. II. Title. III. Series.
HV6439.U5K585 2006
364.1'06'60973—dc22 2005023272

9 8 7 6 5 4 3 2 1

Printed in the United States of America
on acid-free paper

To Father Gregory Boyle, S.J., and the others like him whose perseverance in attempting to change gang lives deserves our appreciation

And to all those police officers who also have persevered in their attempts to control gangs and reduce gang crime

We have little solid evidence to substantiate the positive effects of either approach, but we believe such evidence could be developed, and that is a major goal of this book.

Acknowledgments

A volume like this could only have been written after many years of careful work by other scholars had led to a broad accumulation of knowledge. It could only have been written after many attempts to control street gang problems across the nation had revealed the complexities of the enterprise. We acknowledge with admiration the work of the many gang researchers and practitioners who have brought us to this point, where some integration seems possible. While the names of our predecessors are myriad, we wish to single out a few gang experts who have made the most explicit contributions to our thinking: Scott Decker, Arlen Egley, Finn-Aage Esbensen, Sergeant Wesley McBride, Jody Miller, John Moore and the National Youth Gang Center, James F. Short, Jr., Irving A. Spergel, Terence Thornberry, James D. Vigil, and Elmar G. M. Weitekamp.

Chapter 4 has been greatly enhanced by the perseverance of Monica Whitlock, whose analysis of protective factors has contributed mightily to our recent work.

Chapter 6 is the better for our collaboration on antigang injunctions with Karen Hennigan and David Sloane.

Chapter 8 is a significantly expanded exercise in policy thinking as a result of a special lecture commissioned by Tore Bjorgo for delivery to several Norwegian ministries.

We have for many years benefited from the financial support of the National Institute of Justice and from the Office of Juvenile Justice and Delinquency Prevention, both branches of the U.S. Department of Justice. Other sources of support have aided, but these two agencies deserve very special mention. So, too, does the University of Southern California and its Social Science Research Institute. Letty Baz contributed her excellent skills and unfailing good cheer to the preparation of this manuscript.

Cheryl Maxson can't skip this opportunity to acknowledge three people important to her work. Mac Klein, ever the wonderful colleague and collaborator, showed remarkable forbearance in our work on this project despite our different time frames. Patricia Maxson was ever encouraging and generous with her grace and pride. Brian Robison showed me a boundless reservoir of support and patience. I can't thank you enough.

No one is more aware than we of our debts to the many named and unnamed colleagues whose work is in one form or another included in this volume. We express our gratitude and our hope that we have used their work wisely and well.

Contents

Street Gang Patterns and Policies

INTRODUCTION

This is a book about important patterns that characterize street gangs in contemporary America. It is also a book about important experiments in gang policy, as seen in major programs to reduce or control gang problems. In addition and somewhat uniquely, this is a book about how gang patterns and policies are—or can be—interrelated. This interweaving of patterns and policies, as we will demonstrate in the three chapters of part I, is critical so that we can as a society, as our colleague James D. Vigil has requested, "begin to put to rest the contemporary politically tainted dialogue that interferes with a balanced consideration of the problem. Society needs objective investigations and evidence, not 'moral panic'—in short, facts, not fears" (Vigil, 2002: 14).

As we will note later, the plan of the book is to take the reader through three stages. In part I, we present updated information that strongly suggests that we must revisit our programs and policies for gang control. In part II, we present the information—much of it new—that we believe can provide the foundation for reconsidering programs and policies. Then, in part III, we present a set of program and policy goals and a paradigm for selecting among the many gang control programs that have been offered in the past.

We start this exercise, as we must, with the difficult definitional issue: what *is* a street gang? Does it really matter how we define it? We answer, quite readily, that yes, it does matter. And to be as succinct as possible, we offer the following nominal definition of the street gang with an explanation of how we came to it:[1]

> A street gang is any durable, street-oriented youth group whose involvement in illegal activity is part of its group identity.

Point 1: *Durable* is a bit ambiguous, but at least an existence of several months can be used as a guideline. Many gang-like groups come together and dissipate within a few months. The durability refers to the *group*, which continues despite turnover of members.

Point 2: *Street-oriented* implies spending a lot of group time outside home, work, and school—often on streets, in malls, in parks, in cars, and so on.

Point 3: *Youth* can be ambiguous. Most street gangs are more adolescent than adult, but some include members in their 20s and even 30s. Most have average ages in adolescence or early 20s.

Point 4: *Illegal* generally means delinquent or criminal, not just bothersome.

Point 5: *Identity* refers to the group, not the individual self-image.

This is the consensus nominal definition agreed to by a consortium of more than 100 American and European researchers and policy makers from more than a dozen nations meeting in a series of eight workshops between 1997 and 2005 (the Eurogang program). It represents a minimal approach—the necessary and sufficient defining characteristics—that for most purposes allows us to distinguish street gangs from other troublesome youth groups (of which there are many more).

The components—durable, street oriented, youth group, identity with illegal activity—are definers of street gangs. They are the minimal necessary and sufficient elements to recognize a street gang. Many other characteristics are common descriptors but not definers. One thinks of leadership, cohesiveness, ethnicity, gender, and distinctive argot, clothing, tattoos, or hand signs, for instance. These are variables that help us to capture variations across gangs, but they are not necessary definers of a street gang as we shall deal with it in this book.

A Brief Review of the Definitional Problem

The definitional issue has probably been the stickiest one that gang scholars have had to confront in the almost eight decades since Frederic Thrasher's pioneering efforts in Chicago (1927). All of the attention paid to it has not until now yielded much consensus, a fact which in itself testifies to the complexity of the issue and the need felt by all gang scholars to find a useful and acceptable approach.

Suppose, for the sake of argument, that we were to assess the size and location of America's street gang problems and implicitly lay out the rationales for national gang policy by using a definition of gangs that had essentially no form, which said, essentially, that a gang is any group that you or other responsible people think is a gang. Using such an amorphous definition would make it very difficult to grasp our subject matter, wouldn't it?

Yet this is precisely what has happened. The National Youth Gang Center, on behalf of the U.S. Department of Justice's Office of Juvenile Justice and Delinquency Prevention, has carried out several national, annual surveys of thousands of police and sheriff's jurisdictions. In doing so, they have noted the locations of most gangs and provided a national estimate of the number of gangs and gang members in the United States. Relatively recent figures (National Youth Gang Center, 1999) put these numbers at 30,818 gangs and 846,428 gang members, a level of precision that defies credulity. The instructions to the law enforcement respondents to the gang survey are to include as a youth gang "a group of youths or young adults in your jurisdiction that you or other responsible persons in your agency or community are willing to identify or classify as a 'gang' " (1999: 45).

What sorts of problems does such a nondefinition yield? According to the NYGC report on the 1996 survey (National Youth Gang Center, 1998), 58% of respondents included taggers, 24% included satanic groups, 22% included "posses" and "crews," 20% included stoners, and 5% included terrorist groups. Further, many respondents explicitly failed to exclude "unsupervised youth groups," a term that would include almost any friendship group at some point in its members' adolescence. Twenty-eight percent of respondents in large cities included these friendship groups, as did 33% in suburban counties, 38% in small cities, and 49% in rural counties.

Given these figures, it seems inevitable that the NYGC figures provide a substantial overestimate of gangs and gang members.[2] One would predict that the figures would be particularly suspect in small jurisdictions where minority populations are smaller and would therefore yield unusually high proportions of nonminority gangs. And this is exactly what happened: the figure for white gangs is 14%. Having been alerted to this problem, the NYGC added an item to its third annual national survey. At the very end of the questionnaire, NYGC asked its respondents how many of their gangs would fit under a modified definition that read as follows:

> A group of youths or young adults in your jurisdiction whose involvement in illegal activities over months or years marks them in

> their own view and in the view of the community and police as different from most other youthful groups. Do not include motorcycle gangs, hate or ideology groups, prison gangs, or other exclusively adult gangs. (NYGC, n.d.: 7)

This alternative definition adds durability and criminal identity. NYGC's preliminary analysis of the effect of adopting this modified definition suggests that its previous estimates were somewhat off base. The new data indicated that the number of jurisdictions with gangs was overestimated by 12%, and the number of gangs was overestimated by 26%. These are not trivial differences, and they alert us to the major effects that definitional disparities can yield.

There have been no other, comparable national surveys of the gang situation, although Miller (1980), Spergel (1995), Spergel and Curry (1990), and Maxson and Klein (1995) have used nonrepresentative samples for other research purposes. Thus we cannot know what figures might result from a more narrowly constructed definition of street gangs. Leaving aside antiscientific suggestions that the definitional problem is simply too difficult to merit attention (Horowitz, 1990), we offer what have probably been the most influential attempts to define gangs. Five, in particular, will set the stage for adopting the consensus Eurogang definition as a way to move forward.

The earliest of the five definitions was Thrasher's characterization of a gang as "an interstitial group originally formed spontaneously, and then integrated through conflict" (1927: 57). Thus marginalization, organizational informality, and violence (*conflict* meant intergang fighting here) were seen as central by Thrasher. All three themes are recurrent in more recent gang descriptions.

The second definition was offered by Klein (1971), based on his study of five large clusters of gangs in Los Angeles and on a review of gang structures described in the literature to that date. The definition is of juvenile gangs, specifically, and stresses a social-psychological framework:

> [A juvenile gang is] any denotable adolescent group of youngsters who (a) are generally perceived as a distinct aggregation by others in their neighborhood, (b) recognize themselves as a denotable group (almost invariably with a group name), and (c) have been involved in a sufficient number of delinquent incidents to call forth a consistent negative response from neighborhood residents and/or enforcement agencies. (1971: 13)[3]

Twenty-five years later, Klein (1995a) admitted to so much controversy over this or any other definition that he backed off from his earlier stance to approach the problem in two ways. Emphasizing the term *street gang*, he first excluded certain groups—terrorists, football hooligans, motorcycle gangs, and prison gangs, for instance—and then simply characterized gangs in terms of common descriptors: age, gender, ethnicity, territoriality, and criminal patterns and orientation.

The third much-cited definition was offered by Walter Miller (1980) based on his interviews with police officials, media, and others across the country in the mid-1970s. This definition was basically a distillation of the gang dimensions offered by his informants, almost a popularity poll to determine the most common elements:

> A youth gang is a self-formed association of peers, bound together by mutual interests, with identifiable leadership, well-developed lines of authority, and other organizational features, who act in concert to achieve a specific purpose or purposes which generally include the conduct of illegal activity and control over a particular territory, facility, or type of enterprise. (1980: 121)

This definition captures many of the descriptors of gangs noted by various scholars in addition to Miller's respondents but attributes more formal organizational properties than most scholars might accept. The question of how well organized street gangs are has become one of the more contentious issues between scholars and practitioners.

The reader will note that Thrasher, Klein, and Miller all include involvement in illegal activities as one of their definitional components. This contrasts with the fourth of the commonly cited definitions, that of James F. Short, Jr.:

> Gangs are groups whose members meet together with some regularity, over time, on the basis of group-defined criteria of membership and group-defined organizational characteristics; that is, gangs are non-adult-sponsored, self-determining groups that demonstrate continuity over time. (1996: 5)

Short emphasizes one element common to the Thrasher, Klein, and Miller definitions—self-determination of the group by its members—but significantly and deliberately avoids any connection to illegal activities. The rationale for this exclusion is that retaining illegal behaviors in the definition creates a tautology, a circular argument, in studying gangs in order to understand and predict their illegal behavior. Further, it overestimates the centrality of criminal activity to gang life and concerns.

We can accept the second of these concerns: gangs normally form for reasons of identity, status, need for belonging, and perceived protection, not primarily to commit crimes. But we cannot accept the tautological argument. First, because gangs vary so widely in their criminal orientations and involvement, these can be studied without circularity; i.e., one can readily predict to levels, types, and circumstances of criminal involvement. Second, crime is *not* the only aspect we study and predict. The dependent variables of gang research often include cohesiveness, leadership, organizational sophistication, size, gender, ethnic variations, community embeddedness, and so on. Including criminal involvement or orientation in the definition facilitates rather than hinders such research.

Common to all four of these attempts was a process of deriving definitions inductively from observations and experience with gangs. Each was concerned with specifying critical elements of *informal* groups: gangs don't normally come to us with constitutions and bylaws, charters, organizational charts, or written credos to which members subscribe. Thus, definitional approaches must to some extent be ad hoc and reflective of the definer's experience.

This contrasts starkly with the fifth definition, which was carefully crafted in the late 1980s to serve a specific purpose, the establishment of a *legal* category of gangs in order to enhance the ability of law enforcement to suppress gangs and incarcerate gang members. This definition has become widely accepted by public officials and the media as "real," with some unfortunate consequences. Since copied in many states, that law enforcement definition was originally embodied in the California Penal Code (section 186.22) and legislation known as the Street Terrorism Enforcement and Prevention (S.T.E.P.) Act (enacted January 1, 1993). It referred specifically to "the criminal street gang" as

> any ongoing organization, association, or group of three or more persons, whether formal or informal, having as one of its primary activities the commission of one or more of the criminal acts enumerated in paragraphs (1) to (8), inclusive, of subdivision (E), which has a common name or common identifying sign or symbol, whose members individually or collectively engage in or have engaged in a pattern of criminal gang activity.

The criminal acts referred to included felony assault, robbery, homicide, narcotics offenses, shooting into an inhabited dwelling, arson, witness (or victim) intimidation, and vehicle theft. The legal haziness of "youth gang" or "street gang" is replaced by the critical term *criminal street gang*, and this in turn is defined by reference to the most serious offenses and those that are stereotypical of gang activity. Thus the gang has become reified by police and prosecutors' aims and concerns, with little reference to depictions accumulated over decades by gang research.[4]

As the public has come to accept this definition, street gangs have become demonized as purposefully criminal conspiracies, as violent organizations, and lost their informal, street-corner characterization. Further, any sense of the variations in gang structures and activities is lost in the definition in the S.T.E.P. Act. Reality is replaced by the goals of law enforcement: to label youth as gang members and to incarcerate them for as long as possible. Gangs may not have changed much, but their depiction most certainly has.

As a case in point, consider the suburban California county prosecutor in the case of three white boys who assaulted another during a confrontation at the beach in 1999. The prosecutor offered a plea bargain to the defendants, reducing the charges in exchange for an admission that they were members of a gang. To fit under the rubric of the criminal street gang, the prosecution had to invent a new term—"bully gang"—since the relationships among the defendants did not otherwise fit either the legal or scholarly depictions of street gangs.

These five definitional approaches are far from exhaustive. There are scores of attempts in the professional literature to define street gangs. These five, however, have probably been the most influential and illustrate the very broad dimensions that definitions can take. The consensus Eurogang definition, we think, captures the necessary minimal elements and avoids the complications of a myriad of gang descriptors. This is particularly important as we lay the groundwork for describing variations in gang structures and for encouraging cross-jurisdictional, comparative research and policy. Further, it is our experience to date that this definition, emphasizing durability, street orientation, youth, and self-identity involving illegal behavior, is largely acceptable to research scholars and working practitioners alike. This consensus among both researchers and policy folks is important to our purposes in this book. In this respect, it is our best answer to Ball and Curry (1995), who express their concern about these potentially divergent perspectives as follows:

> Theorists may seek a definition that will provide a term logically integrated into a larger postulatory framework, while researchers seek sufficient standardization to guide them toward the same phenomena and allow for comparisons of findings. Administrators may care less about the theoretical power or empirical applicability of a definition than the fact that it is simple enough to impose bureaucratic standardization for purposes of record keeping, and police may be interested primarily in an expedient definition allowing them to hold the collectivity responsible for criminal acts of individual members or vice versa. (1995: 227)

Street Gang "Control"

Throughout the book, we will for the sake of convenience use the phrase *gang control*, or just *control*, to stand for the myriad of programs and policies designed to reduce street gang problems. It is simply too much of a mouthful to speak each time of gang prevention, intervention, enforcement, and suppression; too much continually to repeat primary prevention, secondary prevention, and tertiary prevention as in public health terminology; too cumbersome to refer always to opportunities provision, social intervention, organizational change, community mobilization, and suppression, these being the five basic strategies implemented nationally as part of the Spergel Model supported by the U.S. Department of Justice. When we speak of gang control, we refer to all of these concepts, to the wide swath of approaches so far undertaken in the United States with, at best, mixed results.

Further, we will use gang control loosely to refer to attempts at individual change, group change, neighborhood or community change, and even societal change. Admittedly, we sacrifice precision for convenience, but we will return to the panoply of program and policy approaches with somewhat more precision in part III of the book. Until then, we beg the reader's indulgence.

Generalizing about Street Gangs

It is our contention, based upon personal field experience and extensive reviews of the gang literature, that street gangs comprise a class of phenomena, that they are more similar to each other than different. This is not to say that "if you've seen one gang, you've seen them all": far from it. There are differences attendant upon structure, gender, ethnicity, geographic location, and social class. But the durable, street-oriented, youthful, illegally toned self-identity of these groups trumps the differences among them. Most comparative gang researchers, though they have been few, have come to a similar conclusion (Fagan, 1989; Sanchez-Jankowski, 1991; J. Miller, 2001; Huff, 1998; Klein, 1995a; Klein, Kerner, Maxson, and Weitekamp, 2001).

This is a critical point. If street gangs did not have enough in common, we could not study them as a class, nor attempt to formulate general policies to respond to them. Further, if they were not sufficiently distinct from other youth groups, we could not reach gang-specific knowledge and policy. Street gangs, in our view, are qualitatively different from other youth groups. The consensus definition we have used here is an attempt to capture this fact. Gangs have reached a "tipping point" in their evolution; they have separated themselves from other groups and are generally seen in their communities as different entities.

The reasons for this are several, and they were captured succinctly by Joan Moore who, earlier in her career as a student of Hispanic gangs only, concluded that Hispanic gangs were different from others. In her foreword to Vigil's 2002 book, *A Rainbow of Gangs*, she recognizes the commonalties across gangs as a function of "street socialization":

> [T]here is an additional factor in the gang that makes street socialization particularly powerful. Actual delinquency—breaking the law—gives gang members an additional reason to keep their activities secret. Each gang cohort develops a deep commitment to secrecy and to the protection of its members from all adults, not just the police, and from outsiders in general. A sense of loyalty becomes a paramount value. Almost all young gang members in this book talk about the gang as family. This implies that the gang commands a much heavier commitment on the part of its members than does the ordinary clique of adolescent friends. Street socialization, then, is probably more intense than is peer socialization in less all-encompassing groups. But the basic point is that the gang, like other adolescent peer groups, is a special group. (2002: xii)

Although the authors of this book have been located in southern California, often dubbed "the gang capital of the nation," the content is not based on that region. To the data from Los Angeles, Long Beach, and San Diego, we will add more from Chicago, Denver, Rochester, Seattle, and a host of other jurisdictions across the country. Indeed, we will on occasion make reference to similar gang problems in various European countries. This is not a book about Crips and Bloods, but about street gangs in general, most of which depart significantly from the stereotypes associated with Crips and Bloods, or with Latin Kings or Gangster Disciples, or with the Jets and Sharks of *West Side Story*. Seventy years of gang research by scores of scholars have finally yielded a fund of generalizable knowledge, and we attempt here to make use of much of it.

Patterns and Policies: Goals

We base this book on several important considerations. First, there is finally a sufficient database about the nature of street gangs so that generalizable patterns can be described. Second, past efforts at gang control have been demonstrably ineffective or—at best—untested for their effectiveness. Third, current gang knowledge, drawn from reliable and valid research, can provide guidelines for useful policies, going beyond the "don't do that" conclusions in which researchers have indulged to date. Fourth, we can serve two important masters: (a) we can update and contextualize pivotal issues of concern to gang researchers at the individual, group, and community levels; and (b) we can also demonstrate to the policy and practitioner audience that accumulated gang knowledge can be joined with experience in gang programming to provide guidelines for more effective gang control.

In part I, we will pull together current data (our own and others') on street gang proliferation and migration, on gang crime patterns both general and specific to violence and drugs, and on the relative ineffectiveness of major gang prevention, intervention, and suppression programs. These three topics will provide more than ample empirical evidence that new thinking about gang control is required.

In part II, we will summarize program-relevant data on individual, group, and community issues. These will include risk and protection factors for joining gangs, data on different forms of gang structure and on the group processes that make gangs qualitatively different from other groups, and data on the city characteristics of gang areas and the community contexts that spawn gangs.

For gang scholars, the data in parts I and II will constitute the most recent compilation of these findings and their importance for understanding the street gang phenomenon. For policy makers and practitioners, they will provide the rationale for more informed gang programming efforts.

In part III, we will lay out alternative goals for gang programming, which are normally not well articulated in the plans for gang control efforts. Then a general model will be presented, and examples of approaches will be offered that respond to these goals, to levels of gang control, and to the issues covered in the data reports in parts I and II. The result will be a panoply of approaches to gang control and attention to how one might select among these or, hopefully, combine some of them.

The content of this volume comes from several sources. The first of these is the authors' own research over several decades. These data will be found principally in the chapters on gang proliferation and migration, crime patterns, program effectiveness, gang structures and group processes, and risk factors.

The second source is the research data from other scholars, with particular emphasis on the longitudinal projects in Rochester, Denver, and Seattle. These will be most relevant to the chapters on crime patterns, group processes, and risk factors.

A third source is the survey data available from the National Youth Gang Center (NYGC), which is most pertinent to the gang proliferation issues and the city contexts. We have had special access both to the longitudinal projects and to the NYGC work as members of their advisory committees. We have employed much of the same interview protocols found in these projects.

Other data supplement these three major sources, but the emphasis is on data from the 1980s on, since this has been the most productive era in gang research, with an increased panoply of research methods applied to an ever-expanding catalog of gang-involved communities.

Both of us, it should be noted, have been involved in intensive gang programming by running programs, evaluating programs, and serving on technical advisory committees for some of the largest gang control efforts. These experiences will inform the volume in ways not readily available to other gang writers.

Chapter Summaries

Chapter 1 will describe and summarize what is known about the proliferation of street gangs across the country and how that relates to the migration of gang members and will suggest some of the implications for thinking about broad-based gang programming.

Chapter 2 will describe and summarize what is known about gang crime patterns, especially their versatility and the realities of gang violence and involvement in drug trafficking. These patterns have implications for many current gang control practices that miss the mark due to failures to appreciate the patterns.

Chapter 3 will take a close look at some of the largest and most prominent attempts at prevention, intervention, and suppression of gang activities. Included will be the Illinois attorney general's program, the L.A. Bridges program in Los Angeles, the national Gang Resistance, Education, and Training program (G.R.E.A.T.), a series of suppression projects mounted in southern California, and the application of the Spergel Model to the national Comprehensive Community-wide Approach to Gang Prevention, Intervention and Suppression program and to the SafeFutures program (both sponsored by the U.S. Department of Justice). The approach here will be to discuss the program failures—in implementation or effectiveness—in terms of political and ideological conventional wisdoms rather than their use of basic gang knowledge.

These three chapters comprise part I of the book, setting the stage for greater attention to the data here and in part II. The seriousness of gang proliferation and crime patterns requires approaches to policy significantly different from those discussed in chapter 3, most of which have demonstrably failed to achieve needed changes in gang activity.

Chapter 4 speaks primarily to the level of the individual gang member. It describes and summarizes data on gang joining, the risk and protection factors that relate to joining, and data on different levels of youth commitment to the gang. Implications for prevention and intervention can be easily identified (and illustrated by reference back to the L.A. Bridges and G.R.E.A.T. programs).

Chapter 5 will describe in some detail our research in developing a typology of gang structure and how the results can inform approaches to gang control. We have published some of this material in several places, but pull it all together here for the first time. Chapter 5 will also include extended discussion of group processes (especially group cohesiveness) in street gangs as these place almost insurmountable barriers to some forms of gang control.

Chapter 6 will discuss both city and community contexts. The distinction between "chronic" and "emergent" gang cities is important here, especially as it relates to gang structures. Ethnicity and other data will be reported. At the community level, the discussion will of necessity be more conceptual than data based and will also describe the use of community-based antigang injunctions and abatements.

The sets of data presented in part II will set the stage for moving to the part III model of approaches to gang programming.

Chapter 7 will discuss the various goals of gang programming, with examples to illustrate the differences between individual versus group change; reducing joining versus encouraging desistance; prevention versus intervention versus suppression. Reference again to the Spergel Model will clarify some of these issues.

Chapter 8 will present a heuristic model, which combines elements of the Spergel Model with the data summaries from chapters 1, 2, 4, 5, and 6. The model will then be expanded to cover both individual and group levels of change. The result will be two tables with 12 (3 × 4) cells each, and the discussion will use these models to elaborate on available and conceivable program approaches. Specific program examples will be offered. At the same time, the complexity of a multilevel approach will become obvious. This chapter, then, will be a combination of specific approaches and guidelines to choosing among programs. Gang control is necessarily very complex, so the greater clarity provided in chapter 8 should be helpful to policy makers anxious to leap into programming.

Part I

Major developments in the growth of street gangs and gang crime, along with the results of large-scale gang control programs, are reviewed and point to the need to rethink our approaches to gang control.

One

GANG PREVALENCE, PROLIFERATION, AND MIGRATION

Since 1980, no single aspect of street gang existence has captured more attention than the emergence of gangs in literally thousands of previously unaffected communities. This chapter addresses the available research information on four types of questions: (1) What do we know about the distribution of gangs in the United States and elsewhere? (2) How have these patterns changed over time? What are the patterns of gang proliferation and desistance? (3) Is proliferation related to gang migration? and (4) How might what we know about new patterns of prevalence, proliferation, and migration inform better gang intervention program and policy choices? We will report the relevant data in the following pages, but first let us suggest some of the implications of a growth in gang-involved cities from fewer than 50 prior to 1960 to an estimated high of 3,850 in 1996, which declined to 2,300 in 2002 (Klein, 1995a; Office of Juvenile Justice and Delinquency Prevention, 1999; Egley, Howell, and Major, 2004):

- Hundreds of thousands of people have been reduced in life efficacy by membership in street gangs.
- Hundreds of thousands of victims, ranging from homicide victims to those in fear of walking in their own neighborhoods, have suffered grief and discomfort, as have their families.
- Thousands of city councils, mayors, and county supervisors have

had to devise political responses and devote precious resources to gang control and victim services.

- Thousands of police departments, prosecutors, and correctional officials have had to develop new organizational units and new strategies for gang problems; state legislatures have had to devise new antigang legislation and build new correctional facilities to aid in the process.
- Thousands of public and private youth service agencies have had to consider the needs and costs of modifying their programs to do gang prevention and intervention programming—or have had to justify avoiding this new clientele.
- Numerous federal agencies—justice, education, health and welfare, housing, and others—have had to accept street gangs as a national phenomenon, requiring either national-level research and action or the enabling of state and local responses.

In short, gang proliferation has changed important aspects of our society and seldom in desirable ways. Thus the extent to which responses are based on inappropriate, conventional wisdom versus accumulated fact-based understandings takes on special importance. We start our journey, therefore, with a review of recent data about this proliferation.

In this chapter, we focus on broad trends in the United States (and occasionally elsewhere). Much research has been devoted to examining individual-level processes and the socioecological features of the environment that might explain why some youth join gangs while others do not. The chapters in part II cover the accumulated knowledge on this issue. In particular, chapter 4 looks at the features of individuals and their family, peer, and school situations that are related to gang involvement. Chapter 6 takes this question to the community level, asking what features about places might generate gangs, including the ebbs as well as the flows of gang proliferation. Studies about gang joining often report the rate of gang membership in the study sample. Before turning to the distribution patterns in gang cities, which constitute the remainder of this chapter, we review the available information on the proportion of youth who join gangs.

Individual Gang-Prevalence Studies

Although studies occasionally use police records to identify an individual's gang membership status (e.g., Katz, Webb, and Schaefer, 2000; Reiner,

1992; Maxson, 1995), police gang files necessarily reflect agency organizational characteristics and recording practices. A far superior method for addressing the prevalence of gang membership within a specific population is the strategy of self-report: asking youth directly, for example with the question: are you a member of a street gang? While there is some concern about whether subjects are totally honest in replying to such a question, and there is considerable variety in the way in which the gang membership question is asked, there is a consensus that valid responses can be obtained when proper research practices are observed in confidential settings.

Two recent studies offer national prevalence estimates. In one representative survey of youth who were 12 to 16 years old at year end 1996, 5% of U.S. youth reported that they had ever belonged to a gang and just 2% belonged in the year prior to the survey (Snyder and Sickmund, 1999). Gottfredson and Gottfredson (2001) surveyed students in a nationally representative sample of secondary schools. Although only 37% of the schools agreed to participate, the prevalence estimate derived is similar to the other national study: 7.1% of males and 3.6% of females reported that they had "belong[ed] to a gang that has a name and engages in fighting, stealing, or selling drugs" in the last 12 months. Every other study we reviewed reported higher levels of gang prevalence, some far higher. Why? As we discuss later in this chapter and in chapter 6, gangs are not evenly distributed in neighborhoods and communities throughout the United States, and researchers often conduct gang studies in areas that have higher concentrations of gangs and risk characteristics for gang activity. It can be difficult to compare one self-report study to the next to get an overall picture of what proportion of youth join gangs because studies often capture different types of samples and use somewhat different research procedures and definitions.

We've selected for review relatively recent studies that employ large samples of youth and that use research methods that are considered by scholars to be appropriate to the question of individual gang member prevalence.[1] The study samples sometimes are drawn from schools, other times from high-risk neighborhoods, and occasionally from arrested or incarcerated populations and may therefore be more or less representative of the general youth population. As noted above, the best estimate of the general U.S. youth gang prevalence is 5% ever-joined, 2% current gang members. How do the more-targeted studies compare with this baseline, and what can we learn from them about patterns of gang participation?[2]

Our first pass through the current literature on gang prevalence asks what should be a straightforward question: what proportion of individuals in any given study population, by their own admission, joins a gang? Table 1.1 lists each study that reports gang prevalence among youth or young adults in community (nonincarcerated) settings, as well as the study characteristics that might help us to compare findings across studies. Nineteen studies are included (analyses of different subsamples within the same study are counted separately), and with one exception (Johnstone, 1981), all derive from work published since 1990. The approaches to measuring gang membership vary in whether current or any (i.e., ever) gang membership is reported, whether restrictions are placed on the nature of the group (i.e., group engages in illegal activity, has a name or has other identifying symbols),[3] and whether the sample design increased risk (disproportionate levels of males, minority subjects, or high-crime areas). Notably, these studies produce 33 different gang prevalence rates.

Clearly, gang definitions and study samples matter a great deal. Three general patterns of variation are evident. Risk-targeted samples report higher rates than the more general samples. Also, restricting the type of group by name or criminal activity considerably decreases the gang prevalence rate (see same-sample comparisons in Bradshaw, 2005; Esbensen and Winfree, 1998; Lahey et al., 1999; Winfree et al., 1992). Particularly in places that don't have a long tradition of gang activity, youth may identify less delinquent and organized social groups as gangs, whereas such friendship groups may not be labeled as such by youth in Los Angeles and Chicago. Finally, and quite obviously, studies that capture movement in and out of gangs throughout adolescence report higher gang prevalence than those that limit the question to current gang membership (see same-sample comparisons in Dukes et al., 1997; Snyder and Sickmund, 1999; Winfree et al., 1992).

If we group the studies by current versus any membership, group definitional restrictions, and sample risk targeting, the range of gang prevalence is narrowed somewhat, but is still considerable. For example, six studies that employ unrestricted definitions in risk-selected populations report ever-involved prevalence of 6% (Eitle et al., 2004, but note that these are retrospective reports of adults), 10% (Johnstone, 1981, data gathered in 1974), 19% (Gordon et al., 2004), and around 30% (Lahey et al., 1999; Thornberry et al., 2003; Winfree et al., 1992). Conversely, the five studies that use restricted definitions among risk-targeted populations (Hill et al., 1999; both Bremen and Denver samples in Huizinga and Schumann, 2001; Lahey et al., 1999; Winfree et al., 1992) reveal more consensus in findings that between 13 and 18% are gang members at some

TABLE 1.1. *Prevalence of Gang Membership in Self-Report Studies, Nonincarcerated Populations*

Source	Location, Date Collected	Sample & Method	N of cases	Sample Characteristics	Gang Definition	Proportion Gang
Bolland & Drummond (1999)	6 public housing developments in Huntsville, Alabama, 1997–1999	survey (NFI), all youth 9–19 years old, public housing residents	562–618 (cross-sectional annual surveys)	males & females 9–19 years "overwhelmingly" African American	currently a member of a gang	1997: 19.9% 1998: 17% 1999: 19.1%
Bradshaw (2005) (Edinburgh Study of Youth Transitions and Crime)	Edinburgh, Scotland, 1999	survey (NFI), all pupils aged 13, in mainstream, special, & independent schools	4,299	males & females 13 years 94% white	current group of friends usually go about with is a gang	19.9%
Bradshaw (2005) (Edinburgh Study of Youth Transitions and Crime)	Edinburgh, Scotland, 1999	survey (NFI), all pupils aged 13, in mainstream, special, & independent schools	4,299	males & females 13 years 94% white	current group of friends usually go about with is a gang with a name and/or special signs or sayings	6.8%
Curry (2000) (Socialization to Gangs)	Chicago, a low-income neighborhood, 1987	survey (NFI) of 6th–8th grade students in 4 middle schools	439	males: 68% black 32% Hispanic	member of a gang	4.6%

(continued)

TABLE 1.1. *Continued*

Source	Location, Date Collected	Sample & Method	N of cases	Sample Characteristics	Gang Definition	Proportion Gang
Curry, Decker, & Egley (2002)	Poor & middle-class neighborhoods in St. Louis, 1996	questionnaire, students in 3 middle & 2 alternative schools	533	53% male 47% female age not given 89% black 11% white	ever belonged to a gang	15%
Dukes, Martinez, & Stein (1997)	Pike's Peak region, Colorado, 1992	questionnaire, all secondary school students in 6 school districts	11,023	males & females age not given 15% black, Hispanic, or Native American 85% white or Asian	ever a member of a gang	10.1%
Dukes, Martinez, & Stein (1997)	Pike's Peak region, Colorado, 1992	questionnaire, all secondary school students in 6 school districts	11,023	males & females age not given 15% black, Hispanic, or Native American 85% white or Asian	currently a member of a gang	5.4%
Eitle, Gunkel, & Van Grundy (2004)	Southern Florida, 1998–2000	personal interview, random sample stratified by race, 6th & 7th grade students in 1990, in 48 Miami-Dade pub-	838	males 18–23 years 25% black 50% Hispanic 25% white	ever in a gang	6%

Esbensen & Huizinga (1993) (Denver Youth Study)	Socially disorganized, high-crime neighborhoods in Denver, 1988–1991	personal interview, youth ages 7, 9, 11, 13, & 15 in 1987, in stratified probability sample of households; repeat measures at annual intervals	1,095 (Wave 4 in 1991)	males & females 12–18 years 36% black 44% Hispanic 10% white 10% other	current member of a street or youth gang that participates in illegal activities	6.7%
Esbensen & Weerman (2005) (G.R.E.A.T.)	11 U.S. cities & counties, 1995	anonymous survey, all 8th grade students in 315 classrooms in 42 public schools offering gang prevention program	5,935	48% male 52% female 29% ≤13 years 60% 14 years 11% ≥15 years 27% black 19% Hispanic 41% white 14% other	currently in a gang that engages in fighting other gangs, stealing cars, stealing in general, or robbing people	7.9%
Esbensen & Weerman (2005) (NSCR School Project)	Southwest region, the Netherlands, 2002	questionnaire, all secondary students in 12 schools in the Hague & 3 smaller cities and villages close by	1,978	55% male 45% female 43% 12–13 yrs. 43% 14–15 yrs. 16% 16–17 yrs. 62% Dutch 7% Surinamese 8% Turkish 5% Moroccan 19% other	belongs to a durable, street-oriented youth group that is substantially involved in illegal activity[a]	5.9%

(continued)

TABLE 1.1. *Continued*

Source	Location, Date Collected	Sample & Method	N of cases	Sample Characteristics	Gang Definition	Proportion Gang
Esbensen & Winfree (1998) (G.R.E.A.T.)	11 U.S. cities & counties, 1995	anonymous survey, all 8th grade students in 315 classrooms in 42 public schools offering gang prevention program	5,935	48% male 52% female 29% ≤13 years 60% 14 years 11% ≥15 years 6% Asian 27% black 19% Hispanic 41% white 8% other	ever in a gang	16.9%
Esbensen & Winfree (1998) (G.R.E.A.T.)	11 U.S. cities & counties, 1995	anonymous survey, all 8th grade students in 315 classrooms in 42 public schools offering gang prevention program	5,935	48% male 52% female 29% ≤13 years 60% 14 years 11% ≥15 years 6% Asian 27% black 19% Hispanic 41% white 8% other	ever in a gang that engaged in fighting other gangs, stealing cars, stealing in general, or robbing people	10.6%

Fagan (1990)	Los Angeles (South-central), San Diego (University Heights), Chicago (Wicker Park), 1984	questionnaire, multi-stage cluster sample of high school students, grades 9–12, & chain referrals of dropouts initiated through local service agencies	1,206	males & females 13–18 years (49% are 17–18) 73% black 20% Hispanic 7% white/Asian/other	belonged to a gang in the year prior to the survey	23%
Gatti, Tremblay, Vitaro, & McDuff (2005) (Montreal Longitudinal Study)	Disadvantaged area of Montreal, 1984–1994	questionnaire, kindergarten boys in 53 low-socioeconomic status schools in 1984, with Canadian-born, French-speaking parents; repeat measures at annual intervals from age 10	756 (those remaining in sample until age 16)	males 14–16 years French Canadian	in the past 12 months, part of group or gang that did reprehensible acts[a]	37%
Gordon et al. (2004) (Pittsburgh Youth Study)	Pittsburgh, 1987–1997	personal interview, 1st & 7th grade students in 1987–1988; oversampled for high risk; repeat measures	858	males young cohort, 6–17 years; older cohort, 12–24 years 57% black 41% white 2% other	ever a member of a gang	19.2%

(*continued*)

TABLE 1.1. *Continued*

Source	Location, Date Collected	Sample & Method	N of cases	Sample Characteristics	Gang Definition	Proportion Gang
Hill et al. (1999) (Seattle Social Development Project)	High-crime neighborhoods in Seattle, 1985–1993	personal interview, 5th grade students (18 schools) in 1985; repeat measures at annual intervals	808	51% male 49% female 13–18 years 21% Asian 24% black 46% white 9% other	ever belonged to a gang with a name	15.3%
Huizinga & Schumann (2001) (Bremen Cohort Study)	Bremen, Germany, 1989–1995	personal interview, all youth that left school after compulsory 9 years, in 1989; repeat measures in 1993 & 1995	380	55% male 45% female 15–18 years (in 1989) 83% white 17% minority	ever a member of a *bande* with a name	13%
Huizinga & Schumann (2001) (Denver Youth Study)	Socially disorganized, high-crime neighborhoods in Denver, 1988–1992	personal interviews, youth aged 13 & 15 in 1987, in stratified probability sample of households; repeat measures at annual intervals	570	males & females 13–20 years 10% white 90% minority	ever a member of a youth or street gang that engages in delinquent behavior and has an identifier such as a name, colors, etc.	14%
Johnstone (1981)	Suburban census tracts (w ≥50 black residents) in Illinois portion of Chicago SMSA, 7 municipal-	questionnaire, youth aged 14–18 years, in stratified sample of black households	454	males & females 14–18 years black	been a member of a street gang since living here	10.3%

(1999) (Pittsburgh Youth Study)	1994	grade students in 1987–1988; oversampled for high risk; repeat measures		12–21 years 59% black 41% white	gang	(weighted population estimate: 24%)
Lahey et al. (1999) (Pittsburgh Youth Study)	Pittsburgh, 1987–1994	personal interview, 7th grade students in 1987–1988; oversampled for high risk; repeat measures	347	males 12–21 years 59% black 41% white	ever a member of a gang whose members engaged in fighting with other gangs, drug sales, robbery, stealing, automobile theft, or homicide	17.9% (weighted population estimate: 16%)
Snyder & Sickmund (1999) (1997 National Longitudinal Survey of Youth)	United States, 1997	personal interview, nationally representative random sample, 12–16 years in December 1996	approx. 9,000	not provided	ever belonged to a gang	5%
Snyder & Sickmund (1999) (1997 National Longitudinal Survey of Youth)	United States, 1997	personal interview, nationally representative random sample, 12–16 years in December 1996	approx. 9,000	not provided	belonged to a gang in last 12 months	2%
Thornberry et al. (2003) (Rochester Youth Development Study)	Rochester, New York, 1988–1992	personal interview, 7th & 8th grade public school students in 1988; stratified for high risk (male & high-crime areas); repeat measures at 6-month intervals, ages 13–17.5	956	73% male 27% female 13–17.5 years 68% black 17% Hispanic 15% white	ever a member of street gang or posse	30.9%

(continued)

TABLE 1.1. *Continued*

Source	Location, Date Collected	Sample & Method	N of cases	Sample Characteristics	Gang Definition	Proportion Gang
Winfree, Fuller, Vigil, & Mays (1992)	Dona Ana County, New Mexico, 1991	questionnaire, stratified (by sex) random sample of 9th and 11th grade students in 4 schools	373	72% male 28% female age not given 75% Hispanic 23% white 2% other	ever member of a gang	27.1%
Winfree, Fuller, Vigil, & Mays (1992)	Dona Ana County, New Mexico, 1991	questionnaire, stratified (by sex) random sample of 9th and 11th grade students in 4 schools	373	72% male 28% female age not given 75% Hispanic 23% white 2% other	ever member of a gang with symbols and initiation	13.1%
Winfree, Fuller, Vigil, & Mays (1992)	Dona Ana County, New Mexico, 1991	questionnaire, stratified (by sex) random sample of 9th and 11th grade students in 4 schools	373	72% male 28% female age not given 75% Hispanic 23% white 2% other	current member of a gang	15%
Winfree, Fuller, Vigil, & Mays (1992)	Dona Ana County, New Mexico, 1991	questionnaire, stratified (by sex) random sample of 9th and 11th grade students in 4 schools	373	72% male 28% female age not given 75% Hispanic 23% white 2% other	current member of a gang with symbols and initiation	8.3%

point. The three studies that employ a restricted definition of current gang membership in a general study population also report a narrow range of 6–8% gang prevalence (Bradshaw, 2005; both the Dutch and U.S. samples in Esbensen and Weerman, 2005). The remaining groups of studies display a wide range of prevalence rates.

This analysis suggests that the variability in gang prevalence cannot be attributed solely to definition or sample design. Table 1.1 includes studies in Scotland, the Netherlands, Canada, and Germany and about two dozen cities or regions in the United States. We see no particular pattern by region or country, suggesting that community characteristics, such as those discussed in chapter 6, rather than location, may be important. Perhaps the strongest message in this research is that even with unrestricted definitions in high-risk populations, most youth—7 or 8 out of 10—do *not* join gangs throughout adolescence.[4] On the other hand, youth in a wide variety of places acknowledge gang membership at levels sufficient to provoke concern regarding the deleterious effects that gangs might have on their lives, their families, and their communities.

We expect that youth who participate in gangs have more contact with the justice system. A small group of prevalence studies have drawn samples from police custody facilities or correctional programs and interviewed individuals in these settings regarding gang membership. As shown in Table 1.2, these studies span various locations (including Canada and the United Kingdom), sample characteristics, and gang definitions. Notwithstanding the LeBlanc and Lanctot (1998) study that likely captured nongang delinquent groups, these gang prevalence figures generally fall within the range reported by other studies of high-risk populations with similar gang definitions. The Decker (2000) figures are in the low-to-medium range of comparable nonincarcerated samples, and the ever-involved estimate by Bennett and Holloway (2004) is in the middle of the range, while the current-member figure is the lowest among comparable studies. Surprisingly, the Katz et al. (2005) study is the sole exemplar of notably higher prevalence rates among arrestees than the community studies in the same categories. Although such studies are too few to be conclusive, it may be that studies that choose a higher-risk sample via justice system contact are comparable in risk levels to those imposed in community studies by limiting the sex, race, or neighborhood characteristics.

Is the variation in gang prevalence that is evident in the studies included in these tables reduced if we limit the demographic range of the population assessed? Perhaps a clearer picture will emerge if we compare the rates of gang joining of females to males, younger adolescents to older

TABLE 1.2. *Prevalence of Gang Membership in Self-Report Studies, Adjudicated or Incarcerated Populations*

Source	Location, Date Collected	Sample & Method	N of cases	Sample Characteristics	Gang Definition	Proportion Gang
Bennett & Holloway (2004) (New English and Welsh Arrestee Drug Abuse Monitoring)	14 police force custody suites, primarily urban areas in England & Wales, 2000–2002	personal interview, all arrestees, during 30-day period, aged 17+	2,666	86% males 14% females 49% 17–24 years 51% 25+ years 78% white 22% ethnic minority	ever belonged to a local gang with a name or other means of identification and covers a particular geographic area or territory	15%
Bennett & Holloway (2004) (New English and Welsh Arrestee Drug Abuse Monitoring)	14 police force custody suites, primarily urban areas in England & Wales, 2000–2002	personal interview, all arrestees during 30-day period, aged 17+	2,666	86% males 14% females 49% 17–24 years 51% 25+ years 78% white 22% ethnic minority	currently belong to a local gang with a name or other means of identification and covers a particular geographic area or territory	4%
Decker (2000) (DUF Gun Addendum)	11 U.S. cities, 1995	personal interview, all arrestees during a 6-month period	8,038	58% adult males 23% adult females 17% juvenile males 2% juvenile females	ever a gang member	11%
Decker (2000) (DUF Gun Addendum)	11 U.S. cities, 1995	personal interview, all arrestees during a 6-month period	8,038	58% adult males 23% adult females 17% juvenile males 2% juvenile females	currently a gang member	7%

Katz, Webb, & Decker (2005) (Arizona ADAM)	Maricopa & Pima counties, Arizona, booking facilities in Phoenix, Tucson, & Mesa, 1999–2003	personal interview, all juveniles (< 18 years) arrested during consecutive 14 days, 4 times per year	939	81% males 19% females 26% ≤ 14 years 20% 15 years 54% 16–17 years 3% American Indian 10% black 45% Hispanic 42% white	ever a member of a gang and could name the gang	22.9%
Katz et al. (2005) (Arizona ADAM)	Maricopa & Pima Counties, Arizona, booking facilities in Phoenix, Tucson, & Mesa, 1999–2003	personal interview, all juveniles (< 18 years) arrested during consecutive 14 days, 4 times per year	939	81% males 19% females 26% ≤ 14 years 20% 15 years 54% 16–17 years 3% American Indian 10% black 45% Hispanic 42% white	currently a member of a gang and could name the gang	15.1%
LeBlanc & Lanctot (1998)	Montreal, 1992–1993	personal interview, population of boys placed on probation or institutionalized	506	boys 12–18 years (71% 15–17)	ever a member of group involved in illegal activities[a]	62%

[a]Note that this definition includes nongang delinquent groups as well as gangs.

teens and adults, blacks to whites, and so on. Fewer studies are available for this analysis because some researchers do not report these demographic breakdowns of gang prevalence, preferring instead to describe demographic characteristics within the gang category (i.e., the proportion of all gang members in the sample who are male versus the proportion of all males who are gang members). Table 1.3 includes 14 studies that report sex, age, or race/ethnicity gang prevalence rates, and with multiple definitional approaches these yield up to 18 cases for analysis.[5] As with the prior analysis, we reviewed the studies grouped by gang definition, the general or risk-delimited nature of the sample, and whether current or ever gang membership was measured. The primary question is whether demographic patterns of gang prevalence are visible in comparable studies.

Virtually all self-report studies find that males join gangs at higher rates than females. Among the six entries in Table 1.3 that capture gang membership over the course of adolescence, four report female gang prevalence rates of 8–12% (Curry et al., 2002; Esbensen and Winfree, 1998; Hill et al., 1999; Johnstone, 1981), a narrow range considering they reflect both general and risk-selected study populations and use both restricted and unrestricted gang definitions. The gang proportions among males in these studies range from 13 to 22%. In contrast, Thornberry and his colleagues (2003) find the highest prevalence among Rochester Youth Development Study females (29%) of any study, only slightly less than the 32% rate the researchers found for males. Snyder and Sickmund's (1999) nationally representative sample reports a low 3% prevalence for females and 6% for males and about half that level for current membership. The six other entries for current gang membership fall in the range of 2–6% among females and 6–10% among males, with two exceptions: the Fagan (1990) and Bolland and Drummond (1999) studies, both using unrestricted definitions with high-risk populations, report female gang membership of 8–15% and male rates of about 30%. The male prevalence rates were one and a half to twice as high as female joining rates in most of the studies we reviewed, a pattern that transcended the different study approaches. While at lower rates than males, females clearly do participate in gangs and should be prominent in any discussion of gang programs and policies.

We see wider ethnic/race differentials in gang joining. The rate of white youth participation in gangs is far lower than among black youths, at least half and often one-third lower. This pattern holds up regardless of gang definition and nature of the sample, although studies with more general samples (Esbensen and Weerman, 2005; Snyder and Sickmund, 1999) generate smaller white-black gang-prevalence differentials. Fewer studies are

TABLE 1.3. *Gang Prevalence within Demographic Categories in Self-Report Studies, Nonincarcerated Populations*

Source	Location, Date Collected	Sample & Method	N of cases	Sample Characteristics	Gang Definition	Category-Specific Prevalence[a]
Bolland & Drummond (1999)	6 public housing developments in Huntsville, Alabama, 1996–1999	survey (NFI), all youth 9–19 years old, public housing residents	562–618 (cross-sectional annual surveys)	males & females 9–19 years "overwhelmingly" African American	currently a member of a gang	M: 28–31% F: 8–13%
Craig et al. (2002)	Low socioeconomic area of a large metro city in Quebec, 1989–1994	questionnaire, boys in kindergarten in 1984, with Canadian-born, French-speaking parents; repeat measures at annual intervals from age 10	933	males 11–14 years French Canadian	in the last 12 months, belonged to a group (gang) who did illegal things[b]	11: 12.6% 12: 14.2% 13: 18% 14: 21.3%
Curry, Decker, & Egley (2002)	Poor & middle-class neighborhoods in St. Louis, 1996	questionnaire, students in 3 middle & 2 alternative schools	533	53% males 47% females age not given 89% black 11% white	ever belonged to a gang	M: 18.1% F: 11.5% B: 15.9% W: 8.2%
Dukes, Martinez, & Stein (1997)	Pike's Peak region, Colorado, 1992	questionnaire, all secondary school students in 6 school districts	11,023	males & females age not given 15% black, Hispanic, or Native American 85% white or Asian	currently member of a gang	M: 8% F: 3% B, H, or AI: 13% W or A: 4%

TABLE 1.3. *Continued*

Source	Location, Date Collected	Sample & Method	N of cases	Sample Characteristics	Gang Definition	Category-Specific Prevalence[a]
Esbensen & Huizinga (1993) (Denver Youth Study)	Socially disorganized, high-crime neighborhoods in Denver, 1988–1991	personal interview, youth ages 7, 9, 11, 13, & 15 in 1987, in stratified probability sample of households; repeat measures at annual intervals	1,095 (Wave 4 in 1991)	males & females 12–18 years 36% black 44% Hispanic 10% white 10% other	current member of a street or youth gang that participates in illegal activities	M: 9.4% F: 2.4% 12: 2% 14: 9% 16: 7% 18: 7% B: 7% H: 7% W: 2% O: 2% [calculated]
Esbensen & Weerman (2005) (G.R.E.A.T.)	11 U.S. cities & counties, 1995	anonymous survey, all 8th grade students in 315 classrooms in 42 public schools offering gang prevention program	5,935	48% males 52% females 29% ≤13 years 60% 14 years 11% ≥15 years 27% black 19% Hispanic 41% white 14% other	currently in a gang that engages in fighting other gangs, stealing cars, stealing in general, or robbing people	M: 10.2% F: 5.6% ≤ 13: 3.8% 14: 7.7% ≥ 15: 19.4% B: 9.2% H: 10.6% W: 4.8% [from authors]

Esbensen & Weerman (2005) (NSCR School Project)	Southwest region, the Netherlands, 2002	questionnaire, all secondary students in 12 schools in the Hague & 3 smaller cities and villages close by	1,978	55% males 45% females 43% 12–13 years 43% 14–15 years 16% 16–17 years 62% Dutch 7% Surinamese 8% Turkish 5% Moroccan 19% other	belongs to a durable, street-oriented youth group that is substantially involved in illegal activity[b]	M: 6.4% F: 5.3% 12–13: 4.1% 14–15: 7.3% 16–17: 6.7% D: 5.8% S: 6.8% T: 2% M: 4% [from authors]
Esbensen & Winfree (1998) (G.R.E.A.T.)	11 U.S. cities & counties, 1995	anonymous survey, all 8th grade students in 315 classrooms in 42 public schools offering gang prevention program	5,935	48% males 52% females 29% ≤13 years 60% 14 years 11% ≥15 years 6% Asian 27% black 19% Hispanic 41% white 8% other	ever in a gang that engaged in fighting other gangs, stealing cars, stealing in general, or robbing people	M: 14% F: 8% ≤13: 6% 14: 11% ≥15: 23% A: 8% B: 12% H: 14% W: 6% O: 20%
Fagan (1990)	Los Angeles (South-central), San Diego (University Heights), Chicago (Wicker Park), 1984	questionnaire, multistage cluster sample of high school students, grades 9–12, & chain referrals of dropouts initiated through local service agencies	1,206	males & females 13–18 years (49% are 17–18) 73% black 20% Hispanic 7% white/Asian/other	belonged to a gang in the past year	M: 31% F: 15% 13–14: 25% 15: 26% 16: 23% 17–18: 22% B: 22% H: 24%

(continued)

TABLE 1.3. *Continued*

Source	Location, Date Collected	Sample & Method	N of cases	Sample Characteristics	Gang Definition	Category-Specific Prevalence[a]
Hill et al. (1999) (Seattle Social Development Project)	High-crime neighborhoods in Seattle, 1985–1993	personal interview, 5th grade students (18 schools) in 1985; repeat measures at annual intervals	808	51% males 49% females 13–18 years 21% Asian 24% black 46% white 9% other	ever belonged to a gang with a name	M: 21.8% F: 8.6% A: 12.4% B: 26.2% W: 10.2% O: 19.7% [calculated]
Hill, Lui, & Hawkins (2001) (Seattle Social Development Project)	High-crime neighborhoods in Seattle, 1985–1993	personal interview, 5th grade students (18 schools)in 1985; repeat measures at annual intervals	808	51% males 49% females 13–18 years 21% Asian 24% black 46% white 9% other	current gang member	13: 2.4% 14: 5% 15: 6% 16: 5% 17: not reported 18: 5%
Johnstone (1981)	Suburban census tracts (w ≥50 black residents) in Illinois portion of Chicago SMSA, 7 municipalities, 1974	questionnaire, youth aged 14–18 years in stratified sample of black households	454	males & females 14–18 years black	been a member of street gang since living here	M: 13.4% F: 8.1%

Lahey et al. (1999) (Pittsburgh Youth Study)	Pittsburgh, 1987–1994	personal interview, 7th grade students in 1987–88; over-sampled for high risk; repeat measures	347	males 12–21 years 59% black 41% white	ever a member of a gang	B: 38.2% W: 11.9% (population estimate: B: 34% W: 8%)
Lahey et al. (1999) (Pittsburgh Youth Study)	Pittsburgh, 1987–1994	personal interview, 7th grade students in 1987–88; over-sampled for high risk; repeat measures	347	males 12–21 years 59% black 41% white	ever a member of a gang whose members engaged in fighting with other gangs, drug sales, robbery, stealing, automobile theft, or homicide	B: 26.5% W: 5.6% (population estimate: B: 24% W: 4%)
Snyder & Sickmund (1999) (1997 National Longitudinal Survey of Youth)	United States, 1997	personal interview, nationally representative, random sample, 12–16 years in December 1996	approx. 9,000	not provided	ever belonged to a gang	M: 6% F: 3% 12–13: 3% 14–15: 6% 16: 6% W: 4% N-W: 7%
Snyder & Sickmund (1999) (1997 National Longitudinal Survey of Youth)	United States, 1997	personal interview, nationally representative, random sample, 12–16 years, in December 1996	approx. 9,000	not provided	belonged to a gang in last 12 months	M: 3% F: 1% 12–13: 2% 14–15: 2% 16: 3% W: 2% N-W: 3%

(continued)

TABLE 1.3. *Continued*

Source	Location, Date Collected	Sample & Method	N of cases	Sample Characteristics	Gang Definition	Category-Specific Prevalence[a]
Thornberry et al. (2003) (Rochester Youth Development Study)	Rochester, New York, 1988–1992	personal interview, 7th & 8th grade public school students in 1988; stratified for high risk (male & high crime areas); repeat measures at 6-month intervals, ages 13–17.5	956	73% males 27% females 13–17.5 years 68% black 17% Hispanic 15% white	ever a member of street gang or posse	M: 32.4% F: 29.3% B: 36.6% H: 27.2% W: 13.3%
Thornberry et al. (2003) (Rochester Youth Development Study)	Rochester, New York, 1988–1992	personal interview, 7th & 8th grade public school students in 1988; stratified for high risk (male & high crime areas); repeat measures at 6-month intervals, ages 13–17.5	956	73% males 27% females 13–17.5 years 68% black 17% Hispanic 15% white	current member of street gang or posse	14: 22.2% 15: 11.5% 16: 6.7% 17: 5.2%

[a]M = male; F = female; A = Asian; B = black; H = Hispanic; W = white; AI = American Indian; O = other; N-W = nonwhite. Where necessary, population proportions for some categories are calculated from within-gang estimates multiplied by sample distribution and therefore may be subject to rounding error.
[b]Note that this definition includes nongang delinquent groups as well as gangs.

able to capture gang joining rates among Hispanic youth, but these appear to approximate the rates of blacks. Study samples rarely generate sufficient numbers of Asian or American Indian youth for comparison.

The issue of age-specific gang prevalence rates is best addressed in studies that ask about current gang membership. Seven of the eight studies in Table 1.3 that report age-specific rates for current involvement find that gang participation is highest at age 14 or 15 years of age; only Snyder and Sickmund (1999) report a higher prevalence rate for 16-year-olds (3%), and younger adolescents are only slightly less likely (2%) to be gang members. Likewise, three other studies (Fagan, 1990; Hill et al., 2001; the Dutch sample in Esbensen and Weerman, 2005) find very little difference in prevalence within the adolescent period, although only Fagan (1990) reports substantial rates of current gang participation (22–25% among 13- to 18-year-olds). Typically, studies that have higher prevalence rates display more variation by age (Craig et al., 2002; Thornberry et al., 2003; the U.S. sample in Esbensen and Weerman, 2005).

Notwithstanding the degree of variation in age-specific rates, the finding that the peak age for gang participation is at 14 or 15 is remarkably consistent across self-report studies, regardless of the risk level of the sample, the restrictiveness of the gang definition, and the location of the study. Gang programs and policies should pay close attention to this pattern: vulnerability to joining gangs is highest among youths from 13 to 15 years and decreases thereafter.

As we turn to discussion of gang proliferation and migration, the primary data source becomes law enforcement, rather than youths. The patterns of prevalence by sex, race, and age as revealed in this remarkable volume of recent work on self-reported gang participation are not mirrored in police-generated data, except in the most general of terms—more males than females, more members of minority groups than whites. The age distribution of police-recorded gang members differs dramatically from those determined by self-report research studies. By all accounts, law enforcement figures underestimate young, white, and female gang members. Why is this?

Police often track numbers of members from year to year and describe the age, race, and sex of the gang members they have in their data banks or estimate from familiarity with the gang situations in their jurisdictions. And just as with self-report surveys of youth, law enforcement respondents' perceptions of what a gang is (i.e., gang definitions) influence their answers to research surveys. Due to their strong orientation toward crime, law enforcement records are more apt to reflect the most active or core members and consequently are less capable than self-report studies of capturing more marginal or transitional gang members.[6] And, of course, police records or estimates only reflect the gang members with whom police have contact. The longer an individual participates in a gang, the more likely he or she is to come to the attention of police. There is some indication in self-report studies that girls join—and leave—gangs at younger ages (Thornberry et al., 2003); such patterns could help explain some of the differences in the depictions of gangs between law enforcement and research studies. Curry (1999) argues that the demographic disparities evident in these two types of studies are attributable to the younger age distributions of gang members found in smaller jurisdictions. Thus, gang and police activity, police gang recording policies and practices, and study samples and methods all contribute to the murky brew of information available on street gang patterns and proliferation.

Distribution of Gangs and Gang Members

Beginning with Walter Miller's (1975) survey efforts in the 1970s, scholars have attempted to gather systematic information about the scope and nature of gang activity across the nation. Miller started this work in the early 1970s by interviewing local service personnel in 12 of the largest cities. During the next 25 years, he continued to compile media reports, conference materials, police reports, and interview data, ultimately folding the National Youth Gang Center's annual survey of police into his database to complete his report on nearly three decades of the growth of gang problems in the United States. Miller prefaced his report with a conclusion shared by virtually every study that charted gang cities in the 1980s to the mid-1990s: "The United States, during a time period comprising roughly the last three decades of the 20th century, experienced gang problems in more identified localities than at any other time in history" (W. Miller, 2001: vi). The five national surveys following Miller's 1970s studies used larger and more-representative samples of police gang experts to feed national policy makers and practitioners with systematic research information that may have appeared pretty obvious to any observer of local or national media outlets: street gangs were surfacing in cities and towns across the nation that previously had viewed the "urban gang problem" as someone else's concern.[7]

In the mid-1990s, the U.S. Department of Justice provided funding for an annual assessment—the National Youth Gang Survey (NYGS)—to be conducted by the National Youth Gang Center (NYGC). The 1995 NYGS built on the samples used by previous studies, but beginning with the 1996 NYGS, all police departments serving populations with at least 2,500 people and all county police and sheriff's departments are represented in the survey pool, either with a total enumeration or a systematic random sample.[8] Because the NYGS captures a broadly representative sample, a laudable survey response rate, and consistent measures of core survey items in each annual survey, it represents the single best source of information about the national scope of gang activity, both now and in the past. But with its strengths, the NYGS also has important limitations. Along with the limitations inherent in any paper survey, such as the potential misunderstanding of questions, these include:

- As noted in the introduction to this volume, without a gang definition provided by the survey researchers, respondents reply for any groups that their jurisdiction considers to be a gang.
- Information provided on the survey is only as good as the information or expertise compiled in each agency; recording practices aside, police respond for the gang situations that come to their attention.
- Duplication of information occurs when gangs are active in multiple or neighboring jurisdictions and thus may be reflected multiple times.

So, it isn't perfect, but it is the best we have, and we rely on NYGS data to report the current picture of street gangs in the United States, as well as trends over recent times.

How many gangs and gang members are there in the United States? The research design of the NYGS permits an extrapolation to provide a national estimate. Recall that these figures are based on survey items that ask officers to rely on agency records of unknown validity or to estimate based on their own familiarity. According to the 2002 NYGS, the most recent information available on this question, about 731,500 gang members and 21,500 gangs were active in the United States (Egley and Major, 2004). Needless to say, nearly three-quarters of a million adolescents and young adults represent a sizable population of gang intervention targets. The NYGS estimates of more than 2,300 cities, along with more than 550 county jurisdictions, represent a lot of places that might want to implement gang intervention and prevention programs.

We'll discuss the question of changes in these national figures—gang proliferation—a bit later in this chapter, but the examination of the distribution of places with gangs can provide a foundation to the issue of proliferation. First and foremost, gang presence is directly related to the size of the place's population, a point we will visit in more detail as we discuss the community context of gangs in chapter 6. In 2002, virtually all NYGS respondents in cities with populations of 250,000 and above reported gang problems, as did 87% of cities with populations between 100,000 and 249,000. At the other end of the population spectrum, just over a fourth of smaller cities (less than 50,000 population) and just 12% of rural counties recognized gang activity. Not unexpectedly, population size is also directly related to the number of gangs and gang members. The most current NYGS report (Egley, 2005) uses the highest figure reported on either the 2002 or 2003 survey to show the difference that population size makes.

As shown in Table 1.4, more than 60% of the largest gang cities had more than 30 gangs and 1,000 gang members, but none of the cities with less than 50,000 population and none of the rural counties report gang

TABLE 1.4. *Annual Maximum Percentage of Gangs and Gang Members Reported in Gang Problem Areas, 2002 or 2003 NYGS*

	Cities 250,000 or more	Cities 100,000–249,999	Cities 50,000–99,999	Cities 2,500–49,999	Suburban Counties	Ru Co
Annual Maximum Number of Gangs Reported, 2002 or 2003 (%)						
No data reported	6.0	7.4	7.2	9.2	12.7	4.
3 or fewer	4.5	8.7	23.2	57.8	27.1	53.
4–6	1.5	17.4	27.9	20.2	18.3	29.
7–15	10.4	30.2	30.4	9.8	21.9	9.
16–30	16.4	21.5	8.3	2.9	10.1	2.
More than 30	61.2	14.8	2.9	0.0	9.8	0.
Annual Maximum Number of Gang Members Reported, 2002 or 2003 (%)						
No data reported	13.4	15.4	18.5	26.0	34.0	18.
50 or fewer	1.5	12.1	26.4	55.5	27.5	59.
51–200	6.0	20.8	29.3	12.7	19.0	21.
201–500	9.0	20.1	13.0	5.8	7.8	1.
501–1,000	9.0	14.8	8.3	0.0	2.9	0.
More than 1,000	61.2	16.8	4.3	0.0	8.8	0.
N	*67*	*149*	*276*	*173*	*306*	*71*

Source: Egley, 2005. Printed by permission from National Youth Gang Center.

presence of this magnitude. If three or fewer gangs and 50 or fewer gang members is too small or too unstable a gang figure to be considered a "problem," then more than half of gang cities with less than 50,000 population and more than half of the gang rural counties would suddenly become nongang places. As we continue reporting the patterns of the distribution of gang places and gang problems, it's important to remember that population size counts: although there are many more smaller places with gangs, the magnitude of the gang problem they face—at least as measured by numbers of gangs and gang members—pales beside the figures reported by more populous jurisdictions. Big cities contribute lots of gang numbers to the national figures; small cities contribute lots of gang places.

A second way of presenting a national depiction of gangs is by the geographic distribution of gang places. A map (such as in Figures 1.1 and 1.2, which appear later in this chapter) would show that there are gang places in every state,[9] but there are concentrations around urban centers, as we would expect from the U.S. population distribution in different regions. An NYGC report from the 1997 survey data clarifies the relative prevalence of gang places by region of the country. Nationally, 51% of all NYGS respondents reported that they had active gangs in 1997 (Office of Juvenile Justice and Delinquency Prevention, 1999). This was very close to the proportion of gang cities reported in the South (49%) and Midwest (52%) regions of the United States. In contrast, jurisdictions located in the West were far more likely to report gangs (74%) and those in the Northeast, far less likely (31%). Dividing these regions into smaller divisions reveals an even higher proportion for the Pacific division (Alaska, California, Hawaii, Oregon, and Washington): 80% of the jurisdictions surveyed in this subregion reported gangs. In particular, California has the most gang cities of any state. According to Walter Miller's tabulation, California had 363 gang cities through 1998, more than 100 more than Illinois, the second-ranked state (2001: Table 26). Clearly, gang programs should more often be sited in California and other geographic areas with more gang places, compared to states like Hawaii and Delaware, with 5 gang cities each.

The NYGS data also reveal information about the demographic patterns of gangs and gang members in the United States. The NYGC publications do not provide information about gang size, for example, the proportion of places that report primarily small groups. A simple calculation from the 2002 national gang estimates yields an average gang size of 34 members. This average masks the great variety of gang structures within gang places, a point we will revisit in chapter 5.

We would expect the demographic description of gang members derived from police perspectives to differ from the picture we get from the youth studies we discussed earlier. After all, the police describe the gang members they know, those who come to the attention of justice system agencies and make their way into agency records. Youth studies reflect the demography of the subject population (especially age and race/ethnicity) and only the area in which they are conducted; they also capture youths' report of gang involvement independent of whether or not police know them. The published national information on age, sex, and race/ethnicity of gang members reflects the NYGS survey information gathered in 1999 and 2000 (Egley, 2002).

Most of the gang members known to the police are adults, and the vast majority are males. According to NYGS police respondents, in 1999, 37% of gang members were under 18 years of age and 63% were adults. According to the 2000 survey, 94% of all gang members were male, 39% of all youth gangs had at least one female, and just 2% of gangs had mostly female members. In the 1999 survey, police reported that 47% of all gang members were Hispanic, 31% African American, 13% white, 7% Asian, and 2% other. The age, sex, and race/ethnicity patterns of gang membership likely vary by region and population size, but these are not reported in the NYGS publications.

Recalling the demographic patterns of gang membership from youth self-report studies (see Table 1.3), we can see that police records substantially undercount females and most likely younger gang members. Given the consistent finding from self-report studies that gang membership peaks at age 14 or 15, the validity of law enforcement accounts that nearly two-thirds of gang members are adults must be questioned.[10] Likewise, self-report studies typically find that from about a quarter to just under half of gang members are female, a striking contrast to the law enforcement estimate of 6%. Race differentials are also noteworthy: for example, one-quarter of the eighth-grade gang members in Esbensen and Winfree's (1998) 11-city sample were white, in contrast to the 13% reported by law enforcement. If white and female adolescents tend to join and leave gangs at earlier ages and younger gang members rarely come to the attention of police, this could explain much of the discrepant demographic information between police and self-report studies. Curry (2000) raised the question of whether there might be two separate gang populations captured by the two sources:

> The alternative possibility . . . would suggest that there are actually two parallel gang problems in U.S. communities—one involving younger, self-identified gang members and their comparatively heavy involvement in minor juvenile offending, and the other involving older, police-identified gang members and their involvement in more serious offenses tracked by law enforcement agencies. (2000: 1254)

The different demographic patterns of gang membership reflected by the two sources could foster quite different intervention profiles. It will be important to consider the appropriate source of data in the assessment of gang patterns in order to match interventions to program target populations.

Thus far, we have focused on the prevalence and pattern of the distribution of gangs in the United States, for it is in America where much of the attention and the bulk of the gang research has occurred. While several reports of gangs in Europe, Africa, Asia, Latin America, and Canada have emerged from time to time, much of this information has not stemmed from firsthand research. There has been little sustained attention to gangs outside the United States until the last decade. Since the mid-1990s, two edited volumes of original research on gangs in Europe have been published (Klein, Kerner, Maxson, and Weitekamp, 2001; Decker and Weerman, 2005), along with a textbook (Covey, 2003) and several briefer publications (see Klein, 2002, for recent review) that compile what is known about gangs around the world. We don't yet have good prevalence estimates of international gang cities (those that we know about are usually the result of individual researchers' attention or media reports) and only rarely do we have estimates of the proportion of youth in these international gang places that join gangs (but see non-U.S. locations in Table 1.1). The definition and data collection issues are challenging, yet examples of systematic comparison between U.S. gangs and those in Europe (Huizinga and Schumann, 2001; Esbensen and Weerman, 2005) are emerging as international researchers begin to document the gang situations in their countries. This recent attention has been spawned by international media coverage, by concern about the diffusion of U.S. gang culture, and by researchers interested in international comparative gang research. While U.S. gangs are far more prevalent and violent (Klein, 2002), similarities in gang structures and other group characteristics raise fundamental questions about gang emergence in the context of economic and cultural marginality and youth status needs. Little is known about the relevance of the current research on the individual, group, and community contexts of gangs, which we review in part II, to gang situations outside the United States. A similar foundation of systematic information is critical to developing effective responses to the emerging gang situation in Europe. The U.S. program failures we describe in chapter 3 may offer guidance to other countries about what *not* to do, but the program paradigms we suggest in part III are derived from the U.S. experience. In the face of limited knowledge about the forms and processes of gangs outside the United States, we can offer few positive directions for gang intervention elsewhere.

Gang Proliferation: Trends over Time

The consistent message from the national surveys prior to the NYGS was that the number of gang places was far larger than previously known. Public awareness and fear were growing—and the press coverage was certainly relentless. At the same time, law enforcement agencies were also increasing their awareness and expertise and beginning to keep better tabs on gangs in their jurisdictions. Using the law enforcement survey responses we gathered in 1992, we constructed a series of four maps showing the number and geographic distribution of cities that developed gang problems through 1960, then through 1970, 1980, and finally, 1992 (Klein, 1995a). The progression of these maps makes the gang proliferation point quite succinctly, but ends the story in 1992. In Figure 1.1, we reprint the 1992 map showing the locations of nearly 800 gang places. Fortunately, Egley and his colleagues (2004) plotted the NYGS respondents (in this case, more than 1,400 law enforcement agencies that reported gang problems in one of the 1999–2001 surveys) on a map, reprinted in Figure 1.2. Despite the different mapping technologies of the two studies, the substantial increase in places with gangs is quite evident. There is still a noted concentration around urban centers and on both coastlines. There are some sparse areas in the West, while the eastern half of the country shows more density in gang places.

By asking respondents when gangs first emerged in their jurisdictions, the NYGS has documented periods of gang proliferation in the United States over the past 30 or more years. And, the story of gang proliferation is really two stories, one for larger cities and one for less populated places. The data from respondents to the NYGS 2000 survey on the year of onset of gang problems, displayed in Figure 1.3, illustrate the difference. On the right-hand side, we can see the familiar pattern of gang prevalence as

FIGURE 1.1. The prevalence of gang cities through 1992. *Source*: Klein, 1995a: 4–5. Printed by permission of Oxford University Press.

FIGURE 1.2. Jurisdictions in the contiguous states reporting youth gang problems in one or more years, 1999–2001 NYGS. *Source:* Reprinted by permission of Waveland Press, Inc., from Egley et al., 2004. All rights reserved.

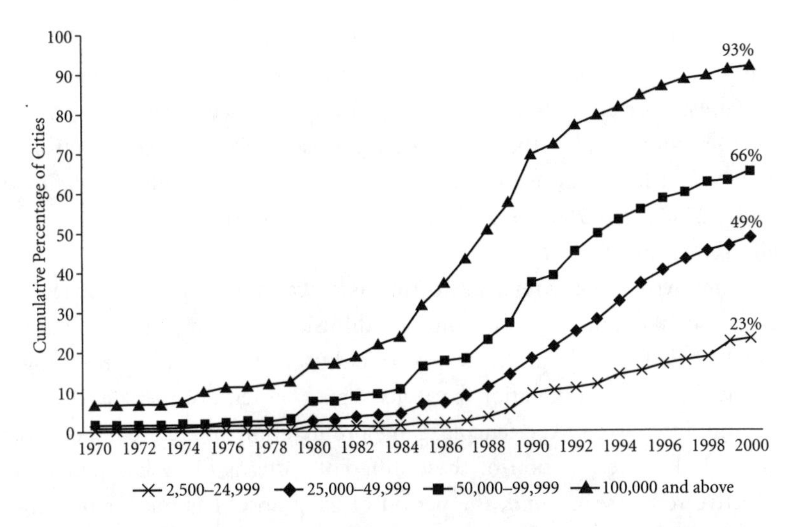

FIGURE 1.3. Patterns of gang proliferation in cities reporting gang activity in 2000 NYGS. *Source*: Reprinted by permission of Waveland Press, Inc., from Egley et al., 2004.

related to the size of the city population. The graph reports cumulative percentages (i.e., cities are included in each year subsequent to the year of reported gang emergence) so the figures on the far right represent the prevalence of cities with gangs in 2000.

There was not much action before 1980; less than 15% of large (100,000 or more) cities had gangs. By 1985, that percentage had doubled, and it increased to about 70% in 1990. A similar trend is evident in the midsized city category (50,000–99,999), though less steep and slightly delayed; there is a slight increase in the first half of the 1980s (to just under 20%) and then a doubling to almost 40% in 1990. More midsized gang cities came online through the next five years, with prevalence reaching about 60% in 1995. An analysis of onset dates in the 1996 NYGS confirms this pattern: the majority of all gang cities and counties with populations over 50,000 reported onset dates before 1991 (Howell, Egley, and Gleason, 2002: Table 1). So this is the first proliferation story: larger cities experienced the steepest rate of gang proliferation in 1986–1990; proliferation in midsized cities was most marked between 1986 and 1995. While the onset of gangs continued thereafter in both categories of cities, the real spurt in proliferation occurred during a relatively brief period.

The second proliferation story took place in smaller cities and towns. The proliferation spurt in small cities (25,000–49,999) happened in the 1991–1995 period when prevalence increased from around 20% to about

40%. In the smallest cities and towns (2,500–24,9999), there is a modest but steady progression from 1985 on—successive increases in five-year increments are about 6–8%. Looking just at gang places within these population groupings, less than 40% of gang jurisdictions between 25,000 and 49,999 and less than a quarter of towns and counties with populations under 25,000 reported gang emergence prior to 1991 (Howell, Egley, and Gleason, 2002: Table 1).

Some writers have referred to this as a "cascading" pattern (Egley et al., 2004: 100), and this term connotes diffusion from large to small cities. We'll tackle this issue in the next section, but for now we note two things about the dual proliferation patterns. First, law enforcement and local communities were experiencing gang proliferation in different periods, and a lack of recognition of these different patterns likely hampered an effective response. Second, the period of gang onset has important ramifications for the nature of local gang patterns today. As we'll show in chapter 6, older gang cities have different gang characteristics than newer gang cities, and this has important implications for intervention.

There is yet another proliferation story masked by these cumulative prevalence percentages. This is the story of gang recession or desistance. Beginning in 1997, the earlier proliferation trend reversed in all of the smaller population categories. There was a marked decline in midsized cities (50,000–99,999; from 82% in 1997 to 66% in 2002), small cities and towns (2,500–49,999; from 37% to 27%), suburban counties (59% to 38%), and rural counties (25% to 12%) (Egley et al., 2004: Figures 1 and 2). However, the pattern in larger cities was essentially stable during this period (100% in cities over 250,000; 85% to 92% in cities with populations of 100,000–249,999).

The 1996 NYGS was the high-water mark for the prevalence of gang cities and counties in the United States and also produced the highest estimate of gangs and gang members. Gangs weren't simply discovered in 1996; the variability in onset dates suggests that NYGC researchers were picking up relatively thoughtful responses from police able to report the emergence of gang problems in the past. How can we account for these patterns in proliferation and recession? Gang migration (i.e., the relocation of gang members from established urban gang centers to the virgin territory of small cities and rural areas) is the oft-cited culprit in proliferation, and we'll assess this explanation in the following section. But what of the recession of gangs in these smaller places? Are there lessons for intervention to be learned?

The vast majority—three-quarters or more—of places with transitory gang problems have few gang members and recent gang onsets. With few exceptions, established gang cities simply don't seem to eradicate their gang problems.[11] Is the reduction in less established gang places due to control practices, either police suppression or community intervention programs? We don't have enough evidence from case studies of such places, but our money is on the gang process explanation. We discuss this more in chapter 5; a combination of factors is probably at play. Enthusiastic or overzealous police officers may have overestimated a new gang problem, but if we take the NYGS assessments at face value, a natural attrition from gang flirtation to desistance took place. Without strong opposition or challenges from other youth gangs, or perhaps without cohesion-building suppressive responses from oppositional authorities, these barely solidified groups probably withered away. Some groups may have been mimicking gang behaviors picked up from the media ("copycats"). Or communities may have activated mechanisms of informal social control (see chapter 6), coupled with multifaceted partnerships with police, schools, and youth-serving agencies to redirect youth to a different path. Other explanations may involve political motivations to underreport gang presence. In any case, we are reminded that gang membership can be a fluid process, and the designation of a youth group as a gang by local practitioners is subject to political as well as experiential factors.

Finally, we note that gang prevalence recorded by a law enforcement agency, i.e., whether or not active gangs are reported in any given survey year, is a blunt instrument with which to gauge fluctuations in gang activity. Tracking trends in numbers of gangs, gang members, and gang crimes also is a risky business. In chapter 2, we will report available data on trends in gang crime within several gang cities. Scholars have often noted that gang activity flows in cycles (Klein, 1995b). Rarely are these systematically assessed by close examination of internal city patterns. We don't know whether decreases in activity are attributable to fewer active gang members (less successful recruitment, more gang exit, natural maturation by older gang members), fewer active gangs, changes in group processes (a hiatus in gang rivalries, a reorientation toward peace and law abidingness), or to interventions.

Large cities contribute vast numbers to the annual national estimates of gangs and gang members provided by the NYGC. Changes in agency record keeping and recording practices (and the internal resources allocated to sustain record systems) can produce year-to-year fluctuations in these numbers that challenge the validity of trend analysis. Consider the following illustrations:

- In the early 1990s, the Los Angeles district attorney's office issued a gang report that included detailed analysis of law enforcement gang databases in the L.A. region (Reiner, 1992). Age- and race-specific comparisons of rostered gang members to U.S. Census figures revealed a whopping 47% of all African-American males between 21 and 24 years old in Los Angeles County were gang members. This figure defies credibility but illustrates how police practices of designating gang members and retention of out-of-date records can produce distorted numbers.
- For many years, the Los Angeles Sheriff's Department (LASD) reported a combined figure of 150,000 gang members for the jurisdictions within Los Angeles County, including the city of Los Angeles. More recently, LASD officials have used a figure of 85,000, citing a stronger reliance on documented gang members and the purging of old gang files as explanations for the reduction. No one suggested a radical decline in gang membership in a single year.
- In the mid-1990s, while trying to explain comparative changes in gang homicide numbers in Los Angeles and Chicago, we interviewed personnel from the Chicago Police Department's crime analysis unit. A new twist was added to our work on the widely recognized distinctions in definitional approaches to gang crime in these two cities when we learned that radical shifts in definitions and recording practices had been implemented. We speculated that Chicago should perhaps be removed from the group of cities employing the "Chicago definition" (Maxson and Klein, 1996: n. 2). Since the cities of Chicago and Los Angeles contribute more than half of the national annual total of gang homicides reported by the NYGS (see Egley and Major, 2004), any change in the recording practices in either of these two cities can have a dramatic impact on our view of the national gang problem.

These are but a few examples that remind us that the information upon which so much gang control policy relies may be as much a reflection of law enforcement activity and recording practices as it is of gang activity.

An Analysis of Conventional Wisdom: The Special Case of Gang Migration

It is our practice to begin discussions of gang migration by quoting claims by local law enforcement and public officials, state and federal task force reports, media sources, and so on regarding the perceived linkages among gang proliferation, the relocation of gang members from urban centers, and the expansion of drug sales and violence (Maxson, 1993; Maxson, Woods, and Klein, 1996). Despite widely disseminated results from our own national gang migration study, as well as analyses of relevant NYGS data from three survey years, the urge to lay blame for new gang problems on the doorstep of big-city gang migrants still remains strong. A smattering of media articles saved for this occasion reflects the endurance of this particular conventional wisdom:

Headline: "Nationwide Spread of L.A. Gangs Is Alarming, FBI Says." This *Los Angeles Times* article from April 24, 1997, reported testimony before the Senate Judiciary Committee. Steven Wiley, head of the FBI's violent crime section, is quoted: "The gang migration 'has set in motion a social phenomenon of violence and . . . defiance among youth' that in turn has 'drastically altered the violent crime problem of communities across the nation' " (Jackson, 1997). The same hearing was the subject of an article in *Crime Control Digest* the next day, which quoted the committee chair, Senator Orrin Hatch:

> Territorial expansion of gangs show they "now more resemble organized crime syndicates than small, romanticized neighborhood street toughs, like those once portrayed in *West Side Story*. Gangs have expanded from state to state and have national, and perhaps even international, networks of illegal activity." By developing cells in different cities to promote illegal activities such as drug trafficking, he said, "Gangs, in a word, have franchised." (Washington Crime News Services, 1997)

Headline: "The Gang's All There: Thousands of L.A. Gang Members Have Fled to Las Vegas, Where a Surge in Crime Has the Police Calling for Enforcement." Here, *Los Angeles Magazine* in August 1998 called forth the authority of the FBI with the boldface inset, "FBI sources estimate that, since the passage of the three-strikes law in 1994, some 5,000 L.A. gang members have picked up and moved to Las Vegas." After reporting on a series of casino heists by gun-toting Crips, drive-by shootings, and property crimes, the reporter stated, "But the real business of L.A.'s gang transplants in Las Vegas has focused on extending their main criminal enterprise: drugs" (Cogan, 1998).

Headline: "Bloods, Crips Infiltrate Ohio: Gangs Migrate to Columbus from Bigger Cities; Members Traffic in Drugs, Guns." This article in the *Lantern: The Student Voice of Ohio State University*, June 4, 2003, quoted Assistant Prosecutor Dave DeVillers, "[T]he increase in gang activity [in 1995 and 1996] was because of people migrating from larger cities, such as Chicago, Detroit and Los Angeles. It was also influenced by the adoption of [the] ideas and mannerisms of gang culture from those cities" (Chinn, 2003).

Headline: "Gangs Making Smaller Cities Home." This "CBS Evening News" report, broadcast on August 21, 2004, continues the long pattern of media reliance on law enforcement informants. After showcasing Durham, North Carolina's "growing gang problem," news correspondent Sharyn Alfonsi announced:

> Gangs who once called the streets of Los Angeles and New York City home are now stretching beyond their big city bases as they find it harder and harder to operate in those big cities. They're bringing their gang-style violence to places such as Tulsa, Denver and the affluent suburbs of Washington, D.C., and New Jersey. "It's kinda like water. They are going to follow the path of least resistance, and go where they feel they can operate under the radar," says Mark Bridgeman of the North Carolina Gang Investigators Association. (CBSNews.com, 2004)

It should be noted that several gang migrant destination cities profiled in this piece reported gang onset dates to us and to the NYGS many years prior to this most recent exemplar of gang migration coverage (Durham in 1995, Denver in 1998, and Tulsa in 1988).

What we don't see in these accounts is the countervailing depiction that is offered from systematic research by scholars in Las Vegas (Miethe and McCorkle, 2002), Columbus and Cleveland (Huff, 1989), St. Louis (Decker and Van Winkle, 1996), Milwaukee (Hagedorn, 1988), Evanston (Rosenbaum and Grant, 1983), San Francisco (Waldorf, 1993), Kenosha (Zevitz and Takata, 1992), and so on. None of these studies rely exclusively on law enforcement reports, but instead these researchers gathered information from gang members, youth, and community informants. The research-based depictions of gang migration, in marked contrast to the accounts of law enforcement and public officials, suggest:

- Primarily home-grown gang problems, likely spawned by local community factors rather than instigated by the direct transfer of gang culture or recruitment by gang migrants.
- Minimal and, when evident, diffuse organizational affiliations with big-city gangs. There are very few examples of shots called by big-city gang leaders; closely connected satellites of major city gangs—Senator Hatch's franchises—are rare.
- Gang culture permeated through the popular media (movies, clothing styles, music) seems to have more influence on local gang activity than do big-city migrants.

We can add national data to these studies of individual cities. In the early 1990s, we conducted a study of gang migration with data derived from mail survey returns from a sample of more than 1,100 cities and towns, interviews with police in 211 cities which reported at least 10 gang migrants in the previous year, interviews with community respondents in 42 cities, and case studies in three migration cities, including interviews with migrant gang members. In all phases of the research, gang migrants were defined as individuals who joined gangs in other locations and relocated for temporary visits for social or criminal purposes or for longer stays, including permanent moves for any reason. Our study findings (Maxson, Woods, and Klein, 1996; Maxson, 1998b) confirmed and expanded on the results listed above from the earlier studies of individual cities. Moreover, the NYGS studies in 1996, 1997, and 1999 used the same definition. When questions were posed the same way, these studies essentially replicated our findings with a nationally representative sample. Since there are few differences among the various years of the NYGS and our findings in the early 1990s, we can list the key results from the national studies together:

- Gang migration is a widespread, yet shallow, phenomenon. Most cities with gangs (more than 80%) report at least some gang migration. In our study, most cities with gang migration reported relatively few migrants (about half reported fewer than 10). The NYGS weighted its respondents' estimated percentage of all gang members in their jurisdictions by the number of gang members reported, and generated a national estimate of all youth gang members in the United States who had migrated from one jurisdiction to another: 21% in 1996; 23% in 1997; 18% in 1999. The unweighted estimates for the three survey years show no consistent differential pattern regarding gang migration by agency type (see Table 1.5). Overall, the percentage of migrants is lower in 1999, except for rural areas. Gang migration to rural areas is rarely studied. Wells and Weisheit (2001) noted the later gang onset dates in rural locations as a possible indicator of diffusion of gangs from urban areas, but found that distance to a metropolitan area was not related to the emergence of gangs in rural areas.

- Los Angeles, Chicago, and Detroit were the most common origin cities; the primary source of migration was typically within 100 miles of the destination location.
- Most gang migrants relocated for social reasons, including family moves for jobs, better housing stock, and to join relatives and friends. Drug market expansion was the primary reason for migration in some cities, but in far fewer cities (about 20% of migration cities) than the publicity suggests.
- Collective gang migration, or several members from the same gang moving to a new city during roughly the same time period, was rare. That is, gangs don't migrate; some gang members do.
- Law enforcement reported no dominant pattern of gang participation by migrants. Migrants joined preexisting local gangs, retained only their old gang affiliations, recruited for their old gangs, or established new branches.
- Law enforcement reported a substantial impact of gang migrants

TABLE 1.5. *Police Estimates of the Proportion of Gang Members Who Are Gang Migrants*

Agency Type	1996 NYGS	1997 NYGS	1999 NYGS
Cities (25,000 plus)	31%	28%	17%
Cities (2,500–24,999)	36%	37%	27%
Suburban counties	31%	31%	20%
Rural counties	30%	32%	34%

> on local crime rates or patterns and also on gang culture. In contrast, gang migrants reported less gang activity in their new locations.

The media portrayals seem correct in identifying Chicago and Los Angeles area gangs as major sources of gang migration in the United States. About one-third of our interviews with gang migrant officers included Chicago among source cities, and two-thirds mentioned a city within a 30-mile radius of Los Angeles. We expected these two cities to generate different migration patterns, but far more similarities than differences were detected (Maxson and Klein, 2002). In both cities, the geographic reach of gang migrants was limited (77% of cities with the most migrants from Los Angeles were located in the West; 91% of cities with the most migrants from Chicago were located in the Midwest). We expected cities with Chicago gang migrants more often to cite drug expansion as the primary reason for migration, but social reasons predominated in both types of cities. Gang participation patterns for migrants in both types of cities were roughly similar.

Another approach in our search for differential patterns of gang migration involved an analysis by primary reason for migration. Although we found that drug expansion was far less frequent than social reasons, we hypothesized that cities with this type of migration might be different. Cities with migrants drawn primarily for drug sales or other criminal opportunities were larger and more likely to be located in the South. Migrants to these cities tended to travel longer distances, stayed shorter periods of time, were older, and were more likely to be black (Maxson et al., 1996).

The three cities selected as special site studies of gang migration varied on the primary reason for migration and the predominant ethnicity of the migrants.[12] These cities were selected from a pool that reported 100 or more gang migrants in 1992. Napa, California, is an exemplar of Hispanic migration for social reasons; Milwaukee of black migration for drug expansion; and Lawndale, California, of black migration for social reasons. During multiple site visits to each location, we interviewed personnel from youth service agencies, schools, law enforcement, and local government. These contacts led us to interviews with about one dozen gang migrants in each site. Neither the sites, nor the interview subjects, were selected to be statistically representative, but they allowed us to take a more nuanced look at some national patterns. In particular, as the summaries provided below suggest, the reasons for gang migration and the impact of migrant activities on destination cities are far more complex than has been portrayed by the media and some law enforcement commentators.

Napa

Napa is located in a valley in the northern California wine country. Seasonal work in the vineyards draws migrant farm workers and their families into the area for fall harvest. At the time of our visit, the city had a population of just over 60,000 white and Hispanic residents. The wine industry is the biggest employer and the engine that drives tourists to the Napa Valley. The image of this bucolic wine country bustling with well-heeled tourists and Old World wine growers belies the undercurrent of ethnic conflict and nativism that surfaced in our interviews with adults and youth.

Police estimated that 200 Latino gang migrants had arrived in the city in 1991, most often for social reasons. The site interviews uniformly confirmed the social reasons for gang members' migration to Napa: not one of the interviewed gang members cited drug sales or other illegal activities as a motive. Instead, gang migrants mentioned getting a job (2), joining family members who lived in Napa (5), moving with parents seeking work (2), a court appointment, release from a youth correctional facility close by, and the desire to "get my life together."

Our analysis revealed two distinct types of gang migrants in Napa. One pattern was gang members from other parts of northern California, who are primarily Mexican Americans whose families generally are not a part of the migrant labor circuit. Mexican immigrants, who in recent years began moving to Napa to join family members who had decided to stay on there, comprise the second type. Upon arrival, these Mexican immigrants are assumed by local youth, both immigrant and native, to be Sureño. The Sureños are the southern California antagonist to the northern California Mexican-American gang alliance known as the Norteños. The Norteños use their status as third- and fourth-generation Americans to distinguish themselves from their first- and second-generation southern rivals. They use inflammatory nativist sentiment as a basis for the rivalry between these two groups. Two gang migrants illustrated this conflict when we asked about the two types of gang migrants:

> We are Sureños, from the south, coming here to do some work. We stick together because we all come from the south. The Nor-

teños don't want us here and try to cause trouble. It's mostly about fighting each other.

Norteños: northern California. Sureños: southern California, wannabe. When they come here they are asking for trouble . . . [which] causes problems. The Sureños cause the trouble.

The volume of gang migrants may have been overestimated as we learned that many southern migrant youth with no previous gang affiliations became Sureños on arrival in defense against this Norteño sentiment. Although the larger gang migrant group consisted of Mexican Americans from other northern California cities, the second type seemed to receive more attention, and some reported hostile attention. We speculated that the small-town nature of Napa contributed to the orientation toward "outsiders" as the source of trouble in town. Outsiders in Napa, a community with a sizable Mexican-American population, were more readily distinguished as those who do not easily blend in—as do other English-speaking Mexican Americans. Even Norteño gang migrants reported that Sureños receive the brunt of harassment and rejection from the police, local gang members, and the community.

The Napa situation illustrates a complex migration model, with macrolevel gang affiliations serving as an overlay to reinforce and perpetuate ethnic antagonism against native Mexicans. All of the community officials we interviewed acknowledged gang migration from northern California cities, but consistently directed discussion toward the north-south conflict. The focus on Mexican immigrants as gang migrants might inadvertently strengthen or encourage gang identity. Just 1 of the 12 youths interviewed had ceased gang activity. Four others retained their old gang affiliations, 3 joined two local Napa gangs, and 4 others said they hung out with Napa gangs, although they had not joined.

Milwaukee

On our visits, we found Milwaukee to be a striking contrast to Napa. A city with a large-scale gang and gang migration experience, Milwaukee was selected because of the reported high number (one survey estimated that 1,400 gang migrants arrived in 1991) of black gang migrants, moving there primarily to exploit drug market opportunities. Hagedorn (1988) described several waves of African-American migration to Milwaukee throughout the twentieth century. The most recent period reflected the loss of manufacturing jobs in northern industrial cities and the deterioration of inner-city neighborhoods. Families, many headed by single women, sought better qualities of life, away from the poverty and violence of inner cities. They moved from Chicago, Gary, and Detroit to suburban areas and cities such as Milwaukee.

The Milwaukee police clearly assessed gang member migration to be driven by the drug market but accorded social reasons a prominent, though secondary, role. Other agency contacts clearly offered family-related motivations as the primary impetus for individual gang members to move to Milwaukee. Although family connections may have been the draw for the movement of gang members, agency personnel suggested that many migrants utilized those same connections to develop networks for drug distribution. By way of contrast, moves with family or to join family were cited a few times, but the modal primary motivation identified by 4 of the 10 gang migrants interviewed was getting away from gang or legal problems. Few of the gang migrants we interviewed cited drug market opportunities as their primary motivation for moving to Milwaukee, although 6 of them stated that drug sales opportunities were an attraction or became an attraction upon arrival in Milwaukee: "I couldn't find a job, so I sold drugs. It was something I did in Chicago as well. After a while, it became an attraction."

A fine line distinguished local and migrant gang members in Milwaukee. Most of our contacts mentioned the strong connections and influence between Chicago and Milwaukee gangs. They cited a lot of movement back and forth between these two cities. The Chicago mystique accompanied these gang migrants, and they achieved a certain level of status and clout in Milwaukee that they may not have had in Chicago. "[They] felt I was some kind of 'god' from Chicago," said one informant. For the most part, gang migrants maintained their same gang affiliations in Milwaukee via the same gang cluster (e.g., Gangster Disciples, Latin Kings). Two subjects joined local Milwaukee gangs, two subjects no longer identified as gang members, and four said they wouldn't join a new gang, "because I'm GD, and I'll be GD until I die." Only one respondent rarely had contact with members of his old gang; six reported frequent contact.

Milwaukee represents a pattern of gang migration which is consistent with one prevailing perception of gang migration—that of big-city gang members moving to other cities and towns while keeping their original gang identity and associations intact. The proximity of Milwaukee to Chicago cannot explain this connection entirely, since half of the Napa migrants we interviewed also came from source cities in close proximity, but they did not maintain their previous gang affiliations.

Milwaukee also challenges the big-city gang spread perception. First, while Chicago gang members may keep their gang identity and ties upon moving to Milwaukee, their migration motivation appeared to rest at the individual or family level rather than at the gang or group level. Second, while the perception was that drug market opportunities were the primary motivation for gang member migration, these interviews suggested that drug selling was an integral aspect of some individuals' lifestyles, an involvement they would likely continue no matter where they relocated. Milwaukee may have had more exploitable drug market opportunities, but drug market participation functioned as a "trade" or "occupation," which was easily transferable.

Lawndale

Lawndale was selected as an illustration of black gang migration for family change of residence. It was estimated that some 300 gang migrants arrived in Lawndale in 1991. Lawndale offered an example of proximal migration, with distances traveled even shorter than those to Milwaukee or Napa. Rather than movement from inner city to outlying suburb, families literally moved to the adjacent town, one that is within the same urban metropolitan area of Los Angeles. This allowed migrant gang members the opportunity to maintain ties with their original gangs and contributed to highly transient gang activity in Lawndale. This was compounded by the city's inclusion in a secondary school district that is also responsible for students in the neighboring town of Hawthorne. The director of security at the local high school stated that many family residential moves were precipitated by incidents resulting in their children getting in trouble with the law or being threatened by other gangs: the family needed to move immediately. Others moved for better qualities of life. Largely a planned community with a population of approximately 28,000, Lawndale is a community of single-family homes with good area schools.

Our site interviews with agency personnel confirmed family moves as the dominant reason for gang migration to Lawndale. Parents often initiated the move in order to get youth away from trouble and into a safer neighborhood:

> My mom just wanted a bigger house when she first came out here. She thought that the school was better. Plus I was getting

> into trouble when I lived with my dad. He worked a lot. My mom thought she could keep a better eye on me.

> We moved to get away from all the activity that was going on over on 55th and Western. It was my gang 'hood. It was the family decision. . . . after my cousin got killed, my mother and father decided to move out here.

Most gang migrants did not claim Lawndale as their territory, and they engaged in most of their gang activity in their old neighborhoods. Of the 12 migrants we interviewed, just 2 joined new gangs. Some gang members considered Lawndale "safe." They expressed relief when they came to Lawndale, that they knew that they would not be involved in any turf issues or other conflicts in their new environment.

> I explain it like this, say like where I lived in Inglewood and I [had] problems with somebody out there. And I moved to Lawndale and won't nobody from Inglewood be over here. I would just be out of a 'hood I don't have to worry about. Lawndale has gang members, but it don't have a gang.

> Like your enemy might be in another territory. You don't have to worry about nothing. It's like a new world coming in. You moved so fast before, you get here and everything slows down.

> It is really safe. Your worst enemy don't really come out here to find you. If you wanted, you can hide out in Lawndale.

In sum, Lawndale was a relatively safe suburb of Los Angeles with no major gang turf issues. It had one local gang that claimed Lawndale; this was a Latino gang, and their antagonists were in the neighboring city of Gardena. Family moves, as the primary motivation for gang member migration to Lawndale, most likely contributed to the decreased gang activity among these migrants. The parents of these youths have taken an activist stance in getting their children away from the negative influences in their old neighborhood, and many of those we interviewed seemed to have a measure of respect for these decisions by their parents.

Lawndale differed from Milwaukee, where although quality of life was the impetus for many moves by families of gang migrants, the environment offered opportunities for criminal and gang-involved distractions that were not much different than those in the cities from which they moved. This appeared to be less true of Lawndale, and the reduction of gang activity for gang migrants to Lawndale was stronger than in the other cities we studied.

The site studies illustrated the range of gang participation patterns among gang migrants: from joining gangs in their new cities, to retaining exclusive identity with their old gangs, to ceasing gang activity altogether. However, cessation was the lesser pattern; we were struck by the strength of the ties to the gang subculture. The decision to disengage from gangs altogether was a much more conscious and challenging choice to make than was the seemingly effortless opportunity to join a new gang or maintain old gang ties.

In Napa, gang migrants became members of local gangs, shedding old gang ties while drawing on similar experiences with new gang affiliates. The Norteño-Sureño distinction solidified gang identities.

This macrolevel gang identity is similar in some ways to the Milwaukee gang migrant experience. Among gangs in the old industrial cities of the Midwest, the notion of gang alliances of Folks and People and the different gangs (such as the Vice Lords, Latin Kings, Gangster Disciples) that ally with each of these two larger identities remain strong. Maintaining the same gang identity wherever one travels in the region is relatively easy, considering the level of movement between Milwaukee and Chicago, the presence of the same gang names in both places, and the degree of familial relationships within these gangs. This makes it difficult to determine whether or not gang migrants are involved with exactly the same gang members of their old gang or with new gang members in a gang of the same name as that of their city of origin.

Lawndale offered a variation on the maintenance-of-gang-identity theme. While California's Crips and Bloods soar in the nation's mythology as highly organized "super-gangs," they are the least of the super-gangs represented in these case studies. The Lawndale gang migrants reflected a more microlevel of gang membership, characterized as numerous discrete sets, be they Crips or Bloods. Like Milwaukee gang migrants, much of the Lawndale gang migrants' maintenance of previous gang affiliations was based on proximity. They maintained ties with their same set in their former location, essentially commuting to gang turf.

Finally, we were struck by the regularity with which the gang migrants we interviewed reported being in less trouble with the law since their moves. This leads us to speculate that "Greyhound therapy" might actually be effective. Although each of the cities exhibited a unique attribute of gang migration, we noted that none of the strategies offered as remedies by law enforcement or other agency personnel appear to be focused on the particular migrant problem, but on gangs in general. For example, diminishing the language and acculturation barriers in Napa might decrease gang violence there. In all sites, programs could be implemented in schools with the help of law enforcement, city administration, and community services to introduce a wide range of alternatives to new transfer students in order to take advantage of the temporary disruption in gang affiliation that is generated by a move.

Gang Migration as the Cause of Gang Proliferation?

We initiated our study of gang migration, in part, to determine whether gang migration was the major culprit in the proliferation of gangs that we were witnessing in the late 1980s and early 1990s. Ultimately, we concluded that migration did not cause proliferation, at least in most newer gang cities and towns. Yes, there was a lot of residential movement from established urban gang centers like Chicago and Los Angeles as well as from other gang cities. And yes, more sophisticated or entrenched gang members from other cities likely affected local crime and gang activity. But the oft-publicized, organized, collective migration of gangs to establish drug franchises is the rare case. It happens, but not all that often, particularly relative to the frequency with which law enforcement and public officials attribute their particular gang problems to gang migrants.

We argue the case against migration as the primary cause of gang proliferation by analyzing the data provided by law enforcement (Maxson, 1998b). Comparing the dates of gang onset with the dates of first gang migration, we find that the development of local, wholly indigenous gangs usually *precedes* gang migration. Furthermore, the primary reasons for gang migration argue against the proliferation hypothesis. Social motivations for migration are just as common in newer gang cities as in more established gang cities. Finally, when asked directly, the vast majority of law enforcement respondents reported that their city would have gangs with or without gang migration.

Ultimately, we advise local policy makers to focus on other potential causes for the rise of gang problems in their cities, of the type covered in part II of this book. Sensationalized press coverage and exaggerated official accounts might accomplish political goals, but they deflect discussion and analysis away from the more fundamental problems and potentially undermine the development of effective gang control policies.

The patterns identified earlier in this chapter add to this consideration of implications for gang control programs and policies. While the best available evidence suggests that the proportion of U.S. youth involved in gangs is quite low, we have shown that in many high-risk neighborhoods, youth join gangs rather frequently—somewhere in the range of 15–30%. Many, although certainly not all, cities and towns are confronting gang problems. A surge in the emergence of gangs in larger cities was evident in the latter part of the 1980s; the pattern for smaller places was a bit later. While gang prevalence in these less-populous areas seems to have diminished, gangs continue to be a striking feature in all large and many midsized cities.

The concentration of gang problems in some neighborhoods in some cities and among certain demographic groups suggests that programs and policies be directed where they are most needed. We should recognize, in fact, celebrate, the distributional variations. Most youth in most neighborhoods won't join gangs. National, broad-based gang prevention programs are unlikely to capture those most at need. Instead, gang programs should be positioned in the locations—whether by virtue of high prevalence rates or the individual, peer, and community factors we will discuss in part II—where the likelihood of gang problems warrants the risk of misfired interventions.

Local assessments are necessary to calibrate a gang program to a specific gang problem. Diverse patterns of gang prevalence are a challenge for a coherent federal gang policy. Within any reasonably sized gang city, there are many types of gang structures, and sex, age, and race distributions vary as well. Presumably, the patterns of who participates, as well as the gang organizational structures, presage different patterns of offending. As we turn in the next chapter to an assessment of current research on gang crime, we continue to lay a foundation for a reconsideration of the programs and policies for gang control—as these may be informed by the patterns revealed by recent research.

Two

GANG CRIME PATTERNS

Gang crime, and particularly violence, is the primary rationale for gang control policy and programs. Recent scholarship has documented the dire consequences of gang participation for those individuals' adult lives: unstable employment, early pregnancy and parenthood, dysfunctional family relationships, poverty, and drug abuse (Hagedorn, 1988; Moore, 1991; Thornberry et al., 2003). However, it is the crimes committed by gang members, the fear that gangs engender in community residents, and the social harm and injury caused by gang involvement that most often is used to justify enormous public expenditure for specialized gang enforcement, prosecution, and punishment, as well as for prevention and intervention programs.

New information about the patterns of gang crime has come to light since the 1990s, research findings that lend new direction to gang policy and programs. In this chapter, we build upon the previous discussion of gang prevalence and proliferation with an overview of recent findings about gang crime and changes in the lethality and patterns of gang violence. This research addresses such issues as the volume and type of gang crime and the sequencing of criminal activity over periods of gang participation and desistance. Gang homicide, gun use, and drug sales are key topics in policy debates about gang crime. Finally, we diverge from our primary focus on criminal offending to look briefly at the crime victimization of gang members and the public's fear of gang crime to offer a different perspective on the impact of gang activity. Our final discussion highlights the implications for gang response strategies of this recent research.

As we move through our presentation of current knowledge on the patterns of gang crime, three points serve as foreground to our discussion. First and foremost, we need to recognize that gang members spend much more time hangin' than bangin'. While observers of gangs note that talk about past and future crime exploits are the coin of the realm of gang membership (Klein, 1995a; Decker and Van Winkle, 1996; Fleisher, 1998), the activity that generates our attention to gangs encompasses a fairly narrow slice of the typical gang member's day or night.

The second point is methodological: how we define and measure gang crime is subject to a panoply of concerns. All of the issues of the definition and measurement of gangs and gang members presented in the introduction and chapter 1 apply directly here, for how are we to grasp the patterns of gang criminal behavior without full recognition of the implications of which groups are called "gangs" and which individuals are deemed "gang members"? This applies equally to studies that rest upon subjects' self-identification of gang membership as to those that utilize law enforcement records. Self-report studies are subject to criticism of their validity and reliability about both gang membership and accounts of criminal behavior. Law enforcement data are limited on both counts as well, exacerbated by the fact that only selected individuals and a small slice of all crime comes to the attention of police. Ethnographic accounts benefit from the expertise of the observer; while they are more limited in producing knowledge that might be generalized, they may suffer less from concerns about the validity of measurement than other approaches.

Coupling gang membership and crime magnifies these definitional, identification, and recording problems. On the law enforcement side, the recording of gang crime is often limited to a narrow range of offenses, those supported by practitioners' wisdom as stereotypically gang. We confronted this practice in a national study on the varieties of gang structures (Klein and Maxson, 1996) that we'll describe in more detail in chapter 5. Our intention of constructing crime profiles on individual gang structures was undermined by the discovery that most departments that maintained records on crimes with gang offenders had limited the crimes tracked to just a handful of offenses, primarily violence. To illustrate the deficit of limited offense recording, Table 2.1 provides the arrest profiles of five gangs sent to us by police agencies in different cities. The first two gangs display the full panoply of offenses we requested, although the patterns differ substantially. The balances of violent to nonviolent offenses seem reasonable, and there is no obvious selectivity for stereotypically gang-like offenses. The other three profiles quite obviously fall short of expectations.

TABLE 2.1. *Illustrative Gang Arrest Profiles for 1994*

Profile #	**339**	**20**	**709**	**462**	**24**
Homicide	2	0	0	0	0
Rape	1	0	0	0	0
Robbery	10	6	12	1	8
Assault	79	9	30	10	8
Burglary	31	10	4	0	0
Larceny/theft	9	7	0	0	2
Motor vehicle theft	5	2	2	0	6
Arson	1	0	0	0	0
Graffiti	43	2	3	5	0
Drug sales	1	2	1	0	9
Use & possession	33	7	22	1	18
Public disorder	79	4	0	0	24
Weapons	24	3	12	7	6
Petty theft	38	13	0	0	2
Forgery, counterfeiting, etc.	42	0	0	0	0
Hate crimes	0	0	0	0	0
Status offenses	217	9	0	0	0
Other	407	0	23	8	0
TOTAL	1,022	74	109	32	83

Source: Klein and Maxson, 1996.

Petty thefts, status offenses, burglary, and larceny are all but nonexistent; imagine gangs whose members engage in none of these activities! By contrast, violence and drug offenses predominate; the stereotype is reflected in the recording practices.

Naturally, one would conclude from analyses such as those derived from the second group of arrest profiles that the vast proportion of gang crime was violent, as some researchers who rely on such reports have inaccurately stated.[1] Such a conclusion would only serve to reinforce the stereotype, unless analyses were based on a wide range of possible offenses, from minor to serious, including property, drug, and public disorder crimes along with weapon use, robberies, assaults, and homicides. Our sense is that for purposes of understanding gang crime, with the exception of gang homicide, the self-report studies are superior. Surveys of youth capture the full range of types of crime, but are limited by the omission of gang crimes committed by adults.

We can add a further methodological quandary: whether to count any crime committed by a gang member—past, present, or future—as a gang crime, or whether only those crimes directly related to gang membership should be counted and studied as gang crime (see Maxson and Klein, 1996; Maxson, 1998a, for a discussion of gang-member versus motive-designation practices). Law enforcement agencies differ in their designation policies, and clearly the approach adopted affects the scope of crime that is used as the basis for depictions of gang crime. This distinction also has implications for the development of legislative approaches to gang control, as with California's S.T.E.P. Act described in the introduction. Illustrating the continued application of this sentencing enhancement law, assistant public defender Denise Gregg argues, "This law isn't used as it should be used. Just because a person is in a gang, then has a fit of temper one night and does something bad, that doesn't mean he deserves a special penalty" (Luna, 2004: B3).

The final point to keep in mind regarding both law enforcement and self-report data on gang crime is that neither type tells us much about patterns of crime on the *group* level. Ethnographic studies, such as Fleisher's (1998) observations of the Fremont Hustlers, contribute vivid accounts of the range of criminal involvement in particular gangs. Self-report and in-depth interview studies sometimes query subjects about illegal activities in their gangs, but patterns are reported by individual, rather than by gang (e.g., Freng and Winfree, 2004; Peterson, Miller, and Esbensen, 2001; J. Miller, 2001; Decker and Van Winkle, 1996). Our frustrated attempt to secure offending profiles for street gangs from law enforcement illustrates the limitations of police records on this topic. Anecdotal comments by law enforcement or correctional officers and portrayals of gang crime in the media don't serve our purposes of a systematic description of current research data for policy purposes. With these caveats stated, we turn first to a discussion of the available research on the patterns of criminal involvement of gang members.

Crime Committed by Gang Members

The most enduring finding in gang research is that youth who join gangs commit more crime than those who do not. If recent studies merely confirmed this pattern, first observed decades ago, we'd have little more to say. This is not the case, as these new studies have taken the analysis of crime patterns much further than in the past: to larger, more-representative samples, to more appropriate and varied comparison groups, to longitudinal approaches that capture changes in offending patterns from early adolescence into young adulthood, and to replications of findings across different studies. The questions addressed with these more-sophisticated methods have become more nuanced. While this work continues, we find a critical mass of evidence on the crime patterns of gang members that should inform policy and programs.

Let's look first at the range of conditions under which the "gang members commit more crime" assertion holds up. Youth who tell researchers that they are gang members at some point in their adolescence report a higher prevalence of committing most types of offenses and committing those offenses more frequently than do other youth, whether the period captured is the previous year or their lifetime (Thornberry et al., 2003; J. Miller, 2001; Huff, 1998; Fagan, 1990; Esbensen and Huizinga, 1993; Esbensen, Winfree, He, and Taylor, 2001; Battin et al., 1998; Maxson, Whitlock, and Klein, 1998; Curry et al., 2002; Gordon et al., 2004, are representative citations from studies with community or school samples in different U.S. cities). This finding holds up in studies of European gang members (Bradshaw, 2005; Esbensen and Weerman, 2005; Huizinga and Schumann, 2001) and Canadian gang members (Gatti et al., 2005; Lacourse, Nagin, Tremblay, Vitaro, and Claes, 2003). It holds up in surveys of incarcerated adolescents and adults in the United States and elsewhere (Bennett and Holloway, 2004; LeBlanc and Lanctot, 1998; Katz et al., 2005; Sheley and Wright, 1995; Decker, 2000; Cox, 1996). Further, it holds up when gang members are compared with highly delinquent, nongang street offenders (Esbensen and Huizinga, 1993; Thornberry, 1998) and with nongang youths with delinquent friends (Battin et al., 1998; Bradshaw, 2005; Gatti et al., 2005; Gordon et al., 2004).

Moreover, the relationship between gangs and offending is robust across a wide variety of definitions of *gang*. As we described in chapter 1, some of the studies cited above constrain the definition to groups involved in illegal activities, with some degree of structural organization, or with group identifiers or symbols, while others use an unrestricted definition.

Specific tests of the gang-crime relationship across different categories of group definitions reveal a progression: the more restricted the definition, the stronger the differences between gang and nongang crime patterns (Esbensen, Winfree, et al., 2001; Bradshaw, 2005; Dukes et al., 1997; cf. Winfree, Fuller, et al., 1992). Similar patterns appear in investigations of varying levels of gang membership or involvement. Individuals who deny gang membership but have gang friends, who identify themselves as wanting to be a gang member or as being a gang "associate," or who engage in symbolic gang activities like throwing gang signs and wearing gang colors have offending profiles that are lower than gang members and higher than noninvolved youth (Dukes et al., 1997; Curry et al., 2002; Katz et al., 2005). Core gang members have the highest offending profiles (Esbensen, Winfree, et al., 2001; Klein, 1995a; cf. Esbensen and Huizinga, 1993).

The relationship is robust across different measurements of offending. The studies cited above all use the subjects' own accounts of criminal involvement, but the gang-crime relationship also holds when arrests are considered: gang members are more likely to have an arrest and also to be arrested multiple times (Battin et al., 1998; Battin-Pearson, Thornberry, Hawkins, and Krohn, 1998; Curry, 2000; Thornberry et al., 2003).

Thornberry (1998) cast new light on the gang-crime relationship by assessing the contribution of gang members to the volume of delinquency reported over the course of adolescence in longitudinal samples in Rochester, Seattle, and Denver. While crimes are grouped in slightly different ways, the analysis reveals that gang members commit a disproportionate share of every type of offense in each city. The highest differentials are evident in the most serious offenses in each city: gang members committed 85% of all robberies reported by the youth sample in Seattle; 79% of all serious, violent crimes and 87% of all drug sales in Denver; and 86% of all serious offenses and 70% of all drug sales events in Rochester. In contrast, results from the National Crime Victimization Survey produce far lower estimates of the proportion of violent crime committed by gang members. Between 1998 and 2003, victims of violent crime perceived that perpetrators were gang members in about 6% of nonfatal violent acts (Harrell, 2005).

But gang members do *not* specialize in violent offending. On the contrary, the cumulative percentage of property offending reported by gang members in Rochester—representing 30% of study youth—is identical to the percentage of violent crimes (68%) and just slightly higher than the percentage of street, public disorder, or alcohol or drug use events (60–

64%; Thornberry, 1998). In a comparison of patterns of offending among gang and nongang youth in Dutch and U.S. youth samples, Esbensen and Weerman (2005) find that gang members are four to six times more likely to engage in minor and serious delinquent acts than nongang youth. Although some research suggests that gangs may be categorized by distinct offending profiles (Fagan, 1989), the current work on this topic confirms that gang member offending is generalist in nature, spanning the range of the cafeteria of delinquency choices (Thompson, Brownfield, and Sorenson, 1996; Esbensen and Huizinga, 1993; Esbensen and Winfree, 1998; Thornberry, 1998; Thornberry et al., 2003; Esbensen, Peterson, Freng, and Taylor, 2002; Curry et al., 2002; Gordon et al., 2004).

The cafeteria pattern appears to transcend sex and race/ethnicity categories. Girls who join gangs display the same variegated pattern of offending as boys. Although the sheer volume of criminal involvement is somewhat lower than that of their male counterparts, gang girls' offending approximates or, in some studies, exceeds that of nongang males (Deschenes and Esbensen, 1999; Esbensen, Deschenes, and Winfree, 1999; Esbensen and Winfree, 1998; Thornberry et al., 2003; Maxson and Whitlock, 2002). Other research suggests that the sex balance within a gang is important in shaping the delinquent activities of gang members. Peterson et al. (2001) found that girls in all-female or mostly female gangs report less delinquency than do girls in gangs that are mixed or majority male. Similarly, males in all-male gangs report less offending than do males in sex-balanced or majority male gangs. Esbensen and his colleagues (1999) note that since the age at which boys and girls participate in gangs may differ (girls are thought to age out of gangs earlier), studies that focus on older adolescents likely underestimate the volume and diversity of female gang offending. In the Rochester study, the age at which either boys or girls joined gangs did not affect either the volume or pattern of offending (Thornberry et al., 2003). This lends further credence to the growing body of evidence that the gang-crime relationship is robust among both girls and boys.

Few study samples have sufficient representations of black, Hispanic, Asian, and white gang members to permit comparisons of offending profiles among gang youth. Two analyses of a multisite sample of 6,000 eighth-grade students found little difference among gang members of different ethnic groups and no evidence of offense specialization (Esbensen and Winfree, 1998; Freng and Winfree, 2004). While other studies have conducted more limited ethnic comparisons, there is no consistent evidence of ethnic differences in self-reported criminal offending by gang members in the literature published since 1990.

Without doubt, gang members within the same gang commit different levels and types of crime, and the crime profiles of individual gangs vary considerably. Nevertheless, our review of the recent research on gang membership and crime shows that "gang" trumps sex or ethnic division. It trumps variations in study samples, gang definitions, and measurement approaches. Youth who participate in gangs commit a wide range of offenses and far more of them than their nongang counterparts.

Modeling the Gang-Crime Relationship

The crime patterns discussed thus far have not differentiated offending during periods of active gang membership as compared with the time before or after gang participation. Thornberry's depiction of the volume of crime attributed to youth who become involved at some point during adolescence in gangs is startling when we reconsider that these longitudinal studies also reveal that the period of gang participation is limited to one year or less for the majority of gang members in these samples. Additional analyses of the Rochester data (Thornberry et al., 2003) establish that gang members contribute disproportionately to the volume of delinquency during each year of active gang membership. Comparisons of offending levels by short-term, or transitional, gang members with more stable gang members confirm the strong association between gang involvement and crime (see Craig et al., 2002, for confirmation in a preadolescent sample in Quebec, Canada). But are the elevated crime profiles observed in gang members solely a function of gang participation?

In 1993, two groups of researchers published initial attempts to sort out the temporal ordering between gang membership and delinquency. Thornberry et al. (1993) offered three models to account for the gang-crime relationship among Rochester youth. Each had a conceptual foundation and prior empirical support to make it a plausible explanation. The *selection* model argues that gangs do not cause delinquency; members bring high offending profiles with them and are in fact recruited for this reason. Offending by gang members would be consistently high before, during, and after active periods of gang participation and higher than among youth who don't join gangs. Alternatively, the *social facilitation* model posits that gang members' offending profiles are similar to other youth before they join the gang, and it is the gangs' group processes, which we elaborate in chapter 5, that elevate criminal activity. When gang members are no longer active, their delinquency patterns should return to nongang rates. The *enhancement* model predicts that both selection and facilitation are at work: gang members will display higher criminality prior to gang participation, but during the active period, offending patterns will increase substantially. When no longer active, this model suggests that offending would decrease but still remain higher than nongang rates.

This is a complex analysis since it requires comparisons between gang and nongang youth as well as individual offending patterns over temporal periods before, during, and after gang participation. Moreover, these researchers replicated the analysis for transient and stable gang members and also assessed patterns of prevalence and the frequency of violent, property, drug use, and drug sales crimes and a combined measure of general delinquency.

The results for general delinquency, violence, drug sales, and drug use were supportive of the social facilitation explanation, particularly for short-term gang members. Thornberry and his colleagues open the door for enhancement as an explanation for general delinquency among stable gang members but emphasize facilitation in interpreting most of the patterns. Consistent and strong evidence for facilitation was apparent in analyses of violent crimes. Property crime patterns did not fit any of the models tested. Overall, the results of this study point to the influence of the gang and criminogenic group processes as the primary generators of crime rather than individual crime propensity.

Esbensen and Huizinga (1993: 567) posed the research question: "Are gang members more delinquent because of their gang affiliation or were they predisposed to delinquent activity prior to their gang affiliation?" Testing both prevalence and individual offending rates, these researchers concluded that gang members in Denver displayed higher levels of crime activity both before and during the period in which they were gang members, but they emphasized that activity was particularly pronounced during the active years of gang involvement. Upon disassociation with the gang, offending decreased but was still higher than that of youths who never belonged to a gang. This pattern was noted in two separate offense scales of serious crimes. In contrast, drug use by gang members was elevated only during the period of active gang involvement. Borrowing Thornberry's model terms, the Denver analyses were most consistent with an enhancement interpretation of the gang-crime relationship, but drug use followed the facilitation pattern.

The Denver and Rochester studies produced somewhat different conclusions. Although neither work found evidence for pure selection, the Rochester team embraced the facilitation model while the Denver researchers determined that both selection and facilitation processes were at work and, hence, fell into the enhancement camp. Science loves conflicting evidence, so during the next decade, researchers mobilized to test these models or to frame interpretations of their findings as supportive of one explanation over the other.

The subsequent direct tests of the three models were conducted with data from Montreal, Pittsburgh, and the Rochester youth samples. Conclusions about the gang-crime interaction in Montreal, however, are obscured by the inclusion of delinquent, nongang groups within the gang status (see chapter 1). In Montreal, one team determined that the mixed, enhancement model best explained the violence patterns among youth who affiliated with delinquent groups relatively early (ages 11–14) in adolescence (Lacourse et al., 2003). However, facilitation appeared the best-fitting model for youth who tended to affiliate with groups later in the teen years (ages 14–17). A later analysis declared support for the enhancement model for both violent and property crimes among stable gang members and for facilitation in transient gang members (Gatti et al., 2005). In this study, none of the models explained the patterns of drug use or sales. An extensive analysis of data from Pittsburgh youth led researchers to conclude that enhancement was the appropriate model for violence, property crime, drug sales, and drug use, although they found more selection effects than did prior studies (Gordon et al., 2004). Finally, further analysis of the Rochester data determined that while some selection effects were evident for general delinquency and violence, strong facilitating effects were the dominant pattern for these types of crimes and particularly for drug sales (Thornberry, 1998; Thornberry et al., 2003). Weak facilitating influences seemed to be operating for drug use.

Other studies have used this model framework to interpret findings about the effects of prior delinquency and delinquent peers among other risk factors for gang membership and for the effect of gang membership on subsequent offending (Battin et al., 1998; Lahey et al., 1999; Hill et al., 1999). Additionally, some studies infer these model processes by assessing offending levels among never-gang-involved individuals, those who would like to be involved or who display other gang behaviors or associations, former gang members, and current gang members (Dukes et al., 1997; Katz et al., 2005). These studies typically find support for the mixed, enhancement model (cf. Katz et al., 2005). The violent victimization of gang members also appears to fit the enhancement pattern (Peterson, Taylor, and Esbensen, 2004).

There's a positive message in the lower offending patterns among former gang members evident in most studies. Criminal activity reduces substantially when youth are no longer active in gangs. These findings call into question the practice of many gang researchers, including this volume's authors, who typically group current and former gang members together for analysis purposes.

This stream of research urges two directions for policy and gang practice. First, there are strong, independent effects of gang membership on crime. Clearly, something goes on within the group context that aggravates offending patterns of all kinds, and thus group process becomes a major area for discussion in chapter 5. Intervention with gang members requires that we recognize and address these group processes in our attempts to reduce levels of gang participation. Second, prior involvement in delinquent behavior is a clear risk factor for gang joining. Whether one interprets this as the active recruitment into gangs of "birds of a feather" or as one dimension of a cluster of social indicators that place youth in a vulnerable position to join gangs, early involvement in delinquency provides a marker of sorts for targeted gang prevention efforts. Not all such youth will join gangs; in fact, as will be shown in our discussion of risk factor research in chapter 4, *most will not.* Thus, gang practitioners need to exercise extreme caution in devising programs that rely on the evidence for the selection component of the enhancement model. One additional cautionary note is appropriate here: much of the data discussed in this section derives from studies in cities that do not have long-standing gang problems. The findings from Rochester, Pittsburgh, Denver, Seattle, and Montreal may not hold for youth in Los Angeles or Chicago.

Other Gang-Crime Issues: Violence, Homicide, Guns, and Drug Sales

Typically, gangs and gang members do not specialize in violent offending, but that is not to deny the centrality of violence to gang membership. Quite the contrary. In his study of 99 active gang members in St. Louis, Decker (1996) notes that violence was mentioned 1,681 times, second only to drugs as the most frequent interview topic. While gang members talk about violence often, and violence serves important symbolic functions within the gang, qualitative studies of gang activity note that collective gang violence is a relatively rare occurrence and is not well organized (Klein, 1995a; Fleisher, 1998; J. Miller, 2001). As Decker summarized, "Such [gang] violence, especially retaliatory violence, is an outgrowth of a collective process that reflects the loose organizational structure of gangs, with diffuse goals, little allegiance among members, and few leaders" (1996: 263). Despite this characterization, gang violence happens often enough to be a focal concern of many public officials, community service practitioners, and researchers. And despite its rarity within the full continuum of gang violence, we may know more about gang homicide than any other form of gang violence. Police investigate homicides more thoroughly than other crimes, and thus more information is available from records to researchers and to national statistical recording systems.

The definitional issues we've noted throughout this book constrain any discussion of a national depiction of the volume and recent trends in gang homicide. The gang circumstances category of the Supplementary Homicide Reports (SHRs) to the FBI's Uniform Crime Reports data system approximates the gang-motivated approach to defining gang homicide. The U.S. Bureau of Justice Statistics' Web site (www.ojp.usdoj.gov/bjs) displays the number of homicides with gang, felony, argument, other, and unknown circumstances from 1976 through 2002 (last revised on September 26, 2004). According to this source and definition, national gang homicides increased from 129 in 1976 to a high of 1,362 in 1993 (with just 4 years within this 18-year period showing a decrease from the previous year). Gang homicides then decreased each year to 834 in 1998, before rising each year to 1,119 in 2002. While this most-recent rise reflects a 34% increase over the recent low point in 1998, the homicides with gang circumstances in 2002 represent slightly less than 7% of all homicides and about 10% of all homicides with known circumstances. Arguments and felony circumstances without gang involvement account for far more homicides in each year reported. In California, Tita and Abrahamse (2004) found that gang killings accounted for 16% of all homicides between 1981 and 2001.

Each year, the National Youth Gang Survey (NYGS) gathers counts of gang homicides from a nationally representative sample of respondents. The NYGS figures are not directly comparable to the SHR system, due to different agency samples and data specifications. For example, the 1997 figure from SHR is 12% higher than the NYGS total of gang-motivated homicides, but the 1998 SHR figure is 8% lower (see Maxson, Curry, and Howell, 2002, for NYGS totals). Analyses of NYGS gang homicide data reveal an expected pattern of concentration in U.S. cities with large populations. The most current NYGS figures are displayed in Table 2.2. In this table, the highest figure reported in either the 2002 or 2003 NYGS is used, due to the large number of agencies that aren't able to report a specific count. Also, we should note that these figures reflect homicides in which gang members were involved, rather than only incidents that were motivated by gang issues. Except for the largest population category, the most frequent response is zero gang homicides. Slightly less than 40% of agencies in cities with 250,000 or more people report at least 10 gang homicides. Other analyses of NYGS homicide data confirm the strong relationship between population size and gang homicides (Maxson et al., 2002; Howell, Egley, and Gleason, 2002).

In their analysis of city-by-city trends using the NYGS and other national surveys, Maxson et al. (2002) note that national trend estimates mask important and sometimes contrasting trends in individual cities. Moreover, a substantial proportion of any national gang homicide figure is driven by the counts from Los Angeles and Chicago. For example, 71% of the decrease in national gang homicides from 1996 to 1998 was derived from declining numbers in these two cities. Tita and Abrahamse (2004) found that 75% of the gang homicides in California over a 21-year period occurred in Los Angeles County. They determined that the increase in statewide homicides from 1999 to 2001 was solely a function of more gang killings in Los Angeles County.

Gang homicide trends are distinct from those evident in other types of homicides. Historically, the proportion of all homicides in Chicago and

TABLE 2.2. *Annual Maximum Percentage of Gang-Related Homicides Reported in Gang Problem Areas, 2002 or 2003 NYGS*

Annual Maximum Number of Gang-Related Homicides Reported, 2002 or 2003	**Cities 250,000 or more**	**Cities 100,000–249,999**	**Cities 50,000–99,999**	**Cities 2,500–49,999**	**Suburban Counties**	**R C**
No data reported	19.4	6.7	5.8	2.9	14.1	11
0	6.0	33.6	60.9	85.0	59.8	76
1 or 2	9.0	27.5	24.6	10.4	14.4	12
3–9	26.9	24.2	8.3	1.7	10.1	0
10 or more	38.8	8.1	0.4	0.0	1.6	0
N	*67*	*149*	*276*	*173*	*306*	*71*

Source: Egley, 2005. Printed by permission from National Youth Gang Center.

Los Angeles has changed from year to year (Block and Block, 1995; Tita and Abrahamse, 2004; Maxson, 1998a). Trends in gang homicide don't seem to be mere mirrors of nonlethal violent gang activity although there is a strong correlation between gang homicides and gang assaults (0.728, as reported in Block and Block, 1995). We don't know the degree to which trends in gang homicide may be attributable to changes in the number of active gang members. While a complete explanation of changes in the volume of lethal gang activity eludes researchers, gang homicides appear to be a function of spurts in gang rivalries, turf battles, and other affiliation challenges.

In a series of studies comparing gang and nongang homicide characteristics in Los Angeles, we have established a wide variety of differences between the two (Maxson, Gordon, and Klein, 1985; Maxson and Klein, 1996; Maxson, 1998). Gang homicides are more likely to take place on the street, to involve firearms, and to have more participants of younger ages, who are more often male. Victims and offenders less often have a clear prior personal relationship in gang cases. Motor vehicles are more often present in gang homicides, and the homicides tend to occur in the late afternoon and evening rather than late at night. The presence of more participants in gang incidents leads to other differences: more injuries and additional violent charges. In general, these differences have also emerged in analyses of the two types of homicides in Chicago (Spergel, 1995) and in St. Louis (Decker and Curry, 2002a; Rosenfeld et al., 1999). However, gang homicides without gang motives looked more like nongang homicides than gang-motivated incidents in St. Louis, while the two types of gang homicides were similar in Los Angeles (Rosenfeld et al., 1999; Maxson and Klein, 1996).

Among the various characteristics that distinguish gang incidents, researchers have taken particular interest in the use of firearms. In an assessment of gang homicides in Los Angeles County between 1979 and 1994, medical researchers determined that the proportion of these incidents where firearms were used increased from 71% to 95% (Hutson et al., 1995). Handguns were the most frequent type of weapon used in these killings, but gang homicide by semiautomatic handguns rose from 5% in 1986 to 44% in 1994. Klein reports a figure of 61% use of firearms in gang homicides in the late 1960s for both Philadelphia and East Los Angeles, and observes, "The contrast with the present is striking. Firearms are now standard. They are easily purchased or borrowed and are more readily available than in the past" (1995a: 73). Noting the absence of reliable data, Fagan (1996) asserted a "broad agreement" of an increased access to gang members in the number and sophistication of firearms, and he cites his own research for evidence that gang members carry guns in anticipation of encountering the "smallest interpersonal slight" (1996: 45). Despite media reports suggesting concerns about gang access to assault weapons, Hutson and his colleagues (1995) determined that they were used in less than 3% of the 7,288 gang homicides they studied. A separate analysis of 1,584 gang drive-by shootings in Los Angeles in 1991 found assault weapons used in just one incident (Hutson, Anglin, and Pratts, 1994).

Increased access to lethal weapons and an increased propensity to carry them for protection and self-defense have no doubt fueled the changes in homicide and other forms of gang violence that have been observed since the 1960s. Several analyses of the Rochester sample have advanced our understanding of these patterns. One study revealed a selection process in protective gun ownership: controlling for factors that might influence both gun ownership and gang membership, Bjerregaard and Lizotte (1995) found that protective gun ownership increased the probability of gang membership by 27%. A later study determined that gang membership is a strong predictor of gun carrying, but only until about age 16 (Lizotte et al., 2000). Beginning at age 17, when gang membership in this sample fell below 7%, a high level of involvement in drug sales was the primary determinant of illegal gun carrying.

Law enforcement officials and some researchers have argued that a nexus among gangs, drug sales, and violence fueled dramatic increases in gang violence from the mid-1980s. In particular, the advent of crack cocaine and police perceptions of widespread gang presence in the street-level distribution of this drug cemented the connection in the minds of many. Analyses of homicide in Los Angeles, as well as work in other cities, challenge this conventional wisdom. Drug motives in homicides involving gang members are far less frequent than conflict relationships between members of different gangs (Maxson and Klein, 1996; Decker and Curry, 2002a; Block and Block, 1995). Our analysis of Los Angeles homicides in the late 1980s found drug motives to be a less-powerful discriminator between gang and nongang homicides than 11 other characteristics (Maxson and Klein, 1996). In a sample of 1992 and 1993 homicides involving adolescents, just 6% were coded with drug motives, less than half of the still-low presence of drug motives in 14% of other homicides (Maxson, Klein, and Sternheimer, 2000). So while police officials often attribute lethal gang encounters to disputes over drug-trafficking issues, this view has rarely been upheld in empirical studies. Tita, Riley, and Greenwood (2003) describe their exercise to address police skepticism about their finding of drug motives in just 10% of gang homicides in the Hollenbeck area of Los Angeles. These researchers reviewed each homicide with the primary investigating detective; as a result, just 4 of the 90 cases were recoded, 3 to include a drug component and 1 to exclude a previously coded drug motive.

We have argued that gang dynamics trump drug issues in the commission of violence, even though the interview studies of youth samples disclose relatively high levels of drug sales by gang members. The adolescent life-course analysis of the Rochester sample by Lizotte and colleagues (2000) suggests that at younger ages, gang members participate in drug sales in a more recreational vein. As youth exit gangs, their drug sales activity drops dramatically. In Rochester, the drug sales–violence connection is much tighter among older youth who have never participated in gangs. The gang–drug sales–violence connection was overstated in the 1980s, and more recent evidence suggests a marked decline in drug-motivated homicide. This decline likely reflects shifts in drug market characteristics more generally (Cohen, Cork, Engberg, and Tita, 1998), but for our focus on gang policy, the gang–drug sales connection to violence now appears to be a dead issue.

Victimization and Fear of Gang Crime

The majority of victims of gang homicides and drive-by shootings are gang members (Maxson and Klein, 1996; Block and Block, 1995; Hutson et al., 1994). More than one dozen of the 99 gang members interviewed in St. Louis were killed within five years of the conclusion of the study (Decker, 1996); by March 2005, 33 had died (Decker, personal communication). Ethnographic and self-report studies of youth find that gang membership is just as strongly associated with violent victimization as it is with offending (Peterson et al., 2004; Vigil, 2002; Decker and Van Winkle, 1996; Curry et al., 2002; J. Miller, 2001; Fleisher, 1998; Freng and Winfree, 2004; Hagedorn, 1988). Gang participation adds to violent victimization risk over and above the additional risk from involvement in violent offending (Peterson et al., 2004). While protection and self-defense loom large among the reasons that gang members cite for joining gangs, it is an unfortunate irony that gang participation so increases victimization risk. Gang members who report they joined gangs to gain protection are just as likely to experience violent victimization as youths who join for other reasons, fully dispelling the notion that gangs provide "a safe haven" (Peterson et al., 2004: 813).

Recent work has focused upon the relative victimization risk of boys and girls in gangs. Joe and Chesney-Lind (1995) find in their Hawaii sample of gang members that the presence of girls depresses violence, but that even for girls, fighting and violence are part and parcel of gang life. In the San Francisco Bay Area, researchers found that the structures of groups to which female gang members belonged was an important determinant of victimization: females in groups that were auxiliaries to male gangs were exposed to violence both within and outside of their gangs, whereas females in the one wholly independent female gang they studied were confronted with violent situations only outside their gang (Hunt and Joe-Laidler, 2001; Joe-Laidler and Hunt, 1997).

Together with various colleagues, Jody Miller's work on the violent victimization experienced by young women in gangs is the most extensive. In a variety of studies, Miller has asserted that the sex composition of gangs shapes both the volume and nature of violent victimization (J. Miller and Brunson, 2000) and that young women employ gendered strategies to reduce their risk of victimization by rival gangs but thereby increase their risk of physical and sexual violence from fellow gang members (J. Miller, 2001, 1998; J. Miller and Decker, 2001). While female gang members experience less victimization than males as a result of lower offending profiles, Miller's interviews in St. Louis document exceptionally high levels of exposure to violence. Nearly all of the girls had seen guns shot (96%) or seen someone shot (89%) or killed (74%), and most had been threatened with a weapon (59%) or attacked (48%; J. Miller and Decker, 2001).

A different perspective on the negative consequences of gang crime is reflected in recent studies that focus on community residents' level of fear and on how fear of gangs may alter participation in community life. Fear of gang crime, like fear of crime more generally, need not flow directly from objective levels of crime. For example, a study of residents in five disadvantaged neighborhoods in San Bernardino, California, found that residents in an area that police had asserted repeatedly had minimal gang activity reported gang-crime fears at comparable levels to residents in areas with very active gangs (Maxson, Hennigan, and Sloane, 2005). Similarly, surveys of residents in Orange County, California, found that concerns about subcultural diversity, disorder, and community decline predicted fear of gang crime in a broad range of neighborhoods (Lane and

Meeker, 2003). A survey of residents in Mesa, Arizona, confirms and expands these results:

> [F]ear of gangs is not simply a consequence of, or in direct relation to, objective threat. As we observed in this study, fear of gangs was unrelated to living in a high-gang area, an area in which we know that gang membership is high and in which we presume that gang crime is also high. (Katz, Webb, and Armstrong, 2003: 123)

A different study employed focus groups of residents in Santa Ana, California, to illustrate how neighborhoods differ in their intensity of gang fear (Lane, 2002). The deleterious effects that gangs can exact on communities are evoked in the following quote from this study:

> In contrast, people living in the lower-income neighborhoods were confronted daily with the possibility of violent victimization by gangs in their own neighborhoods and in others (see Sanchez-Jankowski, 1991). Their fear was more urgent and intense. Each of them could cite personal experience with violent victimization and/or gangs or knew people who had been killed by gangs. They did sometimes have incapacitating fear: They stayed in their homes when it got dark and even during the day. Yet they did not describe their fear as a paralyzing one. Rather, taking precautions had become a normal part of their daily lives: avoiding areas, staying home or in their backyards, putting bars on their windows, restricting their children's activities, and wondering who would be hurt next. (Lane, 2002: 462)

The Orange County studies suggest that public officials' programs to increase community awareness of gang violence and their introduction of gang suppression efforts increased fear levels in community residents (Lane, 2002; Lane and Meeker, 2003). Citing other work regarding general fear of crime, these researchers argue that policy makers could make people feel safer by focusing on building and strengthening community ties rather than on suppressing gang crime. The community level of intervention figures prominently in our proposed framework of gang programs and policies, discussed in the final chapters.

Implications of Gang-Crime Research for Programs and Policy

The information we have about long-term trends in the proliferation of gangs and gang violence reveals a pattern of increased gang participation, fueling a rise in lethal gang activity. Since the mid-1970s, street gangs have exacted a high toll on their victims, their communities, and public resources. Yet gang proliferation and gang homicides appear to have hit a high-water mark in the United States in the mid-1990s; since then, gang activity has ebbed and flowed in patterns we don't fully understand. Theories that attempt to explain these trends might look to broad changes in economic factors, community characteristics, firearm availability, residential mobility, the diffusion of gang culture, and the nature of illegal drug markets, as well as broad trends in public policy. As existing theory does not lend a coherent explanation, what can we draw from the recent research on gang-crime patterns to help direct our discussion of gang programs and policy?

First, efforts that effectively reduce rates of joining gangs, reduce levels of association, or increase desistance from active gang participation would promote large reductions in the volume of youth crime. The research is clear on this point: active participation in street gangs facilitates crime in dramatic fashion. Social policies that have collateral effects of increasing gang participation will increase crime rates, and policies that reduce participation will decrease crime. Further, this research confirms that there is something special about the processes that take place in gangs that distinguish them from other delinquent groups. We'll address this issue more deeply in chapter 5.

Second, there is enough evidence for selection effects to argue that gang prevention efforts need to attack risk characteristics in the youth who join gangs. The challenge for effective programs and policy is to distill out the most powerful risk features that are vulnerable to manipulation and devise efforts to short-circuit the process of joining gangs. The discussion of risk factors and the attractions that gangs hold for youth in chapter 4 will further inform this point.

Third, gang offending is diverse offending. Current policies and programs are increasingly aimed at violence reduction, and while we readily embrace this goal, the focus on violence promotes the inaccurate stereotype of gang members as specialized, violent offenders. Gang members commit a lot of violence but also a lot of other crimes. Yet, an orientation toward violence is a quintessential dimension of the group process in gangs. The issue of violence per se in gang programming should be subject to more careful scrutiny.

Finally, relevant research on community residents reminds us that a narrow focus on gang offending neglects opportunities for intervention at the community level.

Some researchers have argued that we should turn our immediate efforts toward strategies that have been shown to reduce delinquency in other youth populations (Thornberry et al., 2003; Esbensen, 2000). However, such programs have not yet been shown to be effective with youth who join gangs, and if they did, a strict targeting of gang-specific risk factors in clients would be critical. Moreover, such programs fail to address the crime facilitation dimensions of gang participation. Our review of some gang programs in chapter 3 will reveal a history of failure and will highlight our thoughts about how gang research might inform an understanding of failed programs.

Three

SIX MAJOR GANG CONTROL PROGRAMS

In chapters 1 and 2, we offered two reasons that serious discussion of gang control programs must be undertaken. Very simply, gang problems have proliferated enormously, taking hold in many types of American communities. In addition, gang crime has not only become more widespread because of gang proliferation: it has also changed its character. The severity of the crime has grown. In this chapter, we offer a third reason for our effort, mainly, that large-scale gang programs now exist to provide guidance in gang control exercises.

We have selected these six programs in gang control because they are major, organized efforts and because they illustrate a wide range of approaches. In addition, all but one of them were explicitly designed to include full-scale evaluations, making them almost unique in large gang control programs since the 1960s. Evaluated programs yield the sorts of data we need to build more effective programs. They range from efforts at early prevention, to intervention in ongoing gang activity, to outright suppression of gangs and gang crime. All six are multimillion-dollar efforts, dwarfing prior piecemeal projects. All are, as this is written, ongoing efforts or only recently concluded. As such, they represent our national state of the art in major programs of gang control.

To aid in conceptualizing these six programs as to their origins, we will label two of them as ideological, one as political, and three as bureaucratic. These are not pure types. Indeed, one can discern ideological, political, and bureaucratic themes running through each of them. But recognizing the different sources of the programs' intentions helps us to understand why they were developed and why each source implies somewhat different problems for assessing the value of the six programs.

For example, both ideologically based programs were initiated by law enforcement agencies (including corrections, in one case). This gave them a strong police value system even though one was a suppression program and the other a prevention program. In both cases, the law enforcement perspective led to a narrow conception of street gangs and yielded an uncompromising police presence in the program, without recourse to alternative social and community resources. We will report on these two programs first: the "L.A. Plan" and the Gang Resistance, Education, and Training (G.R.E.A.T.) program.

The politically driven program was initiated by the attorney general of Illinois in response to a governor's commission. Attorney General Ryan, later a candidate himself for the governor's office, developed a special staff to mount a gang prevention program. That program consisted of a number of easy-to-swallow social and educational initiatives quite devoid of gang-related reasoning, and then abandoned evaluation attempts that might have assessed the program's success or failure. One gets the impression of more "face" than substance.

The three bureaucratic programs, although emanating from the offices of local or federal elected officials, were shaped and designed to meet the conventional wisdoms of the guiding agencies. In the case of L.A. Bridges, the agency responsible for the program design was a city bureaucracy, the Community Development Department of Los Angeles. In the case of the Spergel Model and SafeFutures programs, the agency was a branch of the U.S. Department of Justice, employing a program design developed at the University of Chicago. In each of these cases, the programs were comprehensive in design, but terribly complex and endangered by the multiple-agency format that each espoused. When confronted by multiple and conflicting agency values and habits, programs tend to develop escape routes through goal displacement and fuzzy conceptualizations that permit but may not guide accommodations among competing interests. All six of these major programs, then, were not simply rational responses to a well-understood gang problem. They were rooted in different origins that shaped their capacities to succeed.

There is, however, another series of control programs the reader may wish to review. Funded within the last decade by several federal agencies, most notably under the Anti-Gang Initiative of the COPS (Community

Oriented Police Services) program funded in 1994, they are mostly smaller and less comprehensive than our six. Many of the available reports are preliminary yet suggest both positive and negative outcomes. They are primarily police-initiated, police-led, or police-driven projects and therefore understandably have a strong emphasis on gang suppression. These projects are reported in Decker (2003). In the lead chapter of that book, Jack Greene comments on the effects of the heavy police presence in these projects:

> Individual officers' behavior and role identification are shaped by departmental organizations rather than by the problems to be solved. This results in the police agency itself being a powerful obstacle to effectively introducing problem solving for youth or other problems. Change in policing and police organizations has occurred at glacial speed. (Greene, 2003: 13)

The placement of our six programs in part I of this book, as with the contents of chapters 1 and 2, is determined by their contribution to the same theme: the need to entertain a new discussion about approaches to gang control. This is because, either by failures in program implementation or program effect, they are proving to be program failures.

What ties these six programs together, beyond their concern with gang problems, is their reliance on conventional wisdom, albeit quite different versions thereof. The term *conventional wisdom* refers to the combination of untested assumptions and relatively unchallenged facts that we normally take to represent truth. In criminology, we have many conventional wisdoms, some of them in direct conflict with each other. We can recognize them easily. They start with the phrase "It is obvious that . . ."

Thus, "it is obvious that" police discriminate against minorities; it is obvious that imprisonment creates more confirmed criminals; and it is obvious that rehabilitation doesn't work. Or, take the example of street gangs in the 1950s and 1960s in the United States. It was "obvious" to policy makers in that era that street gangs could be transformed and turned from their destructive pursuits by dedicated and streetwise workers. While tenets of differential association, culture conflict, and opportunity structure theories were supportive of the street worker approach, any but the most superficial reading of those theories would have warned against the conventional wisdom of street work programs. These theories each had much to say about neighborhood and community structure, about formal institutions of control, and about class-related value systems, but little of this was systematically incorporated into street work programs, which became dependent, instead, on the personal relationships between workers and gang members (Caplan, 1968; Carney, Mattick, and Callaway, 1969). For the most part, these programs, with their conventional wisdoms, became conventional failures (Klein, 1971).

Another gang-related conventional wisdom took hold in the 1980s and has been well entrenched ever since, despite a plethora of evidence that challenges it. It has been "obvious," especially among law enforcement officials, that drug sales and gang violence go hand in hand. As an illustration, we noted in chapter 2 that Braga, Kennedy, and Tita (2002) describe a study result showing that only 8 of 90 gang-motivated homicides included a drug component. But police were skeptical: "These kids are . . . being killed because of [dope]" (278). When this assertion forced a reanalysis of the data, a net of only 2 additional cases were coded as drug related. One can only wish that more conventional wisdoms would be subjected to empirical testing.

Generally in the 1980s, the emerging conventional wisdom concerning street gangs, mirroring the neoclassical writing then in vogue (Wilson, 1975; Van den Haag, 1975) and the sociopolitical conservatism of the Reagan and first Bush administrations, was based on deterrence theory. The gang transformation model was in decline, and the deterrence model in the ascendancy. In the arena of street gangs, this led to emphases on surveillance, parole revocation, violence control, and greater reliance on police and prosecution programs (Maxson and Klein, 1983). Yet, even the most cursory examination of deterrence theory would reveal that these programs, such as the L.A. Plan to be described here, concern themselves *only* with the conventional wisdoms associated with deterrence, not with such theoretical corollaries as have been spelled out by Gibbs (1975), Zimring and Hawkins (1973), and others. Concepts of celerity and certainty of punishment have not penetrated the punishment severity mentality to any significant degree; perceptions of punishment probabilities are assumed rather than manipulated; the communication of detection and conviction consequences remains an untouched policy option.

In the case of both the gang transformation model of street work projects and the deterrence model, the existence of relevant theories reveals the very limited value of the resulting programs because the programs are based principally only on the conventional wisdoms associated with those theories. Ironically, it is the theories which provide the material for exposing the inadequacies for policy of these conventional wisdoms.

American criminologists, far more than their European and other counterparts, have involved themselves in the empirical evaluation of public and private programs of crime control. Indeed, in criminology as well as other areas of social concern, evaluation research has become a significant growth industry in the United States. Taken together with the tendency for significant crime programs to claim themselves as exemplars of various theories, this emphasis on evaluation has greatly advanced our understanding of crime etiology and control. Theories that hold up to empirical test, theories that are modified by reference to program-derived data, and theories that must be largely abandoned because of a failure of empirical validation in field tests all advance our knowledge. They advance it because the programs we evaluate relate explicitly to these theories. Programs which do not relate to the theories can offer little but piecemeal tidbits following their evaluations. If we know more now about community organization, opportunity structures, peer relations, labeling, social bonding, and organizational control procedures, it is to a considerable extent true because we have had the opportunity to view these concepts as they have been articulated in evaluated programs. And it is these concepts, not the programs, that constitute our knowledge in criminology. Yet in the gang arena, programs such as the six described below are weak in theory and based almost exclusively on poorly supported conventional wisdoms.

Two Ideological Programs

The L.A. Plan

Our first program was called the L.A. Plan by a federal agency whose superficial review of gang control efforts in Los Angeles led it to see a set of activities with a consistent, even coordinated set of principles. That view was quite incorrect: there was no "plan," only a collection of suppression efforts supported by similar conventional wisdoms.

In 1980, gang-related homicides reached a then-unprecedented high of 351 throughout Los Angeles County. Alarmed officials initiated a series of relatively uncoordinated activities, most of which had the sole purpose of cracking down on street gang activity. The conventional wisdoms, in this case, were that prevention and social intervention attempts had failed, that gang violence had gotten out of control, and that gang suppression was the only viable approach under these circumstances. It was further believed that gang suppression would deter current and future gang activity. It would be tempting to say that gang suppression was based on the tenets of deterrence theory—severity of punishment, certainty of punishment, quickness of punishment, provision of acceptable alternative activities, credibility of the punishers in the eyes of the punished, and so on—but only severity was stressed, or perhaps seen as even possible, with a street gang population.

In an increasingly conservative political era, suppression had become accepted by many as right and proper and assumed to be successful. Indeed, when gang violence began to decrease in the fall of 1980, but before the Community Youth Gang Services project described below was implemented, the decrease was publicly attributed to CYGS by the member of the county board of supervisors responsible for overseeing the program. Others laid claim to contributing to this decrease as well, but became remarkably silent when gang homicides began their steady increase in 1983 (ending in 1995 with more than 800 gang-related homicides in that year and almost 8,000 after 15 years of suppression). Six activities typify the approach taken.

1. Community Youth Gang Services (CYGS). This was a "youth outreach program" based partially on the standard detached worker services seen in many other cities but with a most significant set of modifications. Street workers were no longer assigned to specific gangs, getting to know their members personally. Rather, they were assigned to broad areas in radio-dispatched cars in a fashion based on a similar Philadelphia project that made unsubstantiated claims for eliminating gang-related homicides in that city. Youth services formerly associated with detached workers were deemphasized in favor of area surveillance, rumor deflection, and conflict resolution. Attention to gang violence, specifically, replaced attention to the far broader range of gang member activities associated with earlier outreach programs. Opportunities to engage in independent evaluations of CYGS were overtly ignored, and it was this failure to evaluate that, after almost 17 years, led to the defunding of CYGS and application of its funding to L.A. Bridges, a program we will describe later.
2. OSS and CRASH. These acronyms refer, respectively, to the greatly expanded gang intelligence and control units in the Los Angeles Sheriff's Department (Operation Safe Streets) and the Los Angeles Police Department (Community Resources against Street Hoodlums). OSS placed more emphasis on gathering long-term gang intelligence for crime investigation purposes and

employed officers in civilian clothes with a mandate to become familiar with both gang members and their neighborhoods. CRASH placed more emphasis on suppression, with officers in uniform and clearly marked patrol cars. They were often rotated after several years without the opportunity to become as familiar with their targets as OSS officers. Thus, the LAPD operation was by design more deterrence-oriented and unabashedly suppressive. Both programs were—and remain today—oriented to cracking down on gang activity, especially gang violence.[1]

3. Operation Hammer. This aptly named LAPD activity used area sweeps to arrest and harass gang members, to "send the message" that gangs did not control their turfs. Operation Hammer started with a sweep of gang areas in south-central Los Angeles by a 1,000-officer force on two weekend nights, with full, planned media coverage and special arrangements to process the hundreds of arrestees that were swept up. As it turns out, many arrestees were not gang members, others were subject to outstanding warrants that could have been served in other ways, and the resulting convictions were few and far between. The police arrested 1,435 people, and 1,350 were released without charges; almost half were not gang members, and less than 2% had felony charges filed (Klein, 1995a). The continuation of Hammer, employing only hundreds of officers, yielded similarly questionable short-term results. No overall evaluation was attempted, but the LAPD slowly abandoned the operation in the face of rising criticism and an inability to document the utility of such massive and complex operations.
4. Operation Hardcore. This was a concentrated effort to build a special prosecution unit within the district attorney's office devoted solely to the conviction of gang leaders and perpetrators of serious gang offenses. As time passed and gang homicides continued to rise, the unit was forced to expend its energies almost completely on homicide cases; that remains its primary function today. Included in Operation Hardcore are vertical prosecution (i.e., one deputy carries the case from initiation to conclusion), avoidance of plea bargains, special expertise in gang search warrants, witness protection programs, and special training in gang matters for Hardcore prosecutors. An early evaluation (Dahmann, 1982) indicated a remarkably high con-

viction rate of Hardcore defendants, but no attempt has been made to assess the effects of the operation on other gang members. It has simply been assumed (as with Operation Hammer) that the deterrence message has been passed.

5. Correctional gang caseloads. Both the Los Angeles Probation Department and the California Youth Authority (in charge of parolees) developed special gang units in which each officer maintained a deliberately reduced caseload of gang members only. These officers' mandates had little to do with reintegrating their clients into the community via employment, schooling, counseling, or other social services. Rather, the mandate was—and still is—to maintain close surveillance on the gang members on their caseload and to "violate" them (send them back to court or incarceration) for failure to abide by their probation or parole provisions. Officers are aided in this process by legislation which permits searches of persons and property without warrants. Often, these officers and the police join together in gang member surveillance and arrests. No independent evaluation of the gang caseload program has been performed to our knowledge.
6. Interagency task force. Early in the life of the above activities, an interagency task force was formed to increase collaboration and coordination among the justice system agencies dealing with gang suppression. As we observed in several task force meetings, they were less about collaboration and coordination and more about sharing information on wanted suspects and fugitives, telling "war stories," and similar informal contacts.[2] Yet it was the existence of this task force that led to the idea that there was an L.A. Plan in the minds of staff at the Office of Juvenile Justice and Delinquency Prevention (OJJDP), an arm of the U.S. Department of Justice. It was the result of this OJJDP observation that led eventually to the comprehensive Spergel Model and SafeFutures programs to be described later in this chapter.

Nothing has driven these activities in Los Angeles more than a conservative ideology, a conventional wisdom that suppressive crackdowns, punishment, and "sending the message" will reduce gang crime. Nothing is built into these activities that acknowledges the special group structures and processes of street gangs (Klein, 1995a; Decker and Van Winkle, 1996;

Moore, 1978, 1991; Hagedorn, 1988; Short and Strodtbeck, 1965). No interest was shown in prevention or treatment responses. No attempt has been made to draw in or collaborate with community resources. No independent evaluations of the Los Angeles efforts have attested to their utility, while rising gang violence provides little support. Yet the programs continue and develop new variations. Among the latter are various pieces of antigang legislation and antigang abatement and injunction programs (see Klein, 1995a; Maxson, Hennigan, and Sloane, 2005), mostly unevaluated. As the old saying goes, "don't confuse me with the facts; my mind's made up." There is comfort in conventional wisdom and ideology.[3]

What the L.A. Plan illustrates for us is that there is a strong need to develop gang control programs that incorporate *knowledge* about gangs. Perhaps 30 years ago that would have been problematic. Gang knowledge was fragmented, city- or gang-specific, and of unknown reliability. This is no longer true. One can turn now to very effective summaries of reliable gang knowledge as noted earlier (Covey, Menard, and Franzese, 1997; Curry and Decker, 1998; Huff, 1990, 1996, 2002; Klein, 1995a; Klein, Maxson, and J. Miller, 1995; J. Miller, Maxson, and Klein, 2001; Spergel, 1995). The chapters in part II of this book are an attempt to lay out yet more recent information about street gangs that makes these groups more understandable and subject to more effective interventions. Gang membership patterns, gang structures and group processes, and community contexts are the subjects of new and often comparative research that we will cover. In addition, comparisons of gang and nongang patterns are now more available, adding some certainty to our assertions about the special nature of street gangs.

The G.R.E.A.T. Program

Like the L.A. Plan, G.R.E.A.T. was initiated primarily by law enforcement agencies, but there the similarities stop. G.R.E.A.T., the acronym for Gang Resistance, Education, and Training, was applied nationwide; it was strictly designed for prevention, not suppression of gang activities. It was clearly based on a prior program—D.A.R.E.—already implemented nationwide. We need to digress briefly to discuss D.A.R.E. (Drug Awareness, Resistance, and Education), a remarkably failed program with a remarkably positive public relations image. The fact that G.R.E.A.T., the gang prevention program, was modeled on a failed program with a positive image is, itself, a study in the application of conventional wisdoms in the face of contrary empirical knowledge.

D.A.R.E. was initiated in 1983 by the Los Angeles Police Department with the collaboration of the Los Angeles Unified Schools. It consisted of a series of in-school lectures, delivered initially in the primary grades, consisting of a general life skills curriculum along with information about the nature of illicit drugs, their effects, and how to resist their temptations (including peer pressure issues). The lessons were delivered in regular classes by specially trained, uniformed police officers. Within 10 years, D.A.R.E. had become less a program than a social movement, finding acceptance in almost 80% of the nation's schools. It had (and in truth still has) a high level of acceptance from teachers, parents, police, and politicians from the local to the federal level. White House and congressional support have been manifest. Yet its content was based largely on another failure, Project Smart in the L.A. schools: "They ripped off our materials," reported Project Smart's developer, Robert Hanson, and "they took a version of the program that we had radically revamped because it wasn't working" (cited in Boyle, 2001: 16).

A common problem arose: D.A.R.E. had failed to arrange for a careful, predesigned or controlled research evaluation. When questions were raised about the program's claims for success in drug use reduction or prevention, some evaluations were funded by federal agencies: two of these were of special importance. In 1993, the Research Triangle Institute undertook a careful meta-analysis of eight existing studies, comparing D.A.R.E.'s outcomes with those from comparable programming (Ennett, Tobler, Ringwalt, and Flewelling, 1994). The results showed almost no short-term effect on drug use and also that the comparable programs fared better. These negative results were dismissed by the D.A.R.E. organization and almost censored by the funding agency. Conventional wisdom abhors contrary data, no matter how valid they may be.

The second study was carried out by Clayton, Cattarello, and Johnstone (1996) in Kentucky schools over a five-year period, using 23 schools for the D.A.R.E. implementation and 8 schools receiving a variety of alternative approaches. This excellently designed research found minimal changes in attitudes and values and even less in drug use, and even these effects eroded over time. The better the research, the less support for D.A.R.E.

When the present authors reported these findings to D.A.R.E. officials in Los Angeles, we were asked by the LAPD to review a compendium of 16 studies gathered by D.A.R.E. America along with another 8 studies. Uniformly, these studies provided by D.A.R.E. were of scientifically weak, even ridiculous quality, the exception being the strong design by Clayton et al. noted above. A later study by Rosenbaum and Hanson (1998) is perhaps the best yet. It was a randomized, longitudinal experiment of 1,800 students followed over six years. There were no long-term effects either on drug use or on its mediating variables. When we reported our review to the LAPD, we heard nothing further from the agency, although the L.A. Police Commission and the city council continue to be approached for D.A.R.E. continuation and expansion to the upper school grades.

The point of this brief digression into the D.A.R.E. experience is that the G.R.E.A.T. program is a kissing cousin of D.A.R.E., but aimed at reducing gang joining rather than drug use. D.A.R.E. was a failed program, based on an earlier failed program. What could one then expect for G.R.E.A.T.?

G.R.E.A.T., unlike D.A.R.E. or the L.A. Plan but in tune with our other programs, had an extensive research evaluation attached to it. Unlike our other ideological program, the L.A. Plan, G.R.E.A.T. was concerned not with the suppression of gang activity but with its prevention. Ideology and conventional wisdom can be found on both ends of the spectrum. In particular G.R.E.A.T., like D.A.R.E., is an example of "primary prevention," i.e., prevention aimed at a wide audience of potentially at-risk youth, not just those most likely to join gangs.

G.R.E.A.T. is best described by its evaluators (Winfree, Lynskey, and Maupin, 1999; Esbensen, Osgood, Taylor, Peterson, and Freng, 2001; Esbensen, 2000). It was initiated by police agencies in the Phoenix, Arizona, metropolitan area, and then it was funded and guided by the federal Bureau of Alcohol, Tobacco, and Firearms (ATF). Uniformed police officers delivered a series of eight standardized lessons to seventh graders, starting in 1991. By January 2000, some 3,500 officers throughout every state had been trained to administer the program. The parallels to D.A.R.E. are obvious. Even the lesson contents, substituting gang issues for drug issues, were similar in stressing life skills, conflict resolution, peer resistance skills, and cultural sensitivity. With the stated objectives (1) "to reduce gang activity" and (2) "to educate a population of young people as to the consequences of gang involvement" (Esbensen, Osgood, et al., 2001: 290), the lessons consisted of the following (Esbensen, Osgood, et al., 2001):

1. Introduction to G.R.E.A.T. and the officer
2. Crimes, victims, and legal rights
3. Cultural sensitivity
4. Conflict resolution approaches

5. Meeting basic individual needs
6. Drugs and their impact
7. Individual responsibilities
8. Goal setting

The reader will note how general these topics are, oriented to general attitudes and values education. But note also the clear absence of gang specificity in the list. Gang resistance was of course discussed by the officers during the lessons, but an emphasis on gangs as a central focus was not in evidence. As Esbensen, Osgood, et al. noted off-hand, "discussion about gangs and their effects on the quality of people's lives are also included" (2001: 88).

The analysis of the program's content by Esbensen and his colleagues, the competitively selected program evaluators, revealed a combination of social learning and social control theories implicit in the lessons, but little directly related to gangs. Gangs, therefore, may have been seen merely as an exaggeration of delinquent propensities, rather than the qualitatively distinct groups suggested by much gang literature (and the data reported in this book). This gangs-as-merely-more-serious-delinquents view is a common conventional wisdom among criminologists, as compared to the findings to be reported in chapter 5. G.R.E.A.T. lessons used little about group processes, gang structures, gang culture, and so on. The hope, rather, was to build general "life skills that empower adolescents with the ability to resist peer pressure to join gangs" (Esbensen, Osgood, et al., 2001: 89). The reader should keep in mind that the program was administered to all seventh graders, not just those deemed more vulnerable to gang recruitment. Since the vast majority of adolescents do not join gangs, program efficiency is not high in any case.[4]

G.R.E.A.T. evaluators were careful to assess program integrity, the degree to which it was implemented as designed. They gave the program high marks on this score. The officer/teachers were uniformly well trained and delivered the lessons as planned, regardless of location around the country. A longitudinal research design then permitted a four-year follow-up period in 22 schools, involving more than 150 classrooms and 3,500 students. Control classrooms, receiving no G.R.E.A.T. lessons, were established in each school. This long-term evaluation was undertaken in six cities: Las Cruces, New Mexico; Lincoln and Omaha, Nebraska; Phoenix, Arizona; Portland, Oregon; and Philadelphia, Pennsylvania.[5]

The results are reported in a 2001 article (Esbensen, Osgood, et al.) which requires careful reading; the narrative offers a far rosier picture than the data seem to warrant. Readers hoping for a positive outcome will be pleased to read:

- "Beneficial program effects emerged gradually over time so that there was, on average, more pro-social change in the attitudes of G.R.E.A.T. students than the non-G.R.E.A.T. students four years following program exposure" (2001: 87).
- "Thus, we conclude that the beneficial direction of the program impact is statistically reliable" (2001: 102).
- "Those students participating in the G.R.E.A.T. program expressed more pro-social attitudes after program completion than did those students who had not been exposed to the G.R.E.A.T. curriculum" (2001: 108).

Elsewhere in this summary article, the evaluators call attention to the downside of the findings: positive findings about attitude change are weak—consistent but weak—while findings about gang matters and delinquency are consistently negative. Changes in various delinquency measures failed to approach any sense of statistical significance (p levels averaging 0.51) while the difference in gang membership over the four years yielded a chance level of 0.771.[6]

The report of significant attitude change requires a closer look. The pre- to postprogram changes (Esbensen, Osgood, et al., 2001: 103, Table 3) are shown for 24 attitudinal variables. Of these, only 4 achieve statistical significance (<0.05). Ordinarily, such a result would be reported as a failure of the program to achieve change. In this case, however, the evaluators seek solace in two supplementary notations. First, they note, even these few significant effects are more than should occur by chance. This is technically correct, but substantively of little value, especially for programmatic recommendations.

Second, the evaluators note that all but 4 effects, over a total of 32 attitudinal and behavioral outcome measures of attitudes, delinquent behavior, and gang membership, are in the "right" or program-positive direction. Again, this is statistically significant and technically correct, yet substantively meaningless. The average significance level across the 32 variables is 0.448. No matter how consistently the directions were in the positive, to claim success on the basis of such consistent weakness seems misleading. G.R.E.A.T. was a multimillion-dollar national effort. The weakness of its impact on attitudes thought to be gang-related cannot fairly be counted as supportive of the program.

But worse yet, G.R.E.A.T. was put forth as a *gang prevention* program, for which the attitudinal variables were presumed to be mediating or even causal protection factors. They turned out *not* to be protective. Six measures of drug abuse and minor, serious, and total delinquency were assessed. None of the changes in these approached statistical significance, the average p value being 0.51. Most discouragingly, the reported difference in gang membership, specifically, yielded a probability level of 0.771. No differences were found over the various measures between students at higher and lower risk of antisocial outcomes, with level of risk determined by pretest and one-year follow-up analysis.

In sum, a multisite, multiyear controlled experiment yielded consistently weak changes in various prosocial attitudes thought to relate to gang membership. Further, the evaluation revealed a totally consistent absence of effect on levels of delinquency and, most centrally to the program, levels of gang membership. We have a failed program based on a prior failed program. What went wrong? We suggest four factors:

1. G.R.E.A.T. was built upon a conventional piece of wisdom that had no empirical formulation, namely, that a D.A.R.E.-type program of police officers delivering didactic lessons was effective.
2. G.R.E.A.T. relied on an unproven conventional wisdom that certain life skills or attitudinal variables underlie the attractiveness of gang membership.
3. The content of the G.R.E.A.T. lessons did not take advantage of the accumulated empirical knowledge about gangs. The content was not gang-specific; it did not take adequate account of gang structures, processes, or culture nor of the connections between gang members and their families and communities.
4. G.R.E.A.T. was not targeted at those more at risk of gang membership. Probably 90% or more of its student participants would not have joined gangs in any case; any positive effect on the most vulnerable could easily have been masked by the diffusion of effects over total participants.

Could a seemingly promising prevention program like G.R.E.A.T. be modified to yield more positive results? Perhaps so. It would need to be more carefully planned in terms of the gang-specific knowledge now available. It would probably benefit from coordination with an array of intervention and perhaps suppression programs in the same communities. The case for all of this will have to be made in the future, of course, but as we will note in chapter 8, there are many options to be considered. Data-based, careful planning is required. Conventional wisdoms have not measured up.

In defense of G.R.E.A.T., two additional points should be made. The first is that—unlike D.A.R.E. through most of its history—the disappointing findings about G.R.E.A.T., when fed back to its funders at ATF, led to change. Three meetings were held in which evaluators and program staff thoroughly reviewed the evaluation findings. This led to plans for a considerable overhaul of the program's curriculum and format. Whether a more successful, new G.R.E.A.T. will emerge is at this point unknown.

The second point, obviously dear to our hearts, is that the G.R.E.A.T. evaluators and others have been mining the data to learn more about street gangs as they were studied in the middle-school years of the gang members. In addition to a number of evaluation analyses, about a dozen papers have emerged on gang issues. Of these, seven deal specifically with gender issues in gang membership and crime. This represents a genuine contribution to a much-neglected area of gang research. We draw particular attention to two of these, one on race and gender comparisons between gang and nongang youth (Esbensen and Winfree, 1998) and one on the effects of gang gender ratios on gang crime (Peterson et al., 2001).

A Political Program: The Illinois Gang Crime Prevention Center

In Illinois, a midwestern state familiar with big-city street gangs but recently faced with a proliferation of gangs in many smaller jurisdictions as well, a governor's commission chaired by the state's attorney general[7] undertook analysis of gang problems and solutions. The commission consisted of about three dozen members, half of whom represented law enforcement. One, only, was a gang scholar. Sixteen public hearings took place across the state, engaging more than 100 witnesses. One, only, was a gang researcher.

To its credit, the commission's report placed a good deal of emphasis on community mobilization for gang control and recommended the implementation of three demonstration projects in community mobilization, but in small communities of 300 residents each. Thereafter, the commission report lost sight of a prevention orientation in favor of gang suppression.

Also to its credit, the commission report led to establishment of a Gang

Crime Prevention Center in the attorney general's office, and the center in turn convened a consultant group composed of gang scholars from across the country. But when the consultants proved critical of the conventional wisdoms and the suppressive approach of recommended programs, they were dismissed without further consultation. Beyond pilot projects in community mobilization, the commission report added other recommendations. These seemed unfortunately to be based on the notions we reported in the G.R.E.A.T. program: that what is good for delinquency reduction will apply to gang reduction as well, that gang crime is merely a more severe form of individual crime. Thus we find:

1. Early identification and programming in the schools, a process that both yields inappropriate labeling of youth as "gang prone" and confusing gang proneness with being at risk of a host of other problems—delinquency, drug use, poor school performance, teen pregnancy, family conflict, and so on. Gang members may or may not exhibit these problems, but most youth who do exhibit them do *not* go on to gang membership.
2. Antitruancy programs, despite the fact that most truants do not become gang members.
3. Mentoring programs, based on the notion that gang members do not have effective adult role models. While this is often true, it is in the nature of gang-involved neighborhoods that many nongang youth also face a deficit of such role models.
4. A firearm possession program, a worthy notion that ignores the nongang firearm issue and the principal sources of firearms—parents and illicit dealers.
5. Regional "boot camps" for gang members, ignoring reams of research and reports even from the U.S. Department of Justice that boot camps have proven no more effective in crime reduction than normal correctional programs. The conventional wisdom about boot camp success, unfortunately, has been reflected even in the White House.
6. The 8% program developed by the Orange County, California, Probation Department, a comprehensive compilation of correctional and community social services applied to the first-time referrals to probation predicted most likely to recidivate. This program has been sold nationwide by certain enthusiasts even while the program was still in its pilot phase, even though a program evaluation had yet to yield its first data, and even

though—for our midwestern state—it was *not* developed with street gangs in mind. Indeed, gang membership is but one of the many predictors used to identify the chronic 8% probationers.

7. Increased gang specializations within law enforcement, which is hardly an innovative recommendation.
8. A long series of legislative proposals, just 2 out of 15 of which were nondeterrent in form and purpose, revealing the commission's almost total loss of its focus on prevention, community mobilization, and the like.

Further evidence of a program based on conventional wisdom rather than concepts directly related to the needs of street gang intervention is provided inadvertently by what should be a positive development. Included in the Gang Crime Prevention Center's mandate was a plan to undertake empirical evaluations of the various program components. But the outline for evaluations of five pilot programs reveals five program components with only tangential relevance to what is known about street gangs (Fearn, Decker, and Curry, 2001).

The first of these was a treatment program for predicted chronic recidivists among first-time probationers. Based on the Orange County 8% program, it had no stated or known relevance to first-time *gang* member probationers. The second was an after-school, evening reporting center designed to bolster various services for convicted juvenile offenders. No special gang targeting seemed to be involved. The third was a tutoring/mentoring program, involving one hour per week, for elementary school pupils who were experiencing moderate behavioral or academic problems. The fourth component provided a mandatory (in lieu of prosecution) training program for the parents of young chronic truants. The fifth and final component was a "covenant" program by which high school students agreed to abide by a series of behavioral and academic standards, for which they would later receive financial assistance toward college or vocational training. There is little question that each of these components has worthy attributes in its own right. But nowhere can one discern any direct relevance to gang as opposed to general youth services.

Preliminary evaluations of the five pilot programs document several critical problems.[8] The first is that these are presumably aimed at gang prevention rather than intervention in ongoing gang activity. This is obviously commendable, but brings with it an extra burden. As with the L.A. Bridges program that we will cover next in this chapter, prevention requires some form of early identification and targeting of those youngsters more at risk of joining gangs. After all, only a small proportion of youths become gang members. Gang prevention for likely nonjoiners makes little sense and is terribly costly of fiscal resources and personnel. However, in developing the five Illinois pilot programs, pregang identification seems to have been ad hoc at best and generally absent as if by design.

The second problem, an extension of the first, is revealed in the five programs as they were eventually implemented. Three of them explicitly disavowed the goal of gang prevention per se. A fourth continued to acknowledge a gang prevention goal. The fifth, the evening reporting center which branched into an intervention mode with known gang members, maintained that gang issues were central to its mission, yet of the first 377 program clients, only 12 acknowledged gang membership. What we see then—common to many programs which tackle difficult problems, recalcitrant clients, or inadequately articulated purposes—is the process of goal displacement. This means that goals not easily achieved are replaced by goals more readily amenable to a measurement of success. Numbers of clients served becomes the goal rather than numbers positively affected, or client satisfaction replaces client change, or general youth services replace focused gang prevention activity. This process makes sense, but it does not serve the original program intentions.

The third problem with the Illinois venture is that the Gang Crime Prevention Center, presumably in light of the goal displacement process, decided after the first six months to change the goals of its program evaluation. It dropped its concern for outcome measures on client change and sought instead to have the evaluation assess how well the programs were implemented. This would then be a measure of how well the center could create and maintain new efforts in various sites in the state. Not only were the goals of the programs displaced, but then the goal of the evaluation was displaced. The attorney general, Scott asserts, in a personal communication, "balked and bridled when faced with [potential] research-based criticisms of his own work."

The three small demonstration projects in community mobilization mentioned earlier presented a somewhat different experience. In his review of this chapter, Scott comments as follows:

> Ultimately we found that local neighborhood residents converted what was truly meant to be a capacity building initiative into a kind of "vigilante justice" intervention, their goal being the ejec-

> tion from the neighborhood of select gang members, drug dealers, vagrants, and other marginalized persons. . . . on the whole, the whole enterprise induced a race to the bottom. (Personal communication)

In sum, this political Illinois effort, it seems to us, failed to give attention to much that is now known about gangs, failed to appreciate the programmatic need to distinguish delinquents from gang members, adopted inappropriate but popular programs, and placed far too much emphasis on law enforcement and deterrence at the expense of long-term prevention and gang reduction. Then the commission's stated stress on community mobilization for gang prevention got lost in the program implementation process, a complex and difficult emphasis replaced by a series of largely inappropriate quick fixes. This is not, the reader may recognize, an unusual situation. Further, the opportunity for effective outcome evaluation was discarded. We know little more now than before.

To make a point that is as obvious as it is generally overlooked, the main problem with street gangs *in the long run* is not the gangs themselves, but the societal and community processes that spawn these gangs. Chicago and Los Angeles are by far the greatest contributors to gang activity. Yet this Illinois program and the L.A. Plan described earlier failed to engage the communities and failed to assess any change in levels of gang membership or activity. Los Angeles County is said to have some 85,000 gang members, a staggering figure. If we were to crack down on and put away these 85,000 gang individuals, within 10 years we'd have another 85,000 to put away. The political solutions have failed because they've dealt with the outcome, not the source.

Three Bureaucratic Programs

L.A. Bridges

For our next example of conventional wisdom winning out against accumulated knowledge, we turn again to the city of Los Angeles. It is estimated by law enforcement that the county of about 9 million people contains about 1,200 street gangs with about 85,000 gang members. The city of Los Angeles is said to contribute somewhat under half of those numbers. Countywide, gang-related homicides rose from just over 200 in 1982 to just over 800 in 1995 (comprising 45% of all homicides in the county in that latter year before declining to about 36% in 1997 and then climbing again to over 55% in the year 2000). Within the city alone, the resurgence of gang homicides in 2001 and 2002 yielded almost 60% of all of the city's homicides. Clearly, no area of the country more desperately needs to engage in effective gang prevention and control.

In September 1995, three-year-old Stephanie Kuhen was killed in the early morning hours in the Cypress Park area of the city. Although one of many little children caught in gang gunfire over the previous decade, Stephanie was a cute, blue-eyed blonde, the only nonminority child in this list of unfortunate youngsters. The result was a huge outcry against gang violence, even occasioning a public statement from President Bill Clinton. Mayor Richard Riordan promised appointment of a city-county antigang task force and a "gang czar," neither of which appointments was made. However, the city council did appoint an ad hoc committee, consisting of four council members, the chief of police, the district attorney, the school superintendent, the city attorney, and 13 community members.

Between February 1 and September 19, 1996, the committee met seven times in public sessions throughout the city. The members attended a two-day workshop on policy management at the University of California at Los Angeles and a one-day intensive workshop on gangs and gang program evaluation at the University of Southern California, which was conducted by the authors of this book. Smaller working-group sessions took all of the accumulated testimony and materials to frame a new, $44 million program called L.A. Bridges, open to public and private agencies in 29 designated higher-crime areas.[9] In addition, it was mandated by the council members that there would be a comprehensive, four- to five-year independent evaluation of the program's success in reducing gang problems. Such a large, evaluated program had great promise for adding to our knowledge of gangs and gang control.

The city council voted to discontinue all currently supported gang intervention programs not located in departmental budgets (e.g., LAPD efforts) because they could not demonstrate success. It then dedicated these same funds and far more to the new effort, L.A. Bridges. The differences were striking:

- L.A. Bridges stressed prevention.
- L.A. Bridges was to be located in 29 sites chosen for their youth crime density (with the exceptions noted later).
- L.A. Bridges promised funding continuity for a minimum of four years.
- L.A. Bridges placed uncommon emphasis on accountability through an independent evaluation of intermediate and outcome

goals, including reduced juvenile crime and gang membership rates.

The charge of developing the L.A. Bridges program was given to the city's Community Development Department (CDD), whose staff had previously monitored other programs roughly characterized as "youth services." The CDD staff had available to it the materials from the ad hoc committee's open community hearings and meetings, written materials provided by committee members and many city departments, the experience of the USC intensive workshop on gangs and gang program evaluations, and of course its own past experience with youth service programs.

In addition, the CDD could and did call upon other departmental staff, such as the LAPD, city attorney, district attorney, L.A. Unified School Districts, the Commission on Children, Youth and Their Families, and the mayor's office. Some members of these groups, plus several ad hoc committee members, were brought together by the CDD into a working group to refine the program for submission to the council for its approval. One of this volume's authors was appointed to the working group, participated early on, and then was excluded from further participation. This exclusion was symptomatic of the CDD's avoidance of academic expertise in program development, although not in development of the approach to program evaluation.

During the process of program formulation, the CDD had to accommodate major changes occasioned by political considerations among members of the city council. The CDD's original recommendation was to locate L.A. Bridges in 18 middle-school areas, targeting youth ages 10–14 primarily because these are the ages of early gang membership. The 18 schools were those, among middle schools in the city, that ranked highest on the LAPD's juvenile violent crime arrests for the reporting districts in which the schools were located (note that these were arrests, not rates of gang-related crime). However, when they saw the list of the 18 areas, several council members objected quite vigorously because schools in *their* areas were not included. The result of this objection was the expansion of the targets to a final total of 29 middle schools. A number of the added schools had relatively low juvenile arrest figures and/or negligible gang activity.

Even with an increase in program funds from $9.1 million to $11.2 million per year, this school expansion clearly threatened to dilute the overall program effect. This was true in part because of the increased numbers, but also because of the character of the added schools. While 5 of them were ranked in violent crime arrests among the highest 25 school reporting districts out of 57, others were ranked 28, 36, 37, 41, 43, and 47. One of the schools reported 1 gang crime in the prior year, and another reported only 8 (as compared to highs of 50, 53, 47, and 45 among the original 18 schools). The original 18 schools averaged 31 reported gang crimes in the prior reporting period used by the working group at the CDD, while the violent crime arrests averaged 301.5. In the added schools, the comparable figures for the same period were 24 and 116. These are lower by 23% and 62%, respectively. This diffusion of appropriate program targets can have a major limiting effect on program evaluation. Significant reductions in criminal or gang activity would be hard to demonstrate in school areas largely untroubled by these problems.

Once the program approach had been worked out by the CDD, a request for proposals (RFP) was announced, seeking responses from the communities surrounding the 29 schools. The responses were to be from consortiums of public and private agencies in each designated community, each headed by a lead agency, which would be responsible for overall interagency coordination and program leadership. All but one of the communities responded to the RFP, and special arrangements later brought in the missing school area. Approximately 160 agencies across the city were identified as partners in the consortium proposals approved.

There were two principal constraints on the community responses, which emanated from the RFP itself. The two are interrelated. First, the RFP was quite specific about the forms that the community programs were to take. These materials required a heavy emphasis on interagency coordination and a program design based on three prongs, labeled (1) actualizing youth achievement, (2) strengthening family foundations, and (3) promoting community action. Further, each prong was broken down into more-specific program components and a number of criteria for success that clearly implied further specific program elements. For communities in need of guidelines, the RFP provided rather clear ones. For communities already accomplished in various aspects of youth services, the specifics of the RFP were found to be constraining and insensitive to some agency and community realities.

The second major constraint is more controversial, but comprises a theme that is central to our discussion. The three-pronged strategy adopted by the CDD—and fully approved by the city council—stressed "youth development" and "youth at risk" (of what is not fully clarified). What it did *not* stress, and almost failed to address at all directly, was the requirement of a *gang* prevention or intervention strategy.

This was a problem we had repeatedly cited both in ad hoc committee meetings, with CDD staff, and in the content of the all-day workshop presented at USC for both groups. Further, the gang theme was truly explicit throughout the city council process. The ad hoc committee was formed in direct response to the gang shooting of Stephanie Kuhen. The original motion (from the office of the legislative analyst for the city of Los Angeles), which went to all heads of city departments, stated that the aim was "to develop strategies to prevent, intervene, and suppress gang violence." The focus on gang issues was reiterated on numerous occasions in public settings by the ad hoc committee's chairperson, Councilman Mark Ridley-Thomas.

It is crucial to state the plight of many lead agencies that responded to the RFP. On the one hand, a major criterion of their success (as well as a legitimate public expectation) was to be a significant reduction in gang activity attributable to the program over four years of funding. Yet the program guidelines were almost silent on gang-specific programming. The word *gang* appeared only six times in 12 pages of orientation materials made available to the community participants.

The CDD may have felt that "youth development" and services for generally "at-risk youth" would automatically apply to those who would normally join gangs. Such a belief—the conventional wisdom noted earlier—should have been dispelled during the USC workshop; it is clearly dispelled by the fact that most youth in gang-involved neighborhoods do *not* join the local gangs. The prevention of gang membership and reduction of gang activity are goals that require the careful targeting of program clients and careful consideration of gang-specific interventions. These points were absent from the RFP and therefore are largely absent from the community programs offered by the lead agencies. The CDD almost studiously avoided street gang content in formulating its program requirements. If gang membership and activity did not decline in the 29 middle-school areas in ways attributable to the program, the fault might well lie with the actions of the CDD and the failure of the city council to pay attention to its product and might therefore not lie within the responding communities.

Almost nowhere in the very extensive literature on street gangs can one find a convincing demonstration of successful gang prevention or intervention. Thus, in its defense, L.A. Bridges could be said to be a pioneering effort. On the other hand, the literature *does* provide a series of inviting suggestions and conclusions about what might be more likely to produce a successful effort. A well-researched and promising model (the Spergel Model, described next in this chapter) developed at the University of Chicago on the basis of a national study was presented to the USC workshop participants from the CDD and other agencies. It was as ignored as the workshop itself. While there may be explanations for the CDD's ignoring of gang-relevant matters, it was a deliberate choice. Insofar as the city council approved the CDD product, the same must be said of the council.

Three components of the failure, and thus three concerns that could seriously hamper the success of L.A. Bridges, are worth some repetition. They are the school area selection, the program RFP guidelines, and the inattention to gang-specific issues.

During the period of proposal development in the middle-school communities, approximately 40 research interviews were carried out with agency personnel by USC students. There were a few agencies that declined interview requests, either because they had little to say at that point, or because they were suspicious of the interviewers' intentions, or because they wanted no publicity. Two school principals in the selected areas said they had never heard of L.A. Bridges.

Nonetheless, a sufficient number of interviews were achieved that we can summarize the problems that the respondents felt they faced:

1. Too little attention in the RFP to gang issues; no specifications of what makes youth at risk of gang involvement; no evidence of gang expertise available to responders.
2. RFP permitted business as usual, i.e., funds could be used to expand current programs rather than to modify them or to create new ones for the task at hand; emphasis on coordination across agencies could translate to doing more of what already was being done.
3. Lack of consensus on program goals (including among public officials connected to the city council).
4. Confusion or lack of information about the program among school officials, including principals of some of the middle schools.
5. Too much emphasis on school issues and not enough attention to community realities and street life.
6. No guidelines for dealing with nonresident students or resident

students attending schools out of the area (in some areas, this latter number is very large).

7. Inadequate attention in the RFP to how proposers would tie program activities to effectiveness measures to be imposed by the CDD.

Clearly, some of these concerns would be faced in the initial year of L.A. Bridges. The concerns of the community respondents are noted here not because they are obstacles but because they emphasize the ambiguity of the stimulus provided by the CDD and the council. It is hard to avoid the conclusion that much of this could have been avoided had the CDD been more open to outside opinions and experience, beyond that taken from other city agencies, such as the police. Instead, it relied on its own conventional wisdom about "at-risk" youth and shied away from the harder realities of street gangs.

The depth of the problem was revealed in a second round of agency interviews undertaken by USC students six months after the first. The following generalizations emerged:

1. A large number of dedicated, caring, and competent social services personnel were being engaged in L.A. Bridges.
2. There was evidence of increased coordination among agencies, although interagency problems were also highlighted.
3. In many instances, L.A. Bridges brought enhanced sources of funding without changes in agency programming, i.e., more money to do what was normally done by agencies not normally in the gang prevention business.
4. There remained a general absence of gang-specific programming and, in some cases, an avoidance of the issue.
5. There was evidence of "creaming," i.e., selecting as clients the kinds of youngsters who are least troublesome and most responsive to agency offerings.
6. There was some, though less, evidence of "net widening," the tendency to expand the client base by drawing into the gang program youngsters who otherwise would not have needed or sought it.

L.A. Bridges *as a program* proved impervious to gang research knowledge. Its evaluation would necessarily reflect that fact. Our genuine fear at its inception, with respect to both program and evaluation, was that a major gang intervention program—the nation's largest in the city with the greatest need—would quickly evolve into nongang programs and have no more to prove its merit in gang reduction than the very city-backed programs that were defunded in order to build L.A. Bridges. It was far less the politics of the city council than the rigidities of the CDD and its conventional wisdoms that produced this situation (although better council oversight would have been helpful).

Nonetheless, there were some adjustments that could have improved the chances for evaluating L.A. Bridges as a gang reduction program. We list four categories that were specifically offered to CDD officials:

1. Better targeting. Although the selection of schools was unlikely to change, the research *evaluation* could concentrate its resources on the more gang-involved school areas. Further, the program evaluation could concentrate on gang-active *neighborhoods*, regardless of whether these are adjacent to the middle schools or not. Most important, program and evaluation could concentrate resources on youth at risk most specifically of gang membership, not general delinquency and other youth problems. Criteria for this were offered to the CDD.
2. Indigenous groups. Most of the agencies engaged in the various Bridges consortiums were formal service agencies. Much emphasis was placed by the CDD on coordination and collaboration among those agencies. More attention could have been given (and was, in fact, in a few consortium proposals) to informal or indigenous groups (such as block clubs) already extant and to helping to create such informal groups among parents, other community residents, and merchants. In the end, it is local *informal* social control of gang-prone youth that may most affect incipient gang membership. Formal agents of control—social services agencies, school officials, and police—often get involved too late with too few resources.
3. Gang intervention. Although the program RFP spoke loosely about gang *intervention* (i.e., work with already-involved gang members), and city council members specifically called for the inclusion of gang intervention in the L.A. Bridges program, it was almost nonexistent in its first year. It is difficult to dissuade potential gang members from joining such groups if the appeals of membership are not visibly counteracted by the disadvantages of joining. More planned and coordinated attention

to gang intervention procedures ("Bridges II") were to be built into community consortiums' plans and included as an evaluation target. Unfortunately, these turned out to be a set of contracts to agencies to do intergang conflict mediation and little more.

4. Gang membership predictors. Because of the group processes that drive so much of gang members' behavior—especially the more violent components—and because gangs are responded to far differently than are individual antisocial youth, it is important to appreciate that gang prevention is not synonymous with delinquency prevention. A gang is more than a collection of individual youths. To turn operations like L.A. Bridges into gang prevention programs that aim to keep kids out of gangs, one needs to concentrate resources not only on gang areas, as suggested above, but also on the youth most vulnerable to gang membership specifically. Among the literally hundreds of variables that can be used to predict youth at risk of some form of trouble, only a few have emerged from modern research as most directly related to gang members as opposed to nongang youth in the same neighborhoods. In chapter 4, we will discuss these fully. The variables, which were derived from recent research in Long Beach, San Diego, Seattle, Denver, and Rochester, New York, with considerable consistency across these five sites, were provided to the CDD. It is worth noting that engagement in standard prosocial activities did not emerge in any of this research. Programs placing heavy emphasis on enrolling gang-prone youth in various recreational and vocational activities may themselves be at risk, since gang members (contrary to the conventional wisdom) are often already as involved as are their nongang counterparts. Because the risk variables for gang membership have emerged from research based on extensive interviews with gang and nongang members, reliable procedures for measuring the variables were available from gang researchers. Ignoring them in targeting gang-prone youth was an active error of omission.[10]

In sum, L.A. Bridges was clearly initiated as a gang prevention program, but the conventional wisdom of its developers threatened to produce severe goal displacement, transforming Bridges into a general youth services program in areas of varied levels of at-risk youth. The saving grace in all of this was the promise of a fully independent, substantially funded four-year evaluation of the program's implementation and outcome in levels of gang membership and activity. But as the reader might have guessed by now, this opportunity was lost, as the evaluation became mired in a bureaucratic maze. A rough outline of this process is as follows:

1. An RFP for the evaluation contract was produced with considerable input from the authors of this book. Only one respectable submission was received. The authors of this submission provided plans for an extensive management information system but failed to respond effectively to the specific gang membership issues implanted in the RFP. This may be explained in part by the lack of gang specificity in the Bridges program materials themselves. It also reflected their unfamiliarity with street gang issues.
2. During the first year of Bridges, in 1997–1998, devoted principally to developing the program in the 29 school sites, the independent evaluation team worked on management information systems and gathered baseline data on approximately 1,000 middle-school youth of varying at-risk levels. A political hassle developed among the evaluator, a politically connected subcontractor, and members of the city council. Allegations of fraud were in the air at the end of the first year, and the evaluators "declined to bid" on the evaluation continuation, as the rumors stated the situation. No back-up evaluation resource was developed.
3. A new evaluation RFP was floated for Bridges I and II in September 1999, meaning that the full second year of data would necessarily be lost. This, plus the complete absence of clear gang relevance in the RFP, essentially doomed Bridges to be an unevaluated, very expensive gang prevention program.
4. In response to the new RFP, new bids were received. One was a modification of a rejected bid from the first year. Another was from the politically connected individual involved in the hassle with the first evaluation. A brouhaha ensued, during which this latter individual and others complained of a "tainted" bid review process that rejected his proposal. Appeals to the city council led to divided votes and no decision. No evaluation was undertaken in the second year.
5. Finally, the office of the city controller was assigned the task of

undertaking an audit of L.A. Bridges. Based both on extensive interviews and fiscal auditing, the city controller produced, in March 2000, a devastating review of the program. There were two basic conclusions: despite the well-meaning efforts of many people, the program failed to meet the goal of developing specific gang prevention efforts, and it also failed to develop the data needed to assess gang prevention. Various fiscal and management irregularities were also unearthed. The city controller recommended that Bridges funding be stopped, pending major changes in the program's concept and operation.

6. On the basis of these findings, the mayor of Los Angeles announced his defunding of Bridges and vetoed the city council's decision to continue the program. Support groups rallied, and the city council members, each of whose districts were sharing the $44 million from Bridges, overrode the mayor's veto by a vote of 12–0.
7. A new evaluation RFP, this time for only a six-month period, was announced in mid-2000. The winning bidder, in the absence of three years of potential data gathering on gang matters, produced a process evaluation relying heavily on "votes" of progress. No meaningful outcome evaluation of changes in gang membership or activity was possible.
8. A resurgence of gang violence from 2000 to 2002 led to new calls from the new mayor and the new police chief for renewed antigang efforts. More money was directed toward L.A. Bridges. After six years and a cost ballooning toward $50 million, another short-term evaluation produced yet more criticism. "Not Meeting Standards" and "Gang Prevention Program Plagued by Problems" headlined the *Los Angeles Times*'s report of this latest evaluation in January 2003. In a separate editorial (January 7, 2003), the *Times* urged that "city leaders should call once again on outside advice on how to refocus anti-gang efforts," adding "and this time the city should listen." The call came six years too late.

What went wrong with the largest, perhaps most-promising government attempt to mount and assess gang prevention efforts? Many things did, but among them the most important to the development of successful gang control may be:

1. Reliance on conventional wisdoms, viewing gang involvement as merely a more extreme form of youth deviance
2. Unfamiliarity with, and then resistance to, available knowledge of factors related to gang joining and activity
3. Beliefs about various youth services of general value, allowing goal displacement to these services and away from gang interventions
4. A failure to develop and maintain a gang-relevant evaluation process
5. An inability to overcome political pressures on government bureaucracies

The Spergel Model

The efforts undertaken by the four programs described up to now were complex, yet in some ways they pale in the face of what has become known as the Spergel Model.[11] The approach is named for its creator, Irving Spergel at the University of Chicago.[12] It is more technically known as the Comprehensive Community-wide Approach to Gang Prevention, Intervention, and Suppression program. The road to the present status of Spergel Model projects is part of the story. We will summarize it briefly and then report on the principal project in some detail.

1. In the mid-1980s, officials from the federal Office of Juvenile Justice and Delinquency Prevention visited Los Angeles to view gang control efforts there. They were very impressed by what they saw and dubbed it the L.A. Plan. We described the components of the "plan" earlier in this chapter. The OJJDP officials returned to Washington, D.C., and began to formulate a program to replicate the plan in various new sites across the country. However, it was pointed out to them that there was no plan, merely a set of uncoordinated gang suppression efforts carried out by agencies whose only joint effort was to meet periodically to share war stories and all-points bulletins. Further, it was noted, the OJJDP was in danger of promoting a major suppression effort whose objective indicator of "success" was a threefold increase in gang homicides. Cooler heads then prevailed at the OJJDP, and a more cautious approach was developed, leading to the second step in this narrative.
2. In 1987, the OJJDP made a cooperative agreement award to Ir-

ving Spergel at the University of Chicago to develop a set of alternative approaches to gang control.[13] Originally, the thought at the OJJDP was to offer these approaches as alternatives among which communities could select to meet their needs. Spergel and his team undertook a national survey of 45 locations, involving 254 respondents from various agencies. He also developed an advisory group of research and practitioner experts to help guide the project. What resulted was not the OJJDP's desired alternative approaches but one, comprehensive approach involving 5 pivotal strategies and 12 "modules," or practice guides, for various groups such as police, probation, courts, schools, indigenous groups, social agencies, and so on. This was the basic framework from which the Spergel Model evolved and was implemented.

3. While still fleshing out the comprehensive approach developed from the national survey and while preparing to propose a multisite implementation of the approach, in 1992 Spergel took advantage of funds from the federal Bureau of Justice Assistance to launch a pilot effort in the Little Village section of Chicago, a traditionally heavily involved gang area. The Little Village project implementation and early promises of success became a guiding force in the ensuing developmental phases.
4. In 1995, while the Little Village project was under way but before any reliable indications of success or failure were available, the OJJDP awarded to Spergel and his team a second cooperative agreement for a three-year period, later extended, to serve as the evaluation team to assess the model's implementation and outcome in five sites. This was the aforementioned Comprehensive Community-wide Approach to Gang Prevention, Intervention, and Suppression project. The sites chosen were Mesa and Tucson, Arizona; Riverside, California; San Antonio, Texas; and Bloomington, Illinois.
5. In 1997, interim reports from the comprehensive project indicated very slow start-up at the sites and some progress in approximating the model but a number of serious implementation problems. Among these, it seems, was a failure to articulate the model sufficiently for the five sites to follow explicitly.[14]
6. In December 1998, the Spergel team together with its OJJDP staff monitor produced what in our view is the first clear artic-

ulation of the Spergel Model, sufficiently concise that it could be used to help the five program sites implement the program in roughly uniform ways. Unfortunately, the statement of the model was produced three and a half years after the programs were initiated (and well after the Little Village prototype had been implemented).[15]

7. By mid-2002, two of the five program site final reports had been drafted by the Spergel team, and a third was produced in October 2003. The remaining two have not been produced by this writing, so our coverage of the Spergel Model projects is limited to the reports on Mesa, Riverside, and Bloomington. In addition, the local evaluator in Riverside reported major successes with respect to overall juvenile arrest rates—not the focus of the program—but disastrous results for program youth compared to a comparison group and various indications of inadequate program implementation.[16]
8. By late 2002, a number of frustrations were noted:
   - An adequate write-up of the model and how to implement it was still not available, although an attempt to obtain it would be made.
   - The OJJDP, two years into the changed federal administration and several years after expected results, would settle for "lesser" reports about the San Antonio and Tucson programs.
   - The complexities of carrying out the comprehensive community-wide approach may have been beyond the capacities of many jurisdictions.
   - The model, to be successfully implemented, requires a competent coordinator on-site and constant monitoring. These were not uniformly available in this five-site project.
   - An unclearly articulated and shifting model (a "moving target") prevented a genuine test of the program's rationale.

What can be said about the Spergel Model program is instructive to our purposes in this book, and yet we must be a bit tentative in the absence of five full final reports. To begin with, we *do* at this point finally have a model for implementing a comprehensive gang control program. We will describe the model briefly below, because it will appear again in our discussion in chapter 8.

Second, we also can identify problems in implementing such a model. Some of these are minor; some amount more to debatable preferences among viewers with different perspectives; and some are quite major. We will discuss these briefly below as well.

Third, we can see in the foregoing timeline of events that a developmental process that was slow might effectively have been even slower. The Chicago group and its funding agencies leaped before they looked. They accepted some conventional wisdoms about collaborative procedures and mounted their programs—Little Village and the five site projects—well before a properly articulated model was developed and well before there were adequate data to justify moving forward with such complex operations. The heavy reliance on the Little Village project to guide the five site projects requires particular attention, and we will provide that below. Continuity is good only when earlier stages provide solid foundations for later stages (a point we shall raise again about our sixth major gang control program, SafeFutures).

The Spergel Model is complex because it attempts at the same time to be both a statement of a conceptual or theoretical approach to gang control and a set of guidelines for implementing that approach. Most important is the phrase "comprehensive community-wide." Unlike the L.A. Plan, which emphasized law enforcement and suppression, or G.R.E.A.T. with its school lessons approach, or the Illinois and L.A. Bridges prevention programs, the Spergel Model wants to do it all. It aims to combine prevention, intervention, and suppression in a single package.

Implementing the model calls for a steering committee in each site composed of both public and private agency administrators, e.g., police, prosecutors, schools, social service agencies, indigenous community groups, and so on. There must be a central lead agency to administer the funds and coordinate the program components. In many cases, the police department is the lead agency, but this is not required. Program contents must consist of implementing each of the five strategies that were developed from the national survey discussed in point 2 in our timeline in the previous pages. The combination of prevention, intervention, and suppression through activation of the five strategies is generally what distinguishes and stamps the Spergel Model as different from others. The five strategies[17] are briefly:

a. Community mobilization. Developing and maintaining an interacting set of public and private agencies, groups, and residents to organize a comprehensive program responsive specifically to the gang problem. (It is worth noting that gangs are most likely to emerge and remain in those communities least competent at community organization.)

b. Social intervention. Developing outreach contacts with gang members and those at higher risk of gang membership. Most typically, this refers to the use of street workers (youth workers, gang workers) who both counsel their targeted youth and provide useful bridges between them and the schools, social services, and criminal justice agencies. Outreach can also be provided by probation, police, and treatment workers.

c. Opportunities provision. Developing access for gang members to employment, job training, educational, and cultural opportunities as alternatives to gang activity.

d. Organizational change and development. Bringing about changes in the policies and practices of public and private agencies to reduce their tendency not to respond positively to gang youth, to help them adopt strategies that will enhance their responsiveness, and to increase interagency collaboration.

e. Suppression. The use principally of police, probation, parole, and the courts to hold youth accountable for their criminal activities. This goes beyond the "normal" criminal justice operations to include special antigang practices, such as police gang units, the use of gang court injunctions, and specialized gang intelligence operations. Other agencies and outreach workers can also become involved in suppression activities.

Implementation of these conceptual model components into a community-wide program involves at least the following steps:

- Direct, continuing involvement of community leaders
- Preproject assessment of the seriousness of the street gang problem
- Establishing precise project goals
- Setting up the steering committee, lead agency, and street worker teams
- Careful selection and targeting of gang and high-risk youth
- Implementing the comprehensive package of prevention, intervention, and suppression practices
- Developing adequate gang data and case management systems useable across agencies

- Ongoing evaluation, monitoring, and implementing project change procedures over time

Finally, the intent is to set matters in place so that the initial project becomes an institutionalized component of the targeted community, with adequate and continuing local support.

This very complex process is both the source of the Spergel Model's strength *and* a prescription for inadequate implementation. Every opportunity to bring about an effective component is at the same time an opportunity for things to go wrong. One must admire the optimism and tenacity of the Spergel team. We offer here just a sampling of the problems they faced.

1. Throughout the five sites, garnering the involvement of various agencies proved problematic. In particular, the police and the schools tended to be resistant or uncooperative. The Spergel team provided relevant information on such issues, but the OJJDP was the principal monitor of program implementation.
2. Similarly, there were very uneven performances by the local evaluation teams.
3. Communities not used to or uncomfortable with the use of outreach workers—i.e., gang workers—sometimes resisted the use of ex-gang members and in some cases hired outreach workers who did not put in time in the evenings or on weekends. These outreach workers are essential to the Spergel Model and have to be in the streets when the gang members are—most notably, evenings and weekends. In some cases, these workers actually had little contact with the gangs.
4. Monitoring of the five sites involved both technical program assistance by the OJJDP and data collection supervision by the Spergel team. The central team in Chicago was unable to provide all of the monitoring necessary due in large part to the extreme complexities in the sites.
5. In each site, various data systems were not up to the standard required by the model. Modifying and improving these systems, as well as establishing access to them, often resulted in major losses in data and costs in program time and resources. Police and school records were common examples.
6. In each site, 11 categories of participants were to be brought together: schools, employment agencies, grassroots organiza-

> tions, community-based youth agencies, community mobilization groups, law enforcement, prosecution, judiciary, probation, corrections, and parole.[18] This required getting everyone "on the same page" in each of the five sites. The goal was laudable, but unlikely of achievement in the absence of a readily accessible, clearly articulated statement of the Spergel Model. Spergel comments that "the key issue was . . . coping with divergent political and organizational interests that often made collaboration by agencies and groups very difficult" (personal communication). We note that this point was made bitterly clear five decades earlier in Boston (W. Miller, 1958).

In addition to these and a list of lesser problems is the issue of the articulated model. For the purposes of this book, we will cite just three pivotal issues: having a clear model in place to guide a program, determining the proper targets for the program, and connecting the conceptual model to program implementations.

As to the model, the reader can glean from the timeline in the previous pages how serious this problem was. The five sites of the comprehensive, community-wide program were asked to implement a model that was not well articulated and whose content was described by the research advisory committee as "a moving target." The model did not emerge clearly from its pilot-testing source starting in 1992 in the Little Village project. It was not a clear model in 1995 when the five sites were to initiate their program development. It was not available at the halfway point in 1997 and only found official articulation in December 1998 in a statement authored jointly by the Spergel team and OJJDP staff. Clearly, it was too late to provide proper guidance to the sites. By late 2002, OJJDP staff still wished for an adequate write-up of the model and wondered out loud who would complete that task.

We can illustrate the problems of not having a clear model with two examples. First, the mechanisms for identifying youth at risk of gang joining were not established with clarity, a problem especially troublesome for the comparison (nonprogram) areas in each of the five sites.[19] It's hard to find and measure effects on youth whose very existence is hard to establish.

A second example has to do with the targeting of gang youth. A stated preference of the Spergel team was to concentrate, especially in the first years of the program, on the older, more seriously gang-involved youth. Without this, it was reasoned, the older, active, negative role models would work against success with younger or at-risk youth. In addition, concentrating on the older gang members, who were already well known as such, would minimize the risk of unfairly or inappropriately labeling youngsters as gang members. This approach was carried over directly from Little Village, an old, established, high-violence gang area of Chicago. But what was not clear in the model was when or how the sites were to progress to prevention and intervention with younger or at-risk gang youth. They are, after all, the potential inheritors of the gang tradition and as such require the same *conceptual* attention as the harder core members.

These are two of many examples wherein the absence of clear model guidelines made program implementation more difficult, which of course would affect whatever evaluation would emerge from this comprehensive program. The place of prevention with younger members in particular resonates with problems already outlined in our review of the Illinois, L.A. Bridges, and G.R.E.A.T. programs.

Another comment flows directly from the failure to specify, and not as a moving target, the elements of the Spergel Model. The model was to have interlocking aspects: its conceptual structure (read: theory, or idea system, or logic model, or paradigm here) and its guidelines for implementation. This connection could not be well made without the clarification of the conceptual structure of the model. We do note, however, that as the Spergel team finally confronted the complex task of program evaluation, it did develop a commendable set of charts: a general change model; a three-dimensional depiction of relationships among the five strategies, the program elements, and some implementation principles; a program evaluation model in the form of a path model; and an analysis model, also in the form of a path model. But these products appeared in December 2000, in a program initiated in 1995.

As these comments are written, we have three draft final reports in hand, provided to us by Spergel.[20] A brief review of these and a few summary comments will address a number of important issues in mounting complex street gang control programs.

In the Bloomington-Normal, Illinois, twin cities, gangs began to emerge in the early 1990s. "Violence occurred sporadically," according to the report, with six African-American gangs containing about 460 members. Drug problems were considered the most serious. This small (population 110,000) city with a moderate gang problem is typical of many such areas around the country—far more typical than the stereotypic gang settings of Los Angeles, Chicago, and other major urban areas.

The report indicates substantial support for the project from community agencies, with a particularly strong suppression element and dominance from probation and police. Youth outreach workers were a weak link in the project, although they are central to the Spergel Model. The report indicates that the site failed to incorporate various elements of the model in favor of beefing up its "pre-existing, pro-active suppression approaches against gangs."

The research evaluation revealed a poor match between program and control youths and no differential effect on arrests between the two groups, but, if anything, increased arrest rates overall. There were also no differences in self-report offending between program and control youths, with both declining somewhat. Program services, however, were associated overall with increased self-report offending. There were, within this generally negative picture, complex differences by type of youth, type of services, and type of self-report offenses. In addition, there were mixed results on growth of gang membership during the project. After some four years of action, the final draft report provides a discouraging picture:

> The Bloomington-Normal Program did not follow the OJJDP model. It emphasized a suppression approach. It did not include grassroots groups, and did not develop an adequate outreach youth-worker approach. Little attention was paid to an appropriate mix of strategies for different youth, to the modification of the roles of the different types of workers, and to how different agency workers were to function together to create an improved, interorganizational, street-level worker structure and process to meet the interests and needs of gang youth, and the needs of the community, within the framework of the Model. The program unfortunately contributed to an increase in arrests for program youth, particularly those youth without prior arrest records. However, there was evidence (based on self-reports) that some parts of the program were useful in reducing subsequent offenses for certain youth. In conclusion, we find that the program had no effect on the gang or delinquency problem at the level of individual youth in the program, compared to similar youth in the comparison site, when appropriate statistical controls are used. (Spergel, 2001: 14–15)

The Riverside program was located in two high–gang crime areas in a larger city with California's highest rate of population growth in the prior 10 years, with a best estimate of about 4,000 gang members. Only an hour's drive from Los Angeles, Riverside could be considered a chronic gang city with a number of traditional gangs well established.

The Riverside program started out with a host of management and research problems, so many that the OJJDP seriously considered canceling it. However, the report indicates that major changes in program leadership and design slowly shifted emphasis from suppression to more coordination of social services, to the point that the Spergel team believed that the eventual model implementation was the best in all five sites. However, we note that only gang youth *on probation* were involved, so that the prevention focus was not strong.

There were some research problems that detracted from the evaluation. Program and control youths were not well matched on prior offenses (the strongest predictor variable). The interviews with the control youth were minimal, with the result that there were no self-report comparisons available, only arrest data. This is particularly unfortunate in a project site that became dominated by police leadership and probation dominance of youth targeting.

Results were mixed, at best. Program youth fared considerably better than controls on measures of serious and less-serious violence arrests and for repeat drug arrests, but not for other types of offenses or for overall arrests. Results were generally better for younger than for older youth and better for those who received more coordinated services. There were no differences in "arrest change" patterns for gang members versus gang associates versus nongang youth. There was no measurable effect on the growth of gang membership.

Here, then, we have an active intervention as opposed to prevention emphasis and a better-than-usual program implementation. With results limited only to police measures of effectiveness, the Riverside project reduced serious violent offenses but not others, not overall offending rates, and not gang membership levels. It seems that little was gained in the most promising setting.

Mesa, like Bloomington-Normal, was a small, emerging gang site, with gangs identified as a criminal justice problem only in the early 1990s. Like Bloomington-Normal, it was thus a more typical situation than was Riverside. Model implementation was mixed. Social intervention activities seemed best, with suppression and total services lagging behind. Outreach and grassroots organizations were poorly involved. Most program youth, as in Riverside, were on probation, but in this case with low levels of violence: serious offenders were not involved. As in Riverside, there was a self-report delinquency problem; these data were collected only in the first two project years for program youth. Thus, results again rest principally upon police data.

Results show an 18% greater reduction in arrests among program than control youths, although in the context of declining youth arrests generally in the Mesa area. In contrast, measures of gang growth indicated increased gang sizes, especially in the program area. Because there was more prevention in this site and less targeting of gang members specifically, according to the report, any success achieved in the Mesa site may have been more delinquency related than street gang related.

In sum, the Mesa site saw only partial implementation of the Spergel Model. There was a good deal of inappropriate youth targeting, and the mixed success is not with a serious or heavily gang-involved youth cohort.

With the foregoing extensive coverage of the comprehensive model, we may be in danger of calling undue attention to it, amid the myriad other gang control programs to be mentioned in the last chapter of this book. Yet its very nature—more comprehensive than any other program, located in several contrasting sites, and given major backing by the federal government—the model and its application provides the best test yet of what truly concentrated effort might yield in reducing street gang problems. Our conclusion, unfortunately, is that the result seems not to have justified the effort (a post hoc conclusion, we freely admit; you can't know until you try). Beyond this, we note several points that emerge from the three site descriptions:

1. There are characteristics of the three programs that are surprising, given the initial intention to develop and apply a major, comprehensive, theory-based approach. The program youth numbers were quite small: 101 in Bloomington, 258 in Mesa, and 182 in Riverside. There was truly wide variation in implementation of the model, despite centralized management systems (the Spergel team and the OJJDP). There appears to have been a surprising dominance of police and probation agencies, given the comprehensive, multiagency character of the model. There were notable differences in the effectiveness (when implemented) of various services, and suppression seems to have fared least well. And in the research arena, the failure to gather self-report delinquency data consistently weakens the faith we can have in project outcomes. Arrest systems yield far fewer offense data and are subject to the biases, intended or not, of the enforcement agencies that were so prominent in the programs.

Inappropriate youth targeting, here too minor and there too serious, also leaves us in a quandary in judging how such programs can be implemented. This issue will loom large in the concluding chapter of this book.

2. In all three cases, the draft final reports suggest that there were no notable differences in program effects on core gang members versus gang associates and nongang members. This is truly surprising, since much of what we know about levels of gang involvement (see chapter 5) suggests such differences should exist, and in a major way. Perhaps, then, the comprehensive program, the Spergel Model as implemented, is really more of a *delinquency* reduction model than a *gang* reduction model. This seems most obvious in the Mesa project. Certainly, the various prevention, intervention, and suppression activities and services were applied to individual youth, with little reported attention to group processes and gang structures. This issue, also, will loom large in our concluding chapter on gang control programs.
3. The three reports show that age, gender, and prior record emerge (as usual) as strong predictors of youth behavior outcomes, stronger certainly than program effects. Further, there were no identifiable reductions in gang size or gang membership measures and only inconsistent effects on recorded offending levels. If enrolled youth and involved gangs showed so little impact from the programs, then it seems obvious to us that nothing was achieved to affect the upcoming generation of gang-prone youth in these communities. These 500-plus enrolled program youth will continue in their adolescent and young adult lives, some benefited and some not by these programs. But the effects are not of such a magnitude that the next cohort of youth is likely to be much affected.

In other words, gang reduction may not have been affected; the communities as responders to gang-spawning situations may not have been much affected. Like most other gang control programs, this one was in the here and now, while gang generation is a matter of the future. This strengthens our view, to be emphasized again in this book, that long-term successful gang control will not be achieved by intervention with youth, but by intervention with the nature of gang-spawning communities. And sadly, modern social science has not demonstrated, as yet, much capacity for such intervention.

SafeFutures

We come now to our third large project under the heading of bureaucratic programs. We do so because it is a direct outgrowth of the projects just covered—Little Village and the five-site, comprehensive community-wide program. We label SafeFutures a bureaucratic program because it was one of several, Spergel Model–inspired projects organized and funded by the U.S. Department of Justice and by the OJJDP in particular. The OJJDP had found a transportable program in which it believed, one that seemed to respond rationally to America's burgeoning street gang problem.

The fact that the OJJDP had not yet procured valid, positive evaluations from the earlier projects simply did not seem to matter, even though it had expended considerable effort to develop such evaluations. As this chapter is being written, and before such evaluations have tested the value of the Spergel Model, the Department of Justice has separately funded or developed combined funding with the Bureau of Justice Assistance for the following:

- the SafeFutures program (in 6 sites)
- the Comprehensive Communities program (currently in 2 sites)
- an Anti-Gang Initiative under the COPS program (in 15 cities)
- the Gang-Free Communities program (in 4 communities)
- the Gang-Free Schools and Communities program (in 4 sites)

Each of these includes a variation on the Spergel Model, often in conjunction with the OJJDP's Comprehensive Strategy for Serious, Violent, and Chronic Youth Offenders. Each is a multimillion-dollar investment in the new conventional wisdom about gang control accepted by the OJJDP on the basis of its own (to date) unevaluated immersion in the Spergel Model. Most of these programs, as of this writing, are in their early stages. SafeFutures, however, was initiated in a number of sites in 1996, typically with a five-year commitment of support from the OJJDP. The experience in one of these programs where preliminary reports are available is instructive, as it relates directly to our earlier statements about the Little Village and five-site implementations of the Spergel Model.

We base our discussion of SafeFutures on its implementation in St. Louis because public reports on its progress are available.[21] The elements of the St. Louis SafeFutures, involving 15 agencies and budgeted by the OJJDP for five years at $1.4 million a year, are clearly derived from the Spergel Model with modifications related to the OJJDP's comprehensive strategy. They are:

1. Reaching agreement among all participants on common goals. This included training on the overall model and staff visits to the Little Village project. Emphasis on the five strategies of the Spergel Model was included.
2. Assessment of the local gang problem.
3. Achieving common definitions of levels of gang membership.
4. Proper identification of gang-involved clients and the services appropriate to them.
5. Ongoing process and outcome evaluations.

Program implementation of these elements did not go well with the exception of the second element, this latter because of the evaluators' prior extensive gang research in St. Louis. The evaluators (Decker et al., 2002) cite the following as major program implementation problems:

1. Among the 15 categories of agencies, there were a number of disparities in goals, some of them seemingly insurmountable. There were also clear failures of information sharing between various agencies.

2. Some pivotal agencies were unwilling to engage gang members as clients, and some proved intolerant of client failures to comply with agency expectations and rules.[22]

3. The St. Louis police refused to participate, and there was some mutual antipathy between community agencies and the police department.

4. Considerable "program drift" developed, i.e., changes in goals, clients, and evaluation requirements. For example, less seriously involved clients got increasing services over time while services for the more serious clients declined. As noted by the evaluators, "the program plan . . . called for 'surrounding' each youth with multiple services," so that the decline in appropriate services was "clearly at variance with the identified goals of the program" (Decker et al., 2002: 56). This problem is certainly not peculiar to SafeFutures: the movement toward easier, "more desirable" clients is common to agencies in many fields.

Another example of program drift was an agency with the goals of providing parental training to gang members and delinquent teen parents. Over time, it adopted practices that "prohibited it from reaching gang members or teen parents. Instead, the primary service group was nongang members who were not prospective or actual teen parents" (Decker et al., 2002: 76).

Two other examples were a jobs-training program that couldn't find job placements and a mentoring program that couldn't find mentors. In both cases, the agency spokesperson claimed they weren't geared up for "that kind of kid." And of course the police felt uncomfortable with "service" to gang-oriented youth and the kinds of agencies that serve them.

5. There was little to the multiple-service aspect of the model. At its peak, the project provided multiple (cross-agency) services to 20.7% of the targeted clients, and only about 10% most of the time. These services were supposed to be the focal component of the program, as reported to us by Decker.

6. The school systems' data proved to be totally inadequate for basic project needs.

7. Budgeting accounting was inadequate and fell way behind time. This seriously affected services funding and delivery.

The frustrations with the project's implementation fairly ooze out of the evaluators' report. We quote directly from their summary:

> We noted the many occasions in which the behavior of one constituent agency failed to meet the expectations of the program model, or areas in which the arrangements between agencies failed to meet the requirements. A primary actor in the response model, the police, has not been integrated into the referral and follow-up process. The public schools, a key player in the identification and referral of problem youth, [were] unable to track students and utilize technology and other resources made available to them. The most successful gang outreach agency was unceremoniously closed, despite considerable objective evidence that the agency was the most successful in the service delivery in meeting the goals of the intervention. In a number of cases serious program drift was observed. The service network was designed to ensure that youths were referred to multiple agencies and that the number of youth[s] served by multiple agencies would increase over time. It failed to achieve either of these goals.
>
> In this context, it may be important to distinguish between a *program* and a group of *services*. The logic model that underlies SafeFutures describes a program, a well-integrated web of interventions in which information, decision-making and youth are shared in a seamless manner across programs. However, Safe-

> Futures in operation more closely resembles a series of services, that are related only because they are funded through the same mechanism and because their members attend the same meetings. The absence of a strong client focus distinguishes programs from services in this regard.
>
> Despite these apparent irrationalities, the program continues to exist. Indeed, in many senses the program appears to be thriving, and is often held up by federal monitors as a successful intervention. Representatives from other sites have been sent to St. Louis to observe the local operation, and in at least two of these sites the program appears to be floundering. There also appears to be estimable support for sustaining the program beyond the flow of federal funding. (Decker and Curry, 2002b: 214)

All of this holds despite the fact that the project started off with a heavy dose of planning data and then received constant feedback of process evaluation data. It holds despite a five-year commitment of substantial funding from the OJJDP (later extended to six years). It holds despite having the experience of Little Village and the five sites established under the Spergel Model. Why should this be so?

One reason goes all the way back in gang intervention history to the Roxbury Project in the 1960s, about which Walter Miller wrote a pivotal article whose title tells the story: "Inter-Institutional Conflict as a Major Impediment to Delinquency Prevention" (Miller, 1958). The Roxbury Project had no measurable impact on the gangs it targeted over several years.

And so, 44 years later, Decker and his colleagues report about SafeFutures, "It may be easier to change the behavior of juveniles than the system of caregivers who provide services to those juveniles" (Decker et al., 2002: 3). Further, they note, "The unwillingness to 'share' clients across agencies may be the greatest failure. . . . in many cases agency boundaries may be more difficult to break than patterns of delinquency" (2002: 82), and "[r]esolving turf issues may be more difficult for rational organizations than it is for loosely structured gangs" (2002: 86).

In a personal communication about this situation, Decker has told us:

> Of course, the SafeFutures model was never implemented. I question whether it could be in a complex city with a large youth violence problem like St. Louis. If the model wasn't implemented,

> how can it be a test of SafeFutures? On the other hand, what *was* implemented was SafeFutures, . . . came to be known as SafeFutures.

The initial outcome data from St. Louis were available on 1,022 program youth and 445 comparison nonprogram controls. Over four and a half years, data collection showed *no* positive effects of the program. In fact, more services led to higher subsequent court referrals. Multiple-agency clients produced higher police contacts and court referrals than did single-agency clients. The controls generally did better than the program youth. In sum, state the authors, "The model was not implemented as it was designed and failed to produce positive outcomes for the target group" (2002: 113).

Implications of Six Failed Programs

It may not be amiss, in this context, to note Spergel and Curry's (1990) finding from their survey of 254 law enforcement and social services agencies in cities across the country. Of the five strategies, two were found to be most effective in chronic gang cities, namely, opportunities provision and community mobilization. Yet these two were the least often employed, while the most common, suppression, was found to be the least effective. We are not, it seems, very clever about mounting appropriate gang control procedures.

Elsewhere (Klein, 1979), we have suggested five tests to assess how adequately intervention programs work out. These tests, in total, provide a rather severe assessment of program adequacy, and yet they must be met to a reasonable degree if progress is to be made. Moon shots, the 1991 Gulf War, polio eradication, remedial reading programs, certain workfare programs, and a number of population control programs have all met the five tests. Why not gang control programs? As can be seen, it all starts with a well-articulated program rationale:

Test 1: Adequacy of Rationale. How adequate is the rationale? Is it logical, internally consistent, parsimonious? Can it be implemented in programs? Is it sufficiently well articulated that it can be debated by reasonable people?

Test 2: Level of Implementation. How fully do the program activities become implemented?

Test 3: Outcome Achievement. How well do program outcomes achieve the criteria established for them, i.e., how much "success" is achieved?

Test 4: Program Integrity. How well and directly do the program activities articulate and flow from the rationale, i.e., how well satisfied are we that these activities represent the operational meaning of the ideas behind the program?

Test 5: Outcome Integrity. To what extent do the program activities lead to the measured outcomes? Were they sufficient to achieve these outcomes? Can we be reasonably certain that they, and not something else, led to the outcomes?

It seems obvious to us that, for the most part, our six programs have failed to meet these tests. The rationales have been a mix of conventional wisdom and poorly articulated conceptual models. The programs have varied widely, and sometimes poorly, in implementation. Outcome success has been either undocumented or largely unattained. Program integrity, to the extent that the rationales are articulated, has been weak. Little evidence exists to support the achievement of outcome integrity.

Our task, however, must go beyond mere descriptions of program failures. The real question for us is: what are the implications to be drawn from these failures? It is to these implications that we now begin to turn.

We began this chapter with a discussion of conventional wisdoms, defining these as "the combination of untested assumptions and relatively unchallenged facts that we normally take to represent truth." The terms *untested* and *unchallenged* are anathema to any science, including criminology. We want to move well beyond the "truths" that are introduced by the phrase "it is obvious that . . ."

In summarizing our journey though these six major programs in gang control, we will pinpoint some of these conventional wisdoms. Then we will suggest some "antidotes," which will be discussed in greater detail in the chapters of part II and which will appear again in chapter 8 as we develop a model for considering options in approaches to gang control. Here are some major conventional wisdoms that served as underlying assumptions of the six programs reviewed here:

1. It is obvious that gang behavior can be deterred by vigilant police, corrections, and court surveillance and sanctions.
2. It is obvious that reductions in gang activity can be increased by cross-agency information sharing and collaboration.

3. It is obvious that early identification of potential gang members can be accomplished and effective preventive actions can be taken.
4. It is obvious that in dealing with street gangs, the police are the most appropriate responders and program leaders because gangs are primarily a crime problem.
5. It is obvious that gang prevention can emerge out of general youth services.
6. It is obvious that gangs and gang members stand at the end of the continuum of delinquency and are otherwise not special or qualitatively different from other groups of delinquents.
7. It is obvious that comprehensive antigang programming is required and that multiagency interaction and some combination of prevention/intervention/suppression will lead to better gang control.
8. It is obvious that what we learn about successful antigang programming in one location can fairly well be applied to other locations.

All of the above conventional wisdoms can be found in connection with the six failed programs we have reviewed. If we can use these six experiences to expose these "wisdoms," then perhaps we can begin to offer some antidotes in the form of accumulated knowledge that can be made relevant to future programming. This is what part II of this book is all about, replacing conventional wisdoms with accumulated facts revealed by some old and especially some new research. The antidotes we propose are those having to do with (a) differential targeting of gang members based on their characteristics as seen in risk factors, (b) different forms of gang structure, (c) pivotal group processes in gangs, and (d) aspects of the community contexts in which gangs are spawned and responded to by local authorities.

One additional comment is critical to our approach: evaluate, evaluate, evaluate. If we have learned too little from past programs because of weak or nonexistent or inadequate research designs, this can be changed. New gang control efforts, based on existing gang knowledge and well-articulated models of intervention, can lead to effective measures of what works less well and what works better. Sustained research efforts which don't drift from their original goals can and must be associated with the initiation of new control efforts.

No aspect of the L.A. Plan had a reasonable evaluation component.

L.A. Bridges failed to sustain an evaluation beyond its first year. The Illinois program backed off from evaluating its impact. The Spergel Model projects and SafeFutures in St. Louis have failed to demonstrate positive outcomes, but at least we can learn from these efforts. G.R.E.A.T. showed us a program that can have a modicum of success on youth attitudes and perceptions, yet none on their gang affiliations and criminal behavior. There is a lesson in this as well. Demonstrated failures teach us what not to do. Now we need to demonstrate a few successes. In the words of Alexander Lebed, "There's got to be a time when you stop stepping on the same rake."

Part II

New data about gang issues at the individual, group, and community levels offer an empirical foundation for better understanding of the nature of street gangs. Carefully considered, such data can be used to organize our thinking about gang control options.

Four

INDIVIDUAL-LEVEL CONTEXT: RISK FACTORS FOR JOINING GANGS

We begin our consideration of the recent substantive literature on gang issues by focusing upon the individual-level context: what distinguishes youth who join gangs from similarly situated youth who don't? Recent studies have identified risk factors for joining gangs by thoroughly investigating the circumstances and histories of these two types of adolescents. Whether the characteristics selected for testing are integral to a theoretical model or reflect likely candidates derived from prior research on the correlates of gang membership, identified risk factors lend practical direction to prevention and intervention efforts. While we've labeled this chapter "individual-level" context to distinguish it from the group and community levels to be addressed in subsequent chapters, risk factors derive from the nested environments in which youths live. Typically, risk factors are grouped within the five ecological domains of individual, family, peer, school, and neighborhood. In this chapter, we consider the research on these characteristics as they are reflected in youths' reports of their circumstances. Our focus here is on *individual gang joining* and not on the process of the emergence of gangs in a community (which will be discussed in chapter 6).

In our terms, a risk factor for gang joining is any characteristic that predicts, or is associated with, gang affiliation. In addition to identifying risk factors, researchers also have searched for protective factors. One approach that has been commonly used is to employ the term *protection* as the opposite position on the continuum of risk. In this usage, youth who don't display a risk factor, or have less of a risk factor, are protected. We prefer the term *low risk* for these youth. Referring to two different poles of the same dimension by different terms does not identify new factors or new directions for practice and also tends to obscure findings. More useful from our point of view is the consideration of protective factors as characteristics or processes that counteract risk. In this usage, the effect of a risk factor on gang joining might be diminished by some other circumstance in an individual's life, which by definition is not an identified risk factor. For example, youth at high risk for joining gangs due to the influence of delinquent peers may be less likely to join if bonded to a positive adult outside the family. Technically, the presence of a positive role model would be a protective factor only if the absence of such a model were not directly predictive of gang joining (i.e., a risk factor). This logic has guided our analyses of juvenile violent offending, but has not been thoroughly tested on the issue of gang joining. With one exception, the published work on gangs reports characteristics that have direct effects, statistically distinguishing joiners from nonjoiners. We refer to these as *risk factors*. The exception is work by Monica Whitlock (2004) that analyzed family characteristics, including both direct and indirect effects on joining.

The risk factors that are investigated are drawn from the broader literature on prediction of delinquent involvement, or more specifically, involvement in serious and chronic offending. While this is a good place to start, we argue that identifying gang-specific risk factors is crucial for the development of good gang intervention policy. Obviously, not all delinquents are gang members. While we've shown that gang members commit a lot of crime, and some very serious crime, not all serious and violent offenders are gang members. Gang programs should be modeled from solid research on the specific factors that predict gang membership and not the conventional wisdom of generic applicability of findings from analyses of crime patterns.

We enter methodologically risky territory in our systematic attempt to synthesize the results of the recent work on gang risk factors. The studies from which we draw have research designs that are particular to each study (see Table 1.1), and these design differences may place limits on our ability to detect general patterns from this body of research. All of the studies we use compare the characteristics of youth who join gangs with those who do not. Thus, we limit this discussion to studies that focus on adolescents rather than adults. Information about the characteristics is derived directly from youths and family members via personal interviews or questionnaires and not from police records. Other methodological issues to keep in mind are:

1. Gang definition and status. As discussed in chapter 1 and illustrated in Table 1.1, the threshold for self-identified gang membership varies from one study to the next. Placement of youths in the "gang" comparison category is affected by the particular definition adopted by each investigator. Comparisons across studies require that we suspend our concerns about these differences in order to distill out generic patterns. Most studies we include here rely on youths' self-identification of gang membership. In addition, studies vary as to whether analysis is limited to current gang members or also include those who exited gangs prior to the study. Since our emphasis here is on differences between those who join and those who don't, we include both types of studies.
2. Nongang comparison groups. Risk factor approaches require that gang members be analytically separated from subjects in a larger sample. In some studies, the sample is representative of all youth who live in a neighborhood or city or attend public schools. In other cases, the sample is limited to high-risk neighborhoods and may not be representative of all youth in those neighborhoods. We include studies that permit appropriate comparisons among youth who live in the same neighborhoods and attend the same schools: comparing gang youth from inner-city slums to upper-class suburban youth reveals more about race, class, and employment levels than about the risks of joining gangs. Furthermore, we rarely include studies that draw their sample from incarcerated populations. Finally, some studies report findings by subcategories of nongang youth, such as gang associate or "wannabe." We include these only when more general gang-nongang differences can be assessed.
3. Cross-sectional versus longitudinal analysis approaches. Several studies employ longitudinal designs that permit the assessment of youth characteristics prior to gang membership, thereby establishing causal ordering or risk. Cross-sectional designs might conflate causes of membership with the effects of gang participation, as if, for example, a youth's participation influences relationships among family members or school performance. We

include both types of studies in order to expand the scope of our analysis and to address the issue of whether risk factor findings in cross-sectional studies differ from those derived from more costly and less frequent longitudinal studies.

4. Measurement of risk characteristics. There is no standardization in the way researchers measure important risk constructs. To simplify our analysis, we have combined similar indicators in several broad categories within each domain, thus sacrificing detail and specificity to provide a more general depiction of the findings from the recent gang risk factor literature. We employ a minimum threshold of three studies that assess a risk characteristic for inclusion in the analysis. We focus here on dynamic risk factors rather than the individual, social, demographic characteristics that are reported in chapter 1 (see Table 1.3). Finally, we exclude consideration of individual delinquent offending as we have already discussed the offending profiles of gang and nongang youth in chapter 2.

Characteristics Associated with Joining Gangs

We identified 20 studies since 1990 that met the desired criteria. The studies are listed in Table 4.1, with study identifiers that link to the summary of findings displayed in Table 4.2.[1] The reader will want to refer back to other study characteristics shown in Tables 1.1 and 1.3, especially the descriptions of samples, gang definitions, and gang prevalence.[2] Surveys of adolescents from the United States, Canada, and a few countries in Europe are included in this rich array of studies.

A quick glance at Table 4.2 reveals the following:

1. Individual, family, and peer characteristics are more often the subject of study than are school and neighborhood characteristics.
2. Although less frequent than cross-sectional designs, longitudinal research results confirm those derived from cross-sectional studies.
3. Multivariate analyses are less common than bivariate analyses. We could learn about the relative strength of specific risk factors if researchers reported multivariate results more often.
4. We've learned a lot about risk factors for joining gangs, but

4.1. *Studies Included in the Gang Risk Factor Synthesis*

Reference	Sample Type	Research Design	Analysis Design
Bjerregaard & Smith (1993)	representative	cross-sectional	multivariate
Bradshaw (2005)	representative	cross-sectional	bivariate
Cox (1996)	nonrepresentative	cross-sectional	bivariate
Craig et al. (2002)	representative	longitudinal	bivariate
Dukes et al. (1997)	representative	cross-sectional	bivariate
Eitle et al. (2004)	representative	cross-sectional	bi & multivariate
Esbensen & Deschenes (1998)	representative	cross-sectional	bi & multivariate
Esbensen, Huizinga, & Weiher (1993); Huizinga, Weiher, et al. (1998)	representative	longitudinal	bivariate
Esbensen & Weerman (2005)	representative	cross-sectional	bivariate
Esbensen, Winfree, et al. (2001)	representative	cross-sectional	bi & multivariate
Fagan (1990)	nonrepresentative	cross-sectional	bivariate
Gatti et al. (2005)	representative	longitudinal	bivariate
Hill et al. (1999)	representative	longitudinal	bivariate
Kent & Felkenes (1998)	nonrepresentative	cross-sectional	bi & multivariate
Lahey et al. (1999)	representative	longitudinal	bi & multivariate
Maxson et al. (1998); Whitlock (2004); Maxson & Whitlock (2002)	nonrepresentative	cross-sectional	bi & multivariate
Maxson Whitlock & Klein (1997)	nonrepresentative	cross-sectional	bi & multivariate
J. Miller (2001)	nonrepresentative	cross-sectional	bivariate
Thornberry et al. (2003)	representative	longitudinal	bi & multivariate
Winfree et al. (1994)	representative	cross-sectional	multivariate

TABLE 4.2. *Gang Risk Factors in Self-Report Studies*

Risk Factor	# Studies	Findings[a]	*Type Measurement & Analysis*				Results Summary
			Cross	Long	Bi	Multi	
Individual (6 longitudinal, 13 cross-sectional)							
Negative life events	3	3 S: 16, 17, 19	√	√	√	√	Consistently support
Self-esteem	10	3 S: 7, 16, 17	√		√		
		7 NS: 1, 3, 5, 6, 8, 14, 19	√	√	√	√	Mostly not support
Internalizing behaviors (anxiety, withdrawal)	6	2 S: 7, 19	√	√	√		
		1 I: 4		√	√		Inconclusive
		3 NS: 11, 13, 16	√	√	√		
Nondelinquent problem behaviors	12	12 S: 2–4, 7–9, 12, 13, 15–17, 19	√	√	√	√	Consistently support
Delinquent beliefs	9	6 S: 7–10, 13, 19	√	√	√	√	
		1 I: 14	√			√	Mostly support
		2 NS: 17, 20	√		√	√	
Involvement in conventional activities	6	2 S: 5, 17	√		√		
		1 I: 16	√		√	√	Inconclusive
		3 NS: 8, 13, 16	√	√	√		
Attitudes toward the future	5	1 S: 5	√		√		
		2 I: 16, 17	√		√	√	Inconclusive
		2 NS: 8, 14	√	√	√	√	

Family (6 longitudinal, 13 cross-sectional)							
Poverty/disadvantage	10	2 S: 2, 13	√	√	√		
		2 I: 6, 19	√	√	√	√	Mostly not support
		6 NS: 1, 12, 15–18	√	√	√	√	
Structure (single parent)	11	4 S: 2, 7, 17, 19	√	√	√	√	
		1 I: 13		√	√		Mostly not support
		6 NS: 6, 10, 12, 15, 16, 18	√	√	√	√	
Attachment	12	4 S: 3, 7, 9, 16	√		√		
		2 I: 17, 19	√	√	√		Mostly not support
		6 NS: 1, 6, 8, 11, 13, 14	√	√	√	√	
Parental supervision	12	8 S: 2, 7–9, 12, 13, 16, 19	√	√	√	√	
		4 NS: 1, 4, 15, 17	√	√	√	√	Mostly support
Parenting style/hostile family environment	10	3 S: 2, 13, 18	√	√	√		
		4 I: 3, 16, 17, 19	√	√	√	√	Inconclusive
		3 NS: 4, 14, 20	√	√	√	√	
Family deviance	5	2 S: 16, 17	√		√	√	
		1 I: 18	√		√		Inconclusive
		2 NS: 6, 13	√	√	√	√	
School (5 longitudinal, 9 cross-sectional)							
Commitment/educational aspirations	11	5 S: 2, 4, 7, 9, 13	√	√	√	√	
		4 I: 8, 16, 17, 19	√	√	√		Inconclusive
		2 NS: 1, 14	√		√	√	

(*continued*)

TABLE 4.2. *Continued*

Risk Factor	# Studies	Findings[a]	*Type Measurement & Analysis*				Results Summary
			Cross	Long	Bi	Multi	
Attachment	6	2 S: 13, 19		√	√		
		2 I: 8, 16	√	√	√		Inconclusive
		2 NS: 14, 17	√	√	√	√	
Academic achievement	7	4 S: 13, 16, 17, 19	√	√	√		
		3 NS: 8, 12, 18	√	√	√		Inconclusive
Unsafe school environment	5	1 S: 7	√		√	√	
		4 NS: 11, 14, 16, 17	√		√		Mostly not support
Peers (6 longitudinal; 10 cross-sectional)							
Characteristics of peer networks	14	14 S: 1, 2, 4, 6–11, 13, 15–17, 19	√	√	√	√	Consistently support
Affective dimensions of networks	11	6 S: 2, 5, 7, 10, 13, 16	√	√	√	√	
		2 I: 8, 17	√	√	√		Mostly support
		3 NS: 3, 11, 14	√		√		
Neighborhood (3 longitudinal, 6 cross-sectional)							
Area crime measures	7	2 S: 13, 16	√	√	√		
		2 I: 17, 19	√	√	√		Inconclusive
		3 NS: 11, 14, 15	√	√	√	√	
Criminogenic neighborhood indicators	9	3 S: 13, 14, 16	√	√	√	√	
		1 I: 18	√		√		Mostly not support
		5 NS: 1, 11, 14, 17, 19	√	√	√	√	

[a]"S" refers to findings of statistically significant (p < 05) differences in gang-nongang comparisons; "NS" = not statistically significant; "I" = inconclusive since

> there is work yet to be done; of the 21 categories, the most frequent conclusion is "inconclusive."

Substantive outcomes of the analysis vary by the domain assessed. Risk factors for gang involvement can be identified in all five domains, as noted by most researchers who conduct such studies. However, the five domains are not equally implicated, as suggested by the weak evidence of risk among school and neighborhood characteristics. While relatively few studies assess neighborhood features, most studies find mixed or no support for these as gang risk factors. It may be that different design and analytic approaches are needed to capture neighborhood risk adequately, and we return to this issue later in this chapter as well as in chapter 6.

Unsurprisingly, the characteristics and dynamics of peer networks receive consistent support in the gang risk factor literature. Developmental researchers have noted that adolescent peer influences exert a strong proximal effect on youth attitudes and behavior during this life stage. Having delinquent friends is a noted risk factor for gang joining and exerts an influence net of other risk factors. Yet, as we noted in chapter 3, gang participation promotes individual delinquency even beyond the effects of having delinquent friends. Researchers continue to parse out the effects of delinquent peer networks and gang membership on offending, but for our purposes here, we emphasize that delinquent peer networks and negative peer influences are consistent predictors of joining gangs. Vigil emphasizes the pervasive socialization effect of delinquent peers:

> When street socialization replaces socialization by conventional caretakers, it becomes a key factor in developing not only different bonds but different aspirations for achievement, levels and intensity of gang participation, and belief patterns. Whom you associate with, what you strive for, how you spend your time, and why you embrace a belief system are strongly connected to street culture. (2002: 2)

Like neighborhood characteristics, youths' experiences in school have not received the same level of attention as peer, family, and individual constructs. Assessments of the school bonding dimensions of commitment and attachment, and academic achievement, yield mixed results. Youths' perceptions of their school environments as safe or unsafe do not surface in most studies as gang risk factors.

Some will be surprised about the lack of importance of family characteristics in youth joining gangs. In the six family categories, only parental supervision and monitoring of the youth's activities receives support. Family poverty or economic disadvantage, having a single parent, and affective attachments among family members are not identified as gang risk factors in most of the studies. Inconclusive results were generated in assessments of parenting styles (including hostile or violent relationships between parents, harsh and inconsistent punishment) and family deviance (primarily parent crime, gang, and substance abuse histories). These findings are confirmed by longitudinal analyses, suggesting that the immediate effects of peer networks might overwhelm perceived family risk factors. These research findings might provoke a reconsideration of the strong emphasis on family issues in many gang programs.

Within the individual domain, three of the seven categories receive support as gang risk factors. Two individual-level dimensions receive uniform positive support from all studies. Nondelinquent problem behaviors, such as reactivity, aggressiveness, and impulsivity (also referred to as externalizing behaviors), consistently emerge as risk factors for gang joining. The second consistent predictor—although captured in just three studies to date—is a youth's experience of a series of negative life events. These stresses are measured across the ecological spectrum and include serious illness, school suspension, and disruption in intimate social relationships. The third individual characteristic that the majority of studies find to be a gang risk factor is youth attitudes toward delinquent behavior.

Self-esteem is often included in studies of gang membership but does not appear to be an important risk factor. There is no firm evidence either supporting or not supporting three other individual characteristics: psychological traits such as anxiety, depression, and social withdrawal (also referred to as internalizing behaviors), attitudes toward the future, and participation in conventional activities. Some studies find them to be risk factors, while others do not.

This synthesis of the risk literature has identified peer factors as important, along with a handful of characteristics from the individual and family domains. There is certainly a need for further research that attempts to resolve the many categories with inconclusive findings and for more multivariate analyses. But what have we learned that is relevant to gang practice? The rich variety of characteristics that have been the subject of many studies can suggest both positive and negative directions for gang prevention and intervention.

First and foremost, characteristics of peer networks are important and should receive attention in most gang programs.

Second, programs that focus exclusively on individual or family risk likely will miss important risk processes deriving from other ecological domains. Within these two domains, externalizing behaviors, positive attitudes toward delinquency, and parental supervision practices are promising areas for intervention.

Our review also points to less-promising directions for gang reduction. Youth self-esteem, family-level poverty, parent-child attachment, school safety, and neighborhood social disorganization/integration do not appear to be fruitful avenues to prevent youth from joining gangs, at least not based on the existing research to date.

We find little evidence to support neighborhood characteristics as predictors for individual-level gang joining. We contend throughout this book, particularly in chapters 6 and 8, that neighborhood and community features deserve more attention from both researchers and practitioners. We argue that communities spawn gangs, and it is these gang-spawning characteristics that should be targeted. Our analysis of the gang risk factor literature does not support this argument at the individual level, and it appears that neighborhood characteristics may be more relevant to understanding the emergence or persistence of gangs in communities. The lack of support for neighborhood influences on individual gang joining may result from the nature of this research. First, as mentioned previously, this is the least-studied aspect of risk factor research, and hierarchical analysis methods might generate more insight. The second issue goes back to the sampling designs of many of the studies we included in our analysis. Some studies sample youths from the same neighborhoods—"similarly situated" youth is our term in the first sentence of this chapter—and other studies sample high-risk neighborhoods disproportionately. This has the effect of reducing the neighborhood variance that might be explained. Our own work suggests that gang and nongang youth view their own (the same) neighborhoods somewhat differently, but perhaps not to a magnitude that overcomes these sampling issues. Hence, we continue to embrace our perspective on the import of neighborhood and community but acknowledge the lack of available evidence in the gang-joining risk factor literature to support this view. This does not, in any way, vitiate the importance of neighborhood and community factors in understanding why gangs emerge (independent of who their members may be).

A Note on Cumulative Risk

A handful of researchers have examined the effect of cumulative risk in both longitudinal (Thornberry et al., 2003; Huizinga et al., 1998; Hill et al., 1999) and cross-sectional (J. Miller, 2001; Whitlock, 2004) samples. Each study has determined that risk of joining gangs increases as risk factors pile upon one another. All five studies find that youth who join gangs appear disproportionately in the highest cumulative risk category. For example, Thornberry and colleagues (2003) calculated a high-risk group that manifested at least 21 of 40 possible characteristics. Among males, 43.5% of subjects falling in this high-risk group are gang members, which exceeds the 32.4% sample gang prevalence. Less emphasized in the work on cumulative risk is the observation that more than half of the youths experiencing a very high magnitude of risk factors from many ecological domains (and even higher proportions in other studies) were *not* gang members. Such analyses remind us that most "gang" risk factors are not particularly strong predictors of gang involvement, either individually or in the cumulative measure. Researchers generally draw from the literature on the prediction of violent and serious delinquency to test candidates for gang risk; the factors indicated in Table 4.2 as the most frequently supported risk factors enjoy broad support in this larger literature (see Hawkins et al., 1998, for a synthesis). However, as we have shown, several predictors of youth violence do not seem to predict particularly well to gang involvement (e.g., family poverty and attachment). Interventions that aim to reduce gang involvement specifically should avoid targeting risk factors that conflate violence and gang membership inappropriately.

Different Risk Factors by Sex or Ethnicity

The 20 studies discussed above provide a reasonable starting point for identifying those features of youths' nested ecological environments that place some youth at higher risk for joining gangs than other adolescents. A far smaller number of studies provide directions for understanding features that might differentiate gang risk for girls, as compared with boys, or for youths from different ethnic or race backgrounds. While it is clear from our discussion in chapter 1 that boys more often join gangs than girls and that there are ethnic differences in participation as well, what can be said about different ecological influences on these patterns of gang participation? Supplemental analyses of risk factors within demographic categories might suggest different programmatic directions or, alternatively, that programs need not customize interventions for girls or for different ethnic groups. Unfortunately, the empirical knowledge accumulated to date is insufficient to direct program specialization in these areas.

Few studies report risk factor analyses separately for girls and boys (Esbensen and Deschenes, 1998; Maxson and Whitlock, 2002; Thornberry et al., 2003).[3] But three findings are consistent across all three studies. First, fewer factors distinguish girls who join gangs from their uninvolved counterparts. This finding may be due to the lower number of gang girls available for analysis: smaller numbers make it more difficult to detect statistically significant differences. It may be that researchers have failed to capture important influences on girls' joining patterns; much academic attention has been focused on boys. On the other hand, it may be that few risk factors have been identified because gang girls are less distinct from other girls than gang boys are from other boys. The increased scholarly and practitioner attention to gang girls may yield a more nuanced understanding in the future.

A second general finding from these studies is that most of the risk factors identified for girls also differentiate boys who join gangs.[4] For example, six of the nine gang girl risk factors identified by Thornberry and his colleagues (2003) also differentiated gang boys from other boys.

The third pattern is that each study produces risk factors unique to girls, which might suggest the need for gender-specific programs. However, we find that none of these special risk factors emerge in more than one study. Risk seeking, lower school commitment, and fewer prosocial peers characterize girl gang members but not boys, according to Esbensen and Deschenes (1998). Maxson and Whitlock (2002) find lower involvement in community sports activities, less attachment to teachers, and less likelihood of receiving an award in school to be related to gang involvement among girls, but not boys. More social disorganization in the neighborhood and lower college aspirations and expectations are risk factors for girls only in Rochester (Thornberry et al., 2003). It is noteworthy that school characteristics surface as unique predictors for girls in each study and also that no family variable emerges as a unique risk factor for girls.

While additional studies are needed to examine this issue further, the research thus far suggests that girls and boys share common risk factors for gang involvement, but that exceptions might be found in the general realm of school experience. The studies completed thus far do not provide compelling evidence for gender-specific intervention.

We have even less to offer regarding the issue of ethnic differences in gang risk factors. Just one cross-sectional study with a nonrepresentative sample of young adolescent males compares risk factors between Latino and black gang and nongang youth (Maxson, Whitlock, and Klein, 1997). In this study, we conducted bivariate analyses on 43 variables separately for the two ethnic groups and found just 2 gang risk factors in common: exposure to violence in the neighborhood and street orientation (i.e., gang youths more often report they enjoy hanging out on the street). We detected 11 risk factors for black youth, but just 6 for Latinos. Again, sample sizes and the cross-sectional design limited our conclusions but offered preliminary evidence that gang risk processes may differ for these two ethnic groups. Further evidence of ethnic difference is offered in a study that tracked level of gang involvement over a school year for a cohort of ninth graders (Walker-Barnes and Mason, 2001). These researchers found that parenting style, specifically higher levels of behavioral control and lower levels of lax and psychological control, was particularly salient in decreasing gang involvement for black—but not Hispanic or white—youths. Other studies have investigated the characterizations of gangs and gang experiences among youth of different ethnic backgrounds (Freng and Winfree, 2004; J. Miller, 2001), but these do not inform our interest in differential risk factors.

Do Risk Characteristics Vary across Level or Type of Membership?

With little assistance available from the risk literature to support customizing programs by sex or ethnic background, are other categories of gang membership more useful for this purpose? Do youths who join gangs at younger ages display different risk characteristics than those who form their gang connections later? Are "core" gang members distinct from other gang members? Do youths who sustain gang membership for longer periods of time display different risk characteristics than more transient gang members? An affirmative answer to any of these questions would help to guide prevention and intervention efforts.

The rate of gang joining varies by age, with the highest levels evident in the early to midteen years (see Table 1.3). We might expect that risk factors would be different for youths who join gangs earlier rather than later because youths experience different social developmental stages throughout adolescence. However, we found no empirical studies that have investigated differential gang risk factors by age.

The next question refers to differences between core and fringe (or peripheral) gang members. Do youth whose behavior and identity are tightly bound to the gang have different risk constellations than those for whom gang membership is less central to their identity? A longitudinal research design is critical to ferreting out characteristics that unambiguously predict these levels of gang membership, but such studies have thus far not addressed this question. Klein (1995a) reviews his earlier work on core and fringe levels of membership and notes little distinction between the two types on sociodemographic variables such as age, family status, economic level, parents' education, and immigration status. However, several psychological and behavioral deficits characterize core members: lower measured intelligence, impulse control, school performance, and desire for change as well as higher group dependence. While these data are cross-sectional, some of these character dimensions likely precede gang joining and may be predictors of core membership.

More recent, although also cross-sectional, data reported by Esbensen, Winfree, and colleagues (2001) confirm the pattern. Youths who placed themselves in the two inner circles of a five-ring concentric circles diagram posed by the researchers as "your gang" were designated as core gang members. Core gang youths reported more antisocial attitudes and behaviors than other gang members, but the two types of gang youth were not different demographically (i.e., sex, race, family structure, or parents' education status). Core and fringe gang youth appear to have different risk constellations, although longitudinal analyses are needed to sort out which social and psychological characteristics precede gang membership, which therefore would be the useful focus of intervention efforts. However, youth likely move in and out of the inner circle of a gang so customizing intervention on this dimension may not be advisable.

Conventional wisdom portrays gang membership as a lifetime affiliation: "Once you're a Crip, you're a Crip for life." The age distribution of gang membership and virtually every study of gangs belies this conventional wisdom, but Decker and Lauritsen (2002) note that active gang members perpetuate the notion because "the viability of their gang depends on the ability of active gang members to maintain the perception that leaving the gang is nearly impossible" (2002: 61). Responding to consistent findings in major longitudinal studies that more than half of youths who join gangs sever these ties within one year (Thornberry, Huizinga, and Loeber, 2004), researchers have conducted risk factor analyses on different samples to see whether transient and stable gang members have distinct risk characteristics. A separate risk profile for short-term versus long-term gang members would permit practitioners to target different strategies to appropriate risk subgroups.

The results from Rochester (Thornberry et al., 2003), Seattle (Battin-Pearson, Guo, et al., 1998; Hill, Lui, and Hawkins, 2001), and Montreal (Craig et al., 2002) are quite consistent. Few variables that were tested distinguish transient from stable gang members, while the two types of gang members are consistently different from youth who don't join gangs. These studies find earlier involvement with antisocial peers, engaging in antisocial behavior (including externalizing and internalizing behaviors, disruptive behavior in school, early violence and drug use, and early dating), and family economic disadvantage to be markers for stable gang membership, but no other family, school, or neighborhood characteristics predicted to length of gang membership. The vast majority of characteristics that predict to gang joining don't appear to affect the durability of gang association.

These findings are confirmed by cross-sectional studies that compare the characteristics of current gang members with those who report prior gang membership at the interview. Few differences are detected in risk characteristics in current and former gang members (Winfree et al., 1992; Dukes et al., 1997; Esbensen, Winfree, et al., 2001), especially in light of the substantial differences between both groups and nongang youth.

Surprisingly little research has been conducted on gang desistance and the processes of leaving gangs. Interviews with former gang members conducted by Decker and Lauritsen suggest that the experience of violence may be a "triggering event" for many, while others simply "drift out" (2002: 66). Youths' experience in the gang may be a more important determinant of when they leave than their attitudes or life circumstances prior to joining. While Katz and his colleagues caution us that "combining past and current gang members into one group [for analysis purposes] might mask important attitudinal and behavioral differences according to the extent of gang association" (2005: 83), we find little evidence of important differences between these two groups in risk factor research. Most gang members do not remain gang members; membership is a transitory status.

Findings from Protective Factor Research

The contributions of risk factor research may be limited by the typical method of investigating only main effects. Researchers argue that risk operates in multiple ecological domains, and attempts have been made to combine or accumulate risk factors to gain better predictive power. The problem is that most risk factors do not individually—or as a group—predict gang joining that well. Dukes and his colleagues put it well:

> Additional analyses . . . revealed that a major difficulty in predicting which respondents were gang members was the fact that many

> students had characteristics of gang members but they were not members. From the nucleus of the model emerged a process by which some at-risk students become mainstreamers and more prosocial. They feel good about their abilities as students, and they translate this self-confidence into educational bonds and an orientation toward education as a ladder to a successful career as an adult. These students generally are not interested in becoming gang members, and their behaviors are less deviant. (1997: 158–159)

Our own research team (Maxson, Whitlock, and Klein, 1997) adopted a different approach. We reasoned that the explanatory power of risk characteristics may be limited by the failure to take into account interactions between variables, and we proceeded to test variables that were directly related to youth violence in combination with characteristics that had no direct predictive value. Our objective was to identify protective factors, which we defined as characteristics that reduced the probability of violence, despite the presence of a risk factor. Our ultimate goal was to inform the development of programs that could increase protection by buffering risk-laden youth. Our results were not encouraging. We detected a modest number of significant interactions—more than one would expect by chance but, given the large number of analyses required by the many combinations of variables available, far fewer than we hoped. Even less encouraging was the subsequent investigation of each significant interaction. The protection dynamic we sought (i.e., the violence probability generated by a high score on a risk factor reduced by a high score on a protective factor) was discernible in a handful of variable pairings, but the interpretation of these "true" protection processes was rarely meaningful at a conceptual level. Moreover, we found protective factors that reduced the probability of violence only among lower-risk youth—not a great help to program providers. Furthermore, we found that several pairings of risk factors with other protective variables appeared to *increase* the probability of violence in a pattern that our group labeled "risky protection." As we continue this work in the youth violence arena, we are humbled by the complexity of risk-protective dynamics.

Whitlock (2004) replicated this procedure, but with gang membership as the outcome, and limited her investigation to family characteristics encompassing structure, management, and deviance. She identified 10 of the 21 variables tested as risk factors, and 5 of these risk factors interacted with 7 other family variables to produce reduced probabilities of joining gangs. For example, a youth at risk for joining gangs due to low parental monitoring is less likely to join if his parents discipline him consistently (i.e., parents do not punish or punish for the same things), but discipline consistency has no effect on youth at low risk for joining gangs due to high parental monitoring. Whitlock identified the same protective pattern for the reliability of punishment (punishment doesn't change with parents' mood) when coupled with the risk factor of low parental monitoring. Punishment consistency also emerged as a protective factor, reducing the risk of gang membership for youths whose family members had a history of incarceration.

In all, Whitlock identified just 8 pairs of variables that produced significant interactions from 110 regression equations. Three of these pairs produced reductions of risk only at the low end of the risk continuum. She notes the limitations of her sample and cross-sectional design as possible barriers to uncovering additional protective factors. The importance of this work rests not on the particular pairings of risk and protective factors but in the demonstration that a protective effect is not simply the absence of risk. This approach to identifying protective factors to buffer risk for gang joining should continue with other samples and longitudinal designs, as it holds some promise for prevention and intervention practice. In the meantime, both researchers and practitioners should exercise more precision in their use of the term *protection*. Labeling lower risk as higher protection does not increase our knowledge about the complex dynamic of joining gangs, or of any other outcome measure.

What Reasons Do Gang Members Give for Joining Gangs?

At its best, risk factor analysis utilizes sophisticated statistical techniques to sort out various contextual influences on youths' participation in street gangs. Many researchers also take the approach of asking gang youths directly for the reasons they join gangs. In our overview of the findings from the current research on this topic, we are most interested in the consistency of results from different studies: are there certain reasons for participation that predominate in different samples of youth? We are interested in patterns of results within subgroups of gang members. For example, do girls express different reasons for joining gangs than boys? Do different ethnic groups offer similar reasons? Are the motivations for joining gangs wholly distinct from the reasons that youths participate in social groups more generally? The answers to these questions could provide guidance to the development of prevention and intervention programs.

Most researchers offer a list of reasons for joining gangs and ask gang members to select which apply to them. In contrast, Thornberry and his colleagues (2003) took the free-form responses of Rochester gang members and classified them into general categories. More than half of these gang youths specified family or friends in the gang as the primary reason they joined. Fewer than one in five gang members voiced the need for protection or attraction to fun or action.

Only "it's my neighborhood" garnered endorsement by a notable majority (65%) of current gang members in St. Louis studied by Decker and Curry (2000). The five other reasons (including family members belong, meet/impress girls, important among my friends, makes me feel important in my neighborhood, and nothing else to do) offered by these scholars were selected by less than one-third of these youths as having anything to do with their joining gangs. Decker and Curry also pursued more qualitative responses and found that "a large number of members of the sample stated that they joined their gang to seek physical protection or to participate in violence" (2000: 476). It would appear that Rochester gang members join due to the influence of friends and family gang associations, whereas St. Louis youths feel threatened and join to find safety or to protect their neighborhoods. As the two studies approached the question in different ways, we can't be sure if the reasons for gang joining would be more similar if the question were asked the same way.

Esbensen and Lynskey (2001) note marked differences in reasons for joining in the 11 diverse research sites included in their national G.R.E.A.T. study. Gang members were asked to circle each separate reason for why they joined, and among all gang members, protection was selected most often (54%), but near-majorities also indicated respect, money, or a friend in the gang as reasons. The range by site on protection varied from 37% to 74%, for money from 29% to 65%, and other common reasons showed comparable ranges.

Do male gang members cite different reasons than do females? Few sex differences were identified among Rochester gang youth (Thornberry et al., 2003) or in the combined G.R.E.A.T. research sites (Esbensen, Deschenes, and Winfree, 1999). In contrast, our own research found that associational ties (family and friends) were the most commonly endorsed reasons among female gang members in San Diego, while gang boys most often joined for excitement, territory, or protection reasons (Maxson and Whitlock, 2002).

Just two studies have examined ethnic patterns in the reasons for joining gangs. In Rochester, Hispanic youth were less likely than black or white youth to join due to family or friends' participation and were more likely to be attracted to the fun or action presented by gangs (Thornberry et al., 2003). Among G.R.E.A.T. gang members, Freng and Winfree (2004) detected significant ethnic differences in five of the six reasons and concluded that white youth more often endorsed all of the motivations except having a sibling in a gang.

In sum, the most common reasons offered by gang members vary by research location, ethnic background, and, perhaps, by sex but not in a patterned way that leads us to generalized explanations. One thing that most of the studies have in common is the relatively low rate at which gang members cite being forced to join as a reason. Unlike the risk factor literature, where we have identified convergence across studies on the importance of some factors, we find no overarching reason expressed by gang youths, nor do we find consistent patterns among subgroups by sex or ethnicity. Until we are better positioned to understand these variegated patterns in the reasons that gang members offer for joining, practitioners should investigate the dynamics within their own communities.

One further question remains regarding the reasons for joining gangs. How different are they from the reasons that any youth might participate in a peer social group? As we've argued throughout this volume that gangs are qualitatively different from other youth groups, we expect the reasons offered by youths to be quite different, although meeting opposite-sex peers or other associational influences might be expected to motivate all adolescents. We tested for differences between gang and nongang youths in the reasons they selected for joining their primary peer groups. We investigated this issue in our studies in San Diego and Long Beach with comparable youth samples and study designs, although Hispanic and black males were sampled in Long Beach while only black males were included in the San Diego data. All youths in both studies were offered the same list of 25 reasons; youths could select as many reasons as they liked. Table 4.3 lists the reasons that generated statistically significant differences between gang and nongang boys in both cities.[5]

The first thing to be noted in Table 4.3 is the number of items; 16 of the 25 reasons generated gang-nongang differences in the two samples, suggesting that gangs and other groups do indeed offer distinct attractions to youth. Just 6 items (not included in Table 4.3) differentiated the two groups in one city but not the other, suggesting more stability between

BLE 4.3. *Reasons for Joining Primary Peer Groups That Significantly Differentiate Gang d Nongang Boys in Both San Diego (Maxson & Whitlock, 2002) and Long Beach axson, Whitlock, & Klein, 1997) Study Samples*

sons More Common for Gang Boys	Reasons More Common for Nongang Boys
tection	Make friends
ve a territory	Participate in (other than illegal) group activities
l a sense of belonging	Keep out of trouble
money or other things	Meet girls easily
end was a member	Prepare for the future
nily member had joined	Share secrets
l important	Get parents' respect
illegal activities	
money from drugs	

these two cities than observed in other studies. The cross-site stability is further confirmed by the relatively close frequencies of these items in the two cities; all but 3 of the 16 reasons were endorsed by a similar percentage of that group in each city, and many were within just a few percentage points. Thus, it was easy to rank the reasons by frequency, and each list has the most common reasons listed first. In these two samples, protection and having a territory and a sense of belonging were the most common reasons offered by gang members for joining these groups. While even the least-frequent gang-joining motive—to get money from drugs—was endorsed by at least a quarter of gang members, protection was mentioned by three-quarters of gang members.

Nongang youths say that they join their social groups to make friends, to participate in group activities, and to keep out of trouble. We found that nongang boys more often join groups to meet girls than do gang boys, showing that occasionally the reasons attributed to gang joining are actually more common among nongang youth. The three reasons that did not distinguish the two groups in either city are noteworthy: joining groups for support or loyalty, to avoid home, or to participate in a group the youth can feel proud of were selected in equal numbers by gang and nongang members. Practitioners have mentioned each of these as a major attraction for gang youths, yet we find that they are more generic social inclinations for youth, regardless of gang affiliation. However, most of the reasons listed in Table 4.3, whether more common for gang or nongang youth, are quite consistent with the previous literature.

Conclusions: Implications for Policies and Programs

What have we learned from the recent research on factors that distinguish youth who join gangs from similarly situated youth who do not? We find convincing evidence of the importance of delinquent friends, nondelinquent problem behaviors, and youths' experience of a series of negative life events. Favorable attitudes about breaking the law, lack of parental supervision and monitoring, and commitment to negative peers also receive considerable support in the gang risk factor literature. Conversely, youths with low self-esteem, family economic disadvantage, a single parent or low attachment to parents, or who live in disorganized neighborhoods or attend unsafe schools do not appear to experience higher risk for joining gangs. Prevention and intervention programs should place emphasis on delinquent peer networks and their socializing influences. Early signs of such problem behaviors as reactivity, aggressiveness, and impulsivity should be addressed with effective programs. Parenting monitoring skills should be developed. Programs and policies should avoid interventions on those characteristics that do not distinguish gang from nongang youths if *gang* reduction is the primary goal.

Girls and boys appear to share many of the gang risk factors, although girls' experience of school requires greater scrutiny. We found little evidence in the risk literature for building specialized programs for girls and boys or for youth from different ethnic backgrounds. Few a priori characteristics separate out youth who participate in gangs for only a brief period of time from those for whom gang membership is more enduring.

Notwithstanding the above implications that we draw from this recent research, our review has uncovered a large number of conflicting results. As researchers continue to investigate these possible gang risk factors, programs that emphasize these should be carefully scrutinized. The protection factor research suggests that intervention on some risk factors may elevate risk or reduce the risk of gang joining only among those youth who are unlikely to join in any case.

Regarding the content of programs, our risk factor review falls squarely within Thornberry's lament: "As is true of virtually all findings from basic research, the present ones identify some of the issues that effective programs need to address but they do not by themselves provide a detailed blueprint of what those programs should look like" (Thornberry et al., 2003: 193). In concluding their study, these scholars argue that the "way forward" is found not in customizing gang programs but in drawing from risk factor research to identify and target the most appropriate program clients. "Our proposal is straightforward: we should steer gang members and youths who are at elevated risk for gang membership into programs that have demonstrated effectiveness in reducing delinquency and promoting social competencies" (2003: 199). The programs we describe in chapter 3 and chapter 8 yield little evidence of effective gang control and notable deficiencies in the appropriate targeting of program clients. Gang risk factor research provides a practical and useful tool for client selection: service providers should use the strongest *gang* risk factors to develop a screening instrument for potential program clientele in order to ensure that high-risk youth are targeted. We know that not all risk factors for delinquency apply equally to gang membership. Targeting by gang risk factors would lead us beyond "regular youth" and beyond mere delinquents to youths who could benefit the most from effective prevention and intervention practice.

Five

GANG STRUCTURES AND GROUP PROCESSES

In chapter 1, we described the far-flung dispersion of street gangs across the country and pointed out that most gangs are *local* phenomena. That is, most street gangs are indigenous developments not generally attributable to criminally motivated migrations or "invasion" from such gang centers as Los Angeles and Chicago. One might anticipate, then, that the forms that gangs take would reflect local or regional characteristics. And, it turns out, this is indeed the case to some extent. There is not one kind of street gang, but several distinguishable kinds within the overall class of the groups we define as street gangs. As Wyrick and Howell have noted, "Gangs in any given locality may be more or less sophisticated in their organization or criminality, but it is critical that communities not attempt to treat all gangs equally based on untested assumptions" (2004: 21). The differences among them have important implications for both research and policy. Unique local forms, however, may be less important than the more-general patterns within which they fit.

In this chapter, we start by discussing why the understanding of the variety of gang structures is important and describe past attempts to develop typologies of street gangs. We note in particular some problems with typologies of gangs by their criminal patterns. We discuss issues in the measurement of gang structure types and then present data on our own foray into this area, which is based on U.S. national surveys (with a brief look at the results as applied to the European gang situation). We then discuss some problems presented by the transformations of gang structures over time and present some cautions about generalizing about the nature of street gangs from data limited to any one time period. The overall theme of this material is as simple as it has been widely ignored: to understand street gangs, one must appreciate *both* their common elements *and* their diversity. Science is built on general principles and reasonable qualifications to them.

We point out elsewhere in this book that ethnic differences among gangs—white, black, Hispanic, Asian—are useful to note but not as important as is often suggested by the media (or law enforcement). The similarities among various categories of ethnic street gangs are far more common than are the differences (Klein, 1995a; Sanchez-Jankowski, 1991; Vigil, 2002). Gang structure and group process trump ethnicity.

Similarly, Hall, Thornberry, and Lizotte (forthcoming) have tested whether the group processes that lead to crime amplification in gangs is mediated by the kind of neighborhood in which the gangs exist. Comparing gangs in more- versus less-disadvantaged neighborhoods in their Rochester longitudinal study, these researchers found no differences. Group-induced crime amplification took place at high rates regardless of the character of the gang neighborhood. Group process trumps neighborhood. Therefore, in the second section of this chapter, we return to the point made in the introduction: there is, overall, a class of phenomena called street gangs, the members of which show common characteristics. Most of all, they share important group processes. These processes must be understood in the development of gang control policies and programs.

The Importance of Structure

The importance of understanding gang structures derives in large part from considering the dimensions of the structures and the relationships of these to other issues of concern. Let us consider several of these dimensions and issues.

Levels of Organization

It is assumed by most laypersons, public officials, and a surprising number of law enforcement officers that street gangs are well organized—cohesive, hierarchically led, with clear codes of conduct. While this may be an accurate depiction of a small proportion of street gangs, it is not true for the large majority. We are misled by the images of such dramatic, fictional accounts as *West Side Story* (great musical, poor social science). In most street gangs, leadership is ephemeral, turnover is often high, and cohesiveness only moderate. Codes of conduct often exist in rhetoric but are easily avoided or broken. Many street gangs are more a loose collection of cliques or networks than a single, coherent whole. Further, in the majority of gangs, median individual membership lasts only about a year. This high level of turnover challenges any notion of stable structure (Esbensen and Huizinga, 1993; Thornberry et al., 2003).

A classical description of limited gang cohesiveness was provided by one of the authors more than 30 years ago (Klein, 1971: 109–123). Little has changed since that time. Decker and Curry have most recently (2000, 2002a) described gangs' organization in St. Louis with respect to leadership, formal meetings, rules, subgroupings, connections to other gangs, and gang versus nongang friends. With the exception of generally accepted rules for behavior, the authors conclude that their street gangs are not well organized. Similar findings are reported by Hagedorn (1988) and Fleisher (1998), among others. In a separate analysis, Decker (2001) compared the two most-organized gangs (according to the police) in San Diego, St. Louis, and Chicago. He found that only one of these, Chicago's Black Gangster Disciples, fit the "organized gang" stereotype.

For the social services worker attempting to establish rapport with a gang, this somewhat amorphous structure of street gangs will require extensive observation and interview before any individual interventions are possible. Detached worker programs often require literally *years* of work before gangs become responsive (which is often long after worker burnout takes over). Examples are found in the heyday of detached worker programs in New York (New York City Youth Board, 1960), Chicago (Carney et al., 1969; Spergel 1966), and Los Angeles (Klein, 1971).

For the gang cop, this loose organization makes intelligence gathering quite idiosyncratic and defeats gang control via the arrest of hardcore leaders or the general harassment of members. Indeed, evidence suggests that concerted efforts at gang dissolution by social services workers or police may inadvertently increase gang cohesiveness through understandable mechanisms introduced elsewhere (Klein 1971, 1995a) and discussed later in this chapter.

For the researcher, perhaps the most unrecognized but common problem raised by this loose gang structure is that gang informants, those willing and interested in bringing the researcher into their world, are likely to be atypical of the general membership. Failure to obtain observations or interviews with a representative sample of a gang's members or relying on archival data on those arrested or convicted are factors guaranteed to yield distorted images of gang structure and behavior. Many of the gang case studies in the criminological literature suffer from these faults.

Heterogeneity of Gang Structures

Later in this chapter, we will describe several different street gang structures that illustrate structural variability. But even within each of these, the range is wide along a number of important dimensions both structural and behavioral, to say nothing of the variations across gang communities and the institutions (social services, police, courts, schools) responding to them. There *are* generalizations that can fairly be made about street gangs—that's what science is for—but they are of value only as we understand the variability that qualifies them. Within each category of street gangs, there can be wide differences in size, age ranges, gender proportions, centralized leadership, accepted codes, criminal behaviors, and so on. And *across* structures, these vary measurably.

The practitioner who ignores the structural variations, who thinks gangs are pretty much alike, will inevitably fail in attempting to intervene in multigang settings. The researcher who fails to seek the structural differences or who studies but one gang or one gang type will publish false generalizations and mislead his or her colleagues. The responses of many gang ethnographers to the narrow depictions offered by Yablonsky (1963), Taylor (1990), and Sanchez-Jankowski (1991) reveal that the levels of violence and of drug entrepreneurialism described by these authors have manifestly misled major public policy initiatives. We don't need more of these errors.

Structures and Functions

Groups persist in part because they fulfill certain needs of their members. In the case of street gangs, most prominent of these needs are the status, sense of identity, and perceived protection from rival groups that derive from membership. Secondarily, street gangs provide access to and social legitimization for antisocial attitudes and behaviors.

For the moment, however, the point to be made is that gang structure and function are interrelated, enough so that to ignore structural differences also yields misunderstanding of functional differences. Some gang structures, most notably the "traditional" and "compressed" forms to be described later, exist more for social than for criminal reasons. Especially in the case of traditional gangs, intergang rivalries and territorial disputes, whether violent or merely rhetorical, are often the hallmarks of gang existence, with criminal behaviors an important but secondary function. To attempt gang control in these instances merely through the enforcement of legal codes clearly misses the point; to attempt an understanding of these gangs through their variegated criminal patterns similarly overlooks the principal sources of their origin and persistence. That is, arrests and convictions usually do little to affect gang structure and function. It is the gang as a *unit* that requires intervention and control: gang structure and function should be the targets.

In a similar but contrasting fashion, there are "specialty" gangs, to be described later, whose principal function originated in or evolved into a primary focus on a narrow criminal pattern. Drug gangs, burglary rings, skinheads, and the like come to exist principally around these more-narrow antisocial interests. This type of gang *can* be effectively controlled through selected enforcement procedures, and they can be understood and described by research using these interests as the focal point (Padilla, 1992; Hamm, 1993; Bjorgo, 1997; Valdez and Sifaneck, 2004). As we will demonstrate later, the contrasting functions bring with them important differences in gang size, leadership, duration, and other structural dimensions often overlooked in both practice and research.

It is our intent in this chapter to go beyond the consensus nominal definition offered in the introduction to more of an operational definition in which the measurement of gang patterns defines their nature. The patterns we choose here are those that reflect the *structural* characteristics of gangs—things like their age distribution, longevity, size, internal subgroupings, and crime patterns. We emphasize these structural components because other attempts to find gang patterns—gang typologies—have not done so and have failed in part due to this omission.

If we are successful in developing a structural typology of street gangs, we can offer an additional useful approach to gang definition. We want to attempt comparisons of gang situations across time and between cities and nations; such a typology might allow us to make progress in these directions. A recent example is the application of the structural typology to gangs in a dozen European cities. Where definitional consensus initially proved to be a barrier, the typology revealed much about the common and disparate gang patterns in these cities and many in the United States (Klein, 1996).

One final note: we recognize full well that in adopting this operational stance, we have not "solved" the definitional problem but merely surmounted it for our particular interest in facilitating street gang comparisons over time and space. For us, such comparisons are pivotal to drawing reliable generalizations about gangs and how to control them. It is a major goal of science, after all, to be able to draw forth generalizations about the phenomena it studies. Be these laws, principles, or patterns, science can neither summarize nor predict without them.

Past Efforts at Gang Typologies

Public images of gangs take some common forms. These include

- a group of youths lounging on the street corner, harassing passersby and disrupting local businesses
- the *West Side Story* image of cohesive, tightly organized rival collectivities whose principal concerns are minor crimes and territorial challenges
- super-gangs, Chicago-style, with memberships in the thousands, in control of neighborhoods and tightly entwined with organized-crime groups
- marauding cliques of a half dozen youths moving freely about other people's neighborhoods, randomly targeting people and facilities in almost senseless attacks "for the fun of it"
- bands of drug-selling, gun-toting thugs

So what does a street gang look like? Most thoughtful scholars have answered, first, that there is no one, single form of gang. Rather, gangs pattern themselves in stable and recognizable forms. It is this pattern of forms that has led to the attempts to typologize gangs. In a sense, the purpose of these typologies, and most certainly the one we shall describe as the result of our recent research, is to achieve an "ostensive definition" as described by Ball and Curry: "Although one has a clear or vivid idea of a thing when one can recognize examples of it immediately, the idea is not yet distinct until one can enumerate one-by-one the features that distinguish the thing from others" (1995: 226).

Attempts at gang typologies fall roughly into two time periods, which we will call the "classical" and "modern" periods of gang study. The former starts with Thrasher's 1927 work and ends with Klein's 1971 review of the classical works. The modern period starts with Walter Miller's mid-1970s national surveys and continues through the present.[1]

These attempts also fall roughly into two descriptive forms: gang typologies that are primarily behavioral and those that are primarily structural. Although some mixing of the two forms can be seen, they are usually quite distinct. The contrast is critical to our exposition later of our own research results. Behavioral typologies typify gangs by their purported tendency to manifest a predominant form of behavior. The most influential of these typologies was that of Cloward and Ohlin (1960), to which we will refer below. It was also typical of the behavioral typologies in that the behaviors noted were specifically criminal rather than more broadly social. The structural typologies, by contrast, largely bypass gang behaviors to find patterns in the social characteristics of the groups. Examples of structural dimensions are race and ethnicity (often used by police and the media), size (from small cliques to the super-gangs of Chicago), and type or level of organization (emphasizing leadership patterns or role differentiation).

The Classical Period

Serious attempts at typologizing started with Thrasher's 1927 work, *The Gang*, a monumental exercise in Chicago to catalog more than 1,000 youth groups through observations, interviews, secondhand reports, and other processes that seem loosely constructed in the hindsight of modern methods. The distinctions made were among (1) diffuse, (2) solidified, (3) conventionalized, (4) criminal, and (5) secret society groups. Four of these, at the least, may be seen as structural, although many of the groups subsumed under them would not today be classified as street gangs, many indeed being little more than common boys' play groups.

The only other original classification of gangs as structural entities during the classical period was that of the New York City Youth Board (1960), which mounted a major detached worker program on the streets of several boroughs. These gangs were (1) vertical, (2) horizontal, (3) self-contained, or (4) disintegrating. Here, the structure had to do principally with organizational features and emerged from the experiences of the street workers rather than any a priori conceptual stance.

Four other classical period depictions, derived inductively from the researchers' observations in the field, stress behavioral rather than structural properties. Thus Cohen and Short (1958) reported a pattern of theft, conflict, and addict gangs based on the predominant crime orientations within the groups. Cloward and Ohlin (1960) followed with their highly influential depiction of criminal, conflict, and retreatist subcultures and gangs with the same emphases within them. Spergel (1964), a student of Ohlin, found a fourfold variation of racket, theft, conflict, and retreatist gangs. His was the only one of a half dozen early attempts at replication to confirm the basic behavioral/criminal pattern noted by his predecessors. Finally, we find Yablonsky's (1963) distinction among social, delinquent, and violent gangs in New York, although his emphasis was clearly on violent gangs as the major problem.

In his 1971 review of these major attempts and other gang writings of the classical period, Klein attempted to summarize the gangs described in both structural and behavioral typologies. He found the gang descriptions to be principally structural, with four dominant patterns: (1) traditional (age-graded subgroups, self-regenerating territorial gangs); (2) spontaneous (age-integrated short-term gangs); (3) specialty (short-term groups with specific rather than general criminal focuses, such as drug involvement); and (4) horizontal (short- or long-term alliances of gangs, usually manifest in times of extreme challenges by rival gangs, as in Chicago's early super-gangs).

Of the various typologies of the classical period, two had major influence. The Cloward and Ohlin typology, being theoretically integrated and based on social and cultural descriptions of lower-class urban life, was very appealing to scholars as a conceptual package. Failures to locate the pattern in other settings (e.g., Short and Strodtbeck, 1965; DeFleur, 1967; Vaz, 1962; Monod, 1967; Sherif and Sherif, 1967; and Downes, 1966) did little to discourage the acceptance of the criminal-conflict-retreatist typology.

The other influential attempt was Yablonsky's, although his social and delinquent gangs quickly faded in memory as his violent gang captured media and lay attention. Titling his dramatically written book *The Violent Gang* helped to solidify the image of street gangs not only as violent, but also as large, marauding congregations held together by megalomaniacal, sociopathic leaders. Focusing on the most feared of the behavioral patterns has set a pattern against which almost all future behavioral gang research has had to do battle. Most writers citing Yablonsky's descriptions have failed to note his exaggerations and the fact that the few gangs he observed were short-lived anomalies whose description has seldom if ever been replicated in any other time or place.

In a point to which we will return later, attempts to define gangs by dominant behaviors—violence, theft, graffiti, or other narrow criminal patterns—raise two problems. First, most gang members' crime is versatile; the members (and thus most of their gangs) engage in a wide variety of crimes. Thus the "violent gang" or the "theft gang" is an inaccurate depiction. Second, if one bases a gang control program on one type of crime, for example, violence, one will miss the true target of crime versatility. False assumptions can lead to misguided programming.

The Modern Period

Walter Miller entered into gang research in the 1950s with an anthropological thrust that distinguished his work from that of the dominant sociological paradigm. He viewed street gangs as reflections of lower working-class culture, rather than as distinct social entities, although his behavioral depictions are more those of traditional, territorial gang structures. Returning to gang work some 20 years later, Miller eschewed the ethnographic methods and undertook a survey of officials in many cities across the nation. He was led by this process to the need to distinguish gangs from other groups that he called "law violating youth groups."

In a strictly ad hoc procedure, W. Miller (1980) offered a list of 20 such groups of which only 3 are labeled "gangs": turf gangs, gain-oriented gangs, and fighting gangs. Most others are called rings, cliques, bands, or crowds, although they would by most scholars also be included as gangs. The arbitrariness of the system is obvious, yet the purpose is laudatory as Miller hoped to delineate group differences that would facilitate comparisons across cities.

The labels applied by Miller to most of his other groups are almost solely behavioral rather than structural: disruptive, looting, burglary, robbery, larceny, extortion, drug dealing, and assaultive. The level of criminal specialization is highly unusual, and as we will indicate later, totally opposed to what has been almost universally demonstrated about gang crime, which is that it is versatile rather than specialized.

Several other behavioral typologies have been suggested during the modern period. Taylor's (1990) scheme for the development of gangs in Detroit, highly related to drug sales, claims an evolution from scavenger gangs to territorial gangs to corporate gangs. Others, such as DiChiara for Hartford, Connecticut (1997), and Salagaev for Kazan, Russia (2001), have similarly described case studies of criminal gang evolution from less- to more-organized states.

Huff (1989) and Fagan (1989) have also offered behavioral typologies. Huff described hedonistic, instrumental, and predatory gangs, while Fagan found younger members to form social, party, conflict, and delinquent gangs. Neither Taylor's, nor Huff's, nor Fagan's schemes articulate well with Miller's types—nor with each other's.

One can well ask how this can be. Especially given the three-city research undertaken by both Huff and Fagan (six cities in all), some general patterns should begin to emerge. That each behavioral typology provides a unique pattern raises two fundamental problems. The first of these is the suspicion that the typologies do *not* emerge naturally from systematic observations and analyses, but rather from some combination of different researcher perspectives, different methods, and unique gang locations. To surmount such problems would require the sharing of data and the coordination of research designs, a process almost unknown in American gang research. Without such coordinated, multisite research, we can expect to continue to see "unique" depictions of common phenomena.

The second problem with the behavioral, mostly crime-driven, typologies—as noted earlier—is that they fly in the face of what is known about crime patterns specifically. Klein's (1971) analysis of 1960s data, expanded from gangs to general delinquency in a later review (Klein, 1984), has since been replicated many times by other scholars to show that most offenders show a versatile rather than a specialized pattern of offending. Gang-specific studies of crime profiles are uniform in finding versatility patterns (Thornberry et al., 2003; Esbensen and Huizinga, 1993; Battin et al., 1998). Typically, youthful offenders *and* gangs show a variety of acts, including status offenses, theft, vandalism, burglary, robbery, drug use and selling, fighting, weapons possession, and assault. Klein referred to it as "cafeteria-style offending" (1995a: 68). Given this absence of specialization, it is illogical to propose that gangs be delimited by any predominant crime pattern. Most gangs cannot be of that sort, although we will indicate later one specific but uncommon form of street gang, the "specialty" gang, that does fit that pattern.

It is precisely these sorts of problems of uncoordinated typologies that have led us to our own work on the structural typology reported in these pages. Interestingly, only one other structural attempt has appeared in the modern period, and it is one that gives us some trouble. From his observations in three major cities, Sanchez-Jankowski (1991) proposed the existence of three street gang structures: vertical, horizontal, and influential. The distinctions were based principally on forms of gang leadership or authority structure. Included as well are member rules and duties and codes of behavior, resulting in the author's claims of three *distinct* models.

One of our problems is that we can't find such distinct models in Jankowski's descriptions. More fundamentally, Jankowski has described rational, planned, organized, sophisticated gangs that defy almost all other researchers' findings, but he does not provide any data to support his position. We are, frankly, not convinced by Jankowski's descriptions that the gangs he observed would be similarly observed by others.

We should add that other researchers certainly have been aware of some of the structural dimensions of street gangs. Recent examples include James D. Vigil, Jody Miller, Scott Decker, and Finn-Aage Esbensen. However, their analyses did not refer to the gangs as *units* and did not attempt to delineate differences among gangs. Thus their descriptions do not help us to typologize gangs.

We are left, in sum, with two basic typological approaches that invite further work. The behavioral approach, despite its popularity, seems illogical given one of the few fully accepted generalizations about delinquency and gang crime: that it is versatile rather than specialized. Further, various scholars seem unable to arrive at common types. The structural typologies seem to us even less data based and, with the exception of Jankowski's proposal, have not emerged during the modern period.

Toward a Structural Typology

To develop a structural street gang typology that is clearly data based, one needs ready access to data on structural dimensions. These might include gang size, age ranges, gender, ethnicity, locations, leadership, subgroupings, cohesiveness, duration over time, and organizational norms. Further, one needs such data on many gangs in many settings in order to develop patterns and generalizations. Where could such data be located?

Ideally, a very large series of planned, coordinated ethnographies of street gangs would yield the structural data needed. A few single ethnographies or groups of long-term field observations have, in the past, provided some structural depictions (Klein, 1971; Moore, 1991; Padilla, 1992; J. Miller, 2001; Fleisher, 1998). But one needs far more than these, based on reasonably representative samples of street gangs, not the convenience samples that have been the rule until now. Such a major enterprise, for now, does not seem realistic.

Alternatively, one could undertake an archival analysis of already reported field studies, such as those listed above. But few of those deliberately collected data on structural dimensions, so that the results would at best be rather haphazard. But we shall return to them later to see what might emerge.

A third procedure would be to undertake large-scale, multisite interview or questionnaire surveys of gang-age respondents. Either household or school-based surveys would suffice, although each approach has problems of access and sampling. At this point, we are aware of only two such surveys. In the research undertaken by Esbensen and his colleagues to evaluate the G.R.E.A.T. program, its formulation did not include a deliberate gang structure investigation. Still the Esbensen model could be at some point adapted to our purpose. Surveys of St. Louis, Chicago, and

San Diego gang members (Decker, 2001; Weisel, Decker, and Bynum, 1997) reveal very ambiguous perceptions of the members' own gang structures, even the highly structured Latin Kings and Black Gangster Disciples. Gang members are often poor informants on their own groups; they know their own cliques far better than the overall gang structure.

A fourth procedure would be to take advantage of the observations of street gang workers at various locations. Where they have existed (W. Miller, 1962; Short and Strodtbeck, 1965; Carney et al., 1969; Klein, 1971; New York City Youth Board, 1960; Spergel, 1966), gang workers have provided rich and often detailed pictures of relationships among gang members and the general characters of their gangs. (As with the ethnographic approach, one would have to mount a very large, planned program, in this case a multigang, multisite gang intervention program with the inclusion of gang workers as both interviewers and data providers. One model in five sites has recently been provided by Spergel, as noted in chapter 3, but that model, for our purposes, would have to be greatly expanded at enormous financial cost.)

While our search for a structural street gang pattern could not be accomplished in any of these forms with our limited resources, another source of appropriate data did seem available, namely, police observations. Clearly, one must approach police gang data with great caution. There are built-in biases, sampling problems, and limited perspectives to be recognized and overcome. Police roles and functions make the task difficult, but these same roles and functions are also unique in providing the data access needed. In every city, the police are the only group with broad exposure to street gangs. Officials in other social services agencies may be familiar with one or several gangs in their catchment areas, but they cannot have close-at-hand, citywide exposure. This is especially true when contrasted with those many police departments that have special gang units or gang officers.

Even with knowledgeable gang officers as respondents, two problems have to be surmounted. The first is that gangs are *informal* groups. They do not provide the police with membership rosters, time cards, dues payment lists, membership cards, organizational charts, or constitutions and bylaws. The police data have to be observational, not inherently organizational. Second, some structural dimensions are more obvious than others; e.g., cohesiveness is less immediately observable than the existence of subgroups. Further, police perspectives sometimes ignore some dimensions—gender ratios is one example—and stereotype others, such as leadership. Thus the structural dimensions to be derived from police experts cannot be comprehensive but must be carefully selected. This is a limitation but not an insurmountable barrier.

Methods

We start by noting several dimensions *not* sought from our police respondents. Earlier interviews with 260 police gang experts across the country had made it clear that their style of thought did not yield consistent or realistic views of several matters. One of these was gang leadership. This tended to be stereotypic in form, stressing serious criminal involvement and older age, and thus missing age-graded leadership and leadership based on verbal capabilities, organizational skills, and athletic or social skills.

A second dimension was level of membership, again yielding rather stereotypical categories, such as core or hardcore and peripheral; actives, associates, and wannabes; confirmed, rostered, or certified. The terminology was not consistent, nor were the criteria for the differences very clear beyond the level of involvement in serious crime.

Most important, a direct question about gang structure proved fruitless. While many police experts correctly noted that street gangs tended to be loosely structured and poorly organized, others reported a dominant pattern of hierarchical structure and clear group rules. The notion of assessing gang cohesiveness, so critical to scholarly depictions of street gang structure, was foreign to many of our experts.

Two additional patterns became clear. In the absence of prior guidelines, police tended to think of street gangs in terms of two characteristics, ethnicity and violence. As to the first, it seemed to our experts that Hispanic gangs differed substantially from black gangs; both were different from Asian gangs; and white gangs were all but nonexistent. Most research data on street gangs did not support these clear distinctions.[2] For instance, Freng and Winfree (2004) found remarkable similarities overall among white, African-American, and Hispanic gang members with respect to their attitudes toward gangs, reasons for joining gangs, gang characteristics, illegal activities, and victimization rates. As we have noted elsewhere, group process trumps ethnicity.

The same is true of the violence issue, in that research data dispute the existence of predominantly violent gangs or violence as a meaningful dimension. Levels of gang violence are strongly correlated with the levels of the *amount* of gang offending. The more they offend, the more the pattern includes the less-common violent acts. This is a statistical pattern rather than a qualifying distinction among types of gangs. That police stress violence is certainly understandable, given their societal role, but it reflects a narrow view of what street gangs are all about.

For our purpose, this discussion meant two things. First, we could not ask police gang experts—"gang cops" in common parlance—to respond *directly* to questions about street gang leadership, levels of membership, structure and cohesiveness, ethnicity, or crime patterns. It also meant, however, that if we could establish gang types by reference to *other* dimensions, then we might be able to correlate these with some of the excluded dimensions in other ways. As will be seen in our data, this was indeed possible to some extent. We turn now to phase I of the research.

The Phase I Sample

Using as a database 792 cities with street gangs identified in our 1992 survey on gang proliferation and migration, a stratified sample of 60 cities was selected. Stratification was by period of gang onset in the cities (1970 and earlier, 1971–1984, and 1985–1992) in order to ensure adequate representation of older gang cities. Fifty-nine of the 60 cities yielded responses to our request for interviews with their best gang experts (some of whom had been our respondents in earlier research). We report here only the data that led to the street gang typology; other questions merely corroborated the problems of stereotypical or inconsistent perspectives alluded to above when questions about the many gangs in each city were posed.

The procedure which succeeded with the gang cops was to ask each to describe the single gang with which he or she was most familiar. Consistently useable responses were obtained on the dimensions of subgroups, size, age range, duration, territoriality, and crime versatility versus specialization. In other words, respondents described their best-known street gang as to whether or not it included significant subgroups, the size of its known membership, the range between youngest and oldest members, how long the gang had been in existence, whether it was a territorial gang or not, and whether its members engaged in a wide variety of offenses or mostly one or two types (and if the latter, what types).

These data came from the experts in the 59 cities, both new and old in their exposure to gangs, and were taken from all sections of the country. They included small, medium, and large jurisdictions, in rough proportion to the data set of 792 cities previously identified in our research. Thus we have some confidence in their national representativeness.

We undertook an analysis of the six dimensions across the 59 cities, looking for patterns of relationships among the dimensions. Five types of street gangs emerged from this analysis, as noted in Table 5.1.

TABLE 5.1. *Characteristics of Five Gang Types*

Type	Sub-groups	Size	Age Range	Duration	Territorial	Cr Ve
Traditional	yes	large (> 100)	wide (20–30 years)	long (> 20 years)	yes	yes
Neotraditional	yes	medium-large (> 50)	no pattern	short (< 10 years)	yes	yes
Compressed	no	small (< 50)	narrow (< 10 years)	short (< 10 years)	no pattern	yes
Collective	no	medium-large (> 50)	medium-wide (> 10 years)	medium (10–15 years)	no pattern	yes
Specialty	no	small (< 50)	narrow (< 10 years)	short (< 10 years)	yes	no

The labels—traditional, neotraditional, compressed, collective, and specialty—represent our attempt to capture the more-distinguishing features of each pattern.[3] The traditional, compressed, and specialty gang patterns correspond well to case descriptions already available in the scholarly literature about street gangs. For example, Weisel's (2002) violent gangs resemble our traditional and neotraditional gangs. Her delinquent gangs resemble our compressed gangs, while her income-generating gangs are similar to our specialty gangs. The neotraditional and collective gang patterns have been alluded to on occasion, but emerge more clearly here. In order to provide more meat to the bones of Table 5.1, we developed the five "gang scenarios" below, which also served in the second research phase to be reported next.

Five Street Gang Scenarios

THE TRADITIONAL GANG Traditional gangs have generally been in existence for 20 or more years: they keep regenerating themselves. They contain fairly clear subgroups, usually separated by age. O.G.s ("Original Gangsters") or Veteranos, Seniors, Juniors, Midgets, and various other names are applied to these different age-based cliques. Sometimes, the cliques are separated by neighborhood rather than age. More than other gangs, traditional gangs tend to have a wide age range of their members, sometimes as wide as from 9 or 10 years of age into the 30s. These are usually very large gangs, numbering a hundred or even several hundred members. Almost always, they are territorial in the sense that they identify strongly with their turf, 'hood, or barrio and claim it as theirs alone.

In sum, this is a large, enduring, territorial gang with a wide age range and several internal cliques based on age or area.

THE NEOTRADITIONAL GANG The neotraditional gang resembles the traditional form, but has not been in existence as long—probably no more than 10 years and often less. It may be of medium size—say 50 to 100 members—or number its members in the hundreds. It probably has developed subgroups or cliques based on age or area, but sometimes may not. Like traditional gangs, it is also very territorial, claiming turf and defending it.

In sum, the neotraditional gang is a newer territorial gang that looks to be on its way to becoming traditional in time. Thus, at this point it is subgrouping, but may or may not have achieved territoriality, and its size suggests that it is evolving into the traditional form.

THE COMPRESSED GANG The compressed gang is small—usually in the size range of up to 50 members—and has not formed subgroups. The age range is probably narrow—10 or fewer years between the younger and older members. The small size, absence of subgroups, and narrow age range may reflect the newness of the group, in existence less than 10 years and maybe for only a few years. Some of these compressed gangs have become territorial, but many have not.

In sum, compressed gangs have a relatively short history, short enough that by size, duration, subgrouping, and territoriality, it is unclear whether they will grow and solidify into the more-traditional forms or simply remain as less-complex groups.

THE COLLECTIVE GANG The collective gang looks like the compressed form, but bigger and with a wider age range—maybe 10 or more years between younger and older members. Size can be under 100 but is probably larger. Surprisingly, given these numbers, it has not developed subgroups and may or may not be a territorial gang. It probably has a 10- to 15-year existence.

In sum, the collective gang resembles a kind of shapeless mass of adolescent and young adult members and has not developed the distinguishing characteristics of other gangs.

THE SPECIALTY GANG Unlike the other gangs, which engage in a wide variety of criminal offenses, crime in this type of group is narrowly focused on a few offenses; the group comes to be characterized by the specialty. The specialty gang tends to be small—usually 50 or fewer members—without any subgroups in most cases (there are exceptions). It probably has a history of less than 10 years but has developed a well-defined territory. Its territory may be either residential or based on the opportunities for the particular form of crime in which it specializes. The age range of most specialty gangs is narrow, but in a few others is broad.

In sum, the specialty gang is crime-focused in a narrow way. Its principal purpose is more criminal than social, and its smaller size and form of territoriality may be a reflection of this focused crime pattern.

The two traditional types share subgroups and a strong territorial orientation. The compressed structure can be distinguished somewhat from the traditional types by smaller size and, most commonly, by more recent onset. The compressed, collective, and specialty types have no subgroups and have briefer durations (except the collective type). The reader will note that we have explicitly avoided mentioning crime patterns except in the case of the specialty type. In fact, crime specialization is what defines this type, and it's important for our research concerns to be able to distinguish drug gangs, burglary rings, and the like from other gang types.

We had some concern about the foundation of these scenarios, as they are built upon the "best-known" gangs. We couldn't assume that they are typical of the gangs in the country, and yet the content of the scenarios seems to make sense and have face validity. One exception is the collective type. Collective gangs are fairly large in size and age range and have been around for 10 to 15 years, yet have no subgroup structure. This was a residual category and that may explain some of the ambiguity in the structural characteristics of this type. Should data collection validate this as a meaningful gang type, it would certainly be interesting to know more about the organizational features that keep these gangs together.

The critical methodological problem with the phase I data was the need to fall back on our respondents' knowledge of the single gang that each knew best. If the attempts to measure the prevalence of the five structures nationally were to yield dissent, we wouldn't know whether to attribute this to structural variability or to the biases inherent in our phase I process. Thus the importance of a second research phase becomes obvious; we needed to validate these five types of groups in a totally independent sample of cities.[4]

The Phase II Sample

If consistent handling of the scenarios were to emerge in phase II, and if the five types did indeed encompass a good proportion of the gangs under the purview of our respondents, then we could feel more secure about the validity of the structural depictions. The phase II interviews allowed for data to invalidate our phase I finding of only five major types, because they sought not only the prevalence of the five types, but explicitly sought the existence of alternative structures as well.

We start our report of the phase II data with two promising results. First, while our phase II respondents did indeed offer descriptions of alternative structures, we found in coding these by the characteristics listed in Table 5.1 that the majority of the "alternative" structures were not alternatives at all; they fit neatly into the five structures. Return phone calls to the respondents revealed that these alternative listings were merely the result of some confusion about our instructions.

The second result is that the remaining alternative structures comprised only 5% of the total numbers of gangs enumerated by our respondents. In other words, the five scenarios representing types of street gangs seemed to have captured the vast bulk of gangs across the nation. We were surprised by how well the typology worked; we are no longer concerned about its derivation from the initial 59 best-known gangs.

The data on gang structure prevalence in phase II are taken from the 201 returns from a random sample of police gang experts in 250 cities out of the almost 800 identified in our earlier research. This return rate of 80%, although below the 90–95% return rate we have had in our prior law enforcement research, is nonetheless very substantial and not a source of concern. The instructions were as follows:

> The enclosed survey should take only a few minutes to complete. The first two pages describe five types of gangs, based upon information we have received from law enforcement gang experts throughout the country. Please read all five descriptions first; then consider which type or types generally describe the gang forms in your city. The fit need not be perfect, but should be substantially correct. Then, answer the questions on page three. If some gangs do not fit any of the five descriptions, the questions on page four

request information about these alternative gang forms. We'd like you to focus on the form or structure of your city's gangs first, without regard to crime. After you have completed page four, please turn the page and respond to the questions about crime on page five and about your records (page 6). Then, return the survey to us in the enclosed envelope.

Table 5.2 provides a summary of gang structures prevalence data for 2,860 gangs in 201 cities. We call attention to the following:

- In row 1, cities containing compressed gangs are the most common, and those with collective structures the least. Since most of the classic gang literature of the 1950s and 1960s was based principally on traditional, not compressed structures, it is immediately clear that a reconsideration of gang "knowledge" is called for in the modern era.
- In row 2, cities that are *predominantly* of one type of gang reveal an even stronger pattern of compressed gang prevalence. Both rows 1 and 2 reveal that most cities will typically be more familiar with non-subgrouped gangs.
- In row 3 (reading the percentages horizontally), we see that this general pattern also applies to the number of gangs. Gangs with age-graded or geographically based subgroups are less common than the three more homogeneous structural forms, particularly the compressed type.
- In the five subrows on ethnicity (now reading the percentages vertically), we see that, in line with most scholarly reports, the vast majority of gangs are composed of minority groups, principally and equally Hispanic and black. The marginal percentages (i.e., the final column) are 30% Hispanic, 31% black, 10% white, 13% Asian, and 16% mixed. The largest single percentage is for Hispanics in the traditional structure (57%), yet even here other ethnic groups are found in this structure. Neotraditional and compressed structures, the two most common types, show fairly similar patterns of ethnic composition, with Hispanics and blacks predominating as they do generally. Clearly the common stereotype among police and media reports of a generalized "black gang" or "Hispanic gang" form is incorrect and misleading. As we note repeatedly, group process trumps ethnicity in the world of street gangs.

TABLE 5.2. *Gang Structures in 201 Cities*

	Traditional	Neo-traditional	Compressed	Collective	Specialty	Totals
# cities	75	100	149	40	76*	
# cities with predominance**	15	24	86	6	14	
# of gangs across cities	316 (11%)	686 (24%)	1,111 (39%)	264 (9%)	483 (17%)	2,860
· Hispanic	179 (57%)	229 (33%)	292 (26%)	62 (23%)	95 (20%)	857 (30%)
· black	63 (20%)	191 (28%)	340 (31%)	125 (47%)	155 (32%)	874 (31%)
· white	38 (12%)	34 (5%	152 (14%)	10 (4%)	49 (10%)	283 (10%)
· Asian	15 (5%)	73 (11%)	156 (14%)	49 (19%)	85 (18%)	378 (13%)
· mixed & other	21 (7%)	159 (23%)	171 (15%)	18 (7%)	99 (20%)	468 (16%)

*Specialty focus: drugs (24), graffiti (20), assault (17). Others included burglary, auto, theft, robbery.

**Fifty-six cities showed no predominance of one gang structure, defined as a type appearing twice as often as any other.

- In the first table note (*), we list for cities with specialty gangs what their predominant crime type was (asked only with respect to specialty structures). Drug gangs, while a bit more prominent than other specialty types, certainly do not dominate the picture to the extent that law enforcement and media reports would suggest. Respondents in the 24 cities with drug gangs were asked how many such gangs there were; the result is an estimated maximum of 244 gangs with a drug focus, or about 8.5% of the 2,860 gangs reported in total. These data are at considerable variance with widely circulated reports in the media and many public statements made by prominent law enforcement officials and legislative members, state and federal, to the effect that street gangs have taken over much of the drug trade. They are in line, however, with other data produced by our earlier national surveys.

Not shown in Table 5.2 but of some interest is the relative "purity" of cities with respect to the five types of gang structure. Only one city reported having none of the five structures (but having an alternative structure). Fully a third of all cities reported having only one gang form, and another third reported two of the forms. Thus two-thirds of all 201 cities were relatively homogeneous with respect to the structural types. An additional 1 in 6 reported three types, and the rest reported four or all five types. A search for common pairings or groupings of structural types was not revealing, i.e., no pattern of combinations occurred that would not be predictable from their overall totals.

The five scenarios presented to our respondents, which encapsulate the "definers" of the five gang structures, do not include leadership patterns because we had little confidence in police views of gang leadership. They do not include the important dimension of group cohesiveness, because police responses on this dimension proved ambiguous; cohesiveness was not a common conception for our officers. Yet, other data were gathered that give us confidence that the five types are different in meaningful, indeed in validating, ways.

The ethnic differences, as suggested in Table 5.2, are in some cases very substantial. As we noted above, traditional gangs are more likely to be Hispanic while the collective and specialty gangs are more commonly composed of black members. We also noted that the two most common types—neotraditional and compressed—show far less ethnic or racial predominance.

Average gang size is another differentiating variable, as seen in Table 5.3. We note in particular the predicted large size of traditional gangs and small size of specialty gangs. Year of gang emergence in the city is somewhat differentiating (traditional gangs tend to be located in early onset cities), although not fully at the level we expected. The explosion in gang onsets in the 1980s probably puts limits on these differences. Size of the city shows some differences, but the common existence of two or more structures in the same city sets limits for these differences. The ambiguous collective gang is significantly a product of the largest cities.

The volume of crime attributed to the structures is also important, with the traditional and neotraditional gangs contributing the most, and specialty gangs contributing the least. Of course, this is a function of average gang size. If we control for size as in the last row of Table 5.3, we see a considerable reversal; the average traditional gang member contributes the lowest number of reported arrests and the specialty gang member the highest. Specialty gangs, it should be remembered, are very much organized around their preferred crime type, be it drug sales, burglary, or some other, and are subjected to specialized law enforcement surveillance and pursuit. By contrast, the more crime-versatile traditional gang members engage in many activities which are of relatively little concern to the police. Thus, the reversed patterns of gang volume and per-member arrest rates are quite understandable and help to validate the nature of these gang structures.

We should draw special attention to the subgrouping that is typical of traditional and neotraditional gangs. In his studies of traditional gangs in Los Angeles in the 1960s, Klein (1971) based his conclusions on data describing 5 large gangs. He noted, however, that he preferred the term "gang cluster" because each contained several subgroups. If these separate cliques had been enumerated (each had its own separate name), Klein could have claimed the study not of 5 gangs but of 24 gangs.[5] Thirty years later, Alonzo's comprehensive report on the Crips and Bloods in Los Angeles, one of the very few studies of the modern era to note the special subgrouping nature of traditional gangs, noted the same, continuing pattern:

> As a first step in identifying and counting gangs for this study, I identified general identities that were aligned with one of the two broad gang affiliations in Los Angeles; the Bloods or the Crips. . . . There were more specific identities observed within the gang called *clicks*. These subgroups were part of the larger gang or set.

TABLE 5.3. *Selected Structural Dimensions*

	Traditional	Neotraditional	Compressed	Collective	Specialty
Average size	182	72	35	56	24
Year of onset*					
Through 1970	24%	13%	9%	15%	7%
1971–1984	28%	18%	16%	28%	15%
1985 & beyond	49%	68%	75%	56%	78%
City size >100,000	35%	36%	28%	52%	33%
Average monthly arrests	10.9	9.2	6.1	7.4	5.7
Average monthly per member arrests	.16	.20	.22	.17	.29

*Year of onset refers to the year any gangs first appeared.

> The territoriality of this analysis is based on the gang or set, not the individual subgroups or clicks. In Black gang culture of Los Angeles, a gang will develop subgroups within the gang to either distinguish different groups based on age in a hierarchical structure or based on geographic areas within the one gang. This analysis did not identify the subgroups or clicks as separate gangs and they should not be, but from reading the graffiti of these clicks, it would appear to the novice that multiple gangs were operating in any given area, when in fact all the different specific identities fall under one gang. For example the Grape Street Crips in Watts are the same gang as the Watts Baby Loco Crips, but the latter represents a subgroup that is based on a younger group of members. The Park Village Crips in Compton have a click of younger members that operate under the name Original Tiny Gangsters that is also a part of the same gang. Gangs with large territories will also form subgroups to identify different geographic areas in the gang. For example the Eight Tray Gangster Crips divided their territory into four areas in the winter of 1980; the North Side, South Side, West Side and East Side. These specific identities were part of the larger gang and are not counted as independent groups. Similarly the East Coast Crips in Carson had different clicks based on streets, such as Tillman Ave Crips, and Leapwood Ave Crips, but these represent clicks in a non-hierarchical structure within the main gang of the Del Amo Block East Coast Crips. In some cases law enforcement will count a sub-click as a gang because it has reached a level of notoriety, and for this reason my gang counts may not be consistent with what the Los Angeles Police Department (LAPD) or the Los Angeles Sheriff's Department (LASD) have determined. (Alonso, 1999: 61–62)

We should also report that several variables do *not* reveal differences in our data. Most important, perhaps, is that our respondents did not report much of a difference in average arrests for serious crimes. We omit the data because, as we learned later in this project, their reports are necessarily based on inadequate data, as noted already in chapter 2. Region of the country did not differ; more gangs are to be found in the West and fewest in the Northeast, but this is true of all five gang types.

Additionally, we must recognize that with some of the variables noted above, including those we list as differentiating among the five types, statistical significance is not always achieved. We report the larger differences because this is an exploratory study overall, which clearly calls for further cross-validation of its findings. Equally important, many of the data are taken from police expert reports—these are *perceptions* of gang size, ethnicity, crime patterns, and so on. An officer reporting 5, 50, or 500 gangs in his jurisdiction cannot be close to a lot of the raw data at the street level. Differences that emerge do so over a miasma of informational noise and uncertainty. Those that emerge seem to "make sense"; they have construct validity, but they call for validation with other forms of data—gang by gang by gang. Such validation will prove to be expensive.

To say this does not mitigate the distinctions among the five gang structures. Rather, it calls attention to the need to assess what variables *reliably* characterize those structures. It also calls for considerable thought about the policy implications that derive from the very fact that there is a variety of structures. We will return to such implications in chapter 8. Suffice to say at this point that to label a group a street gang does little to advance understanding of its nature or its impact in the community. Variety, not homogeneity, is the hallmark of the modern American gang.

For further clarification, it is worth noting certain kinds of gangs that do not fit within this typology of street gangs. Prison gangs do not; motorcycle gangs do not; terrorist groups do not; organized crime groups do not.

We emphasize this last group in particular because enforcement officials and the media too often place street gangs in the same category as drug cartels, La Cosa Nostra, the Mafia (Sicilian or Russian), and expanded prison gangs such as the Mexican Mafia ("la EME"). Street gangs are for the most part incapable of behaving like organized-crime groups, although there are a few large street gangs that occasionally bridge this gap, most notably Chicago's Black Gangster Disciples, Vice Lords, Latin Kings, and Black P Stone Nation or El Rukn (see Chicago Crime Commission, 1995, for a sensationalized version of these street gangs as organized-crime groups).

Organized-crime groups require mature, professionalized members—at least in the higher echelons—with organizational skills, well-defined leadership and specialized group roles, codes of conduct with clearly understood sanctions, and financial treasuries or other locations for profits to be used for group purposes; to survive, such crime groups often develop special relationships with legitimate businesses as well as political and legal institutions. Decker's (2001) comparison of street gangs and organized crime mentions a series of such characteristics of organized criminal gangs and how poorly they apply to street gangs in San Diego, St. Louis, and even Chicago. A common orientation to crime is, despite the narrow enforcement viewpoint, hardly sufficient to classify street gangs as organized criminal groups or to suggest that forms of intervention or control for the latter are appropriate to the former.

Further Validation

Without developing new data on gangs to assess how well they are described and encompassed by our fivefold typology, we can provide tests by reviewing existing descriptions of street gangs. We do so by reference to two sets, the first from the United States and the second from Europe.

The first of these sets of descriptions are to be found in various American studies in which the authors have provided sufficient *structural* detail to allow an ex post facto categorization. Our reading of the descriptions by Klein (1971) in Los Angeles, Moore (1978) in East Los Angeles, Vigil (1988) in East Los Angeles, Short and Strodtbeck (1965) in Chicago, W. Miller (1962) in Boston, the New York City Youth Board (1960) in New York, Sanders (1994) in San Diego, and Hagedorn (1988) in Milwaukee all yield the common features of the traditional gang. The picture provided by Decker and Van Winkle (1996) in St. Louis suggests neotraditional gangs. Fleisher's (1998) ethnography of Kansas City male and female gang members provides a rare glimpse at a collective gang. Padilla's depiction of a Puerto Rican drug-selling gang in Chicago (1992), the Brightwood Gang in Indianapolis described by McGarrell and Chermak (2003), the description of a small group of Dominican drug sellers by Williams (1989), the depiction of drug gangs in south Texas offered by Valdez and Sifaneck (2004), and the unique financial analysis of a drug gang's operations in Chicago over four years presented by Venkatesh (1999b) and Levitt and Venkatesh (1999) clearly illustrate the structure of specialty gangs. Jody Miller (2001), describing female-involved gangs in Columbus and St. Louis, deliberately applied the typology to the groups in those two cities to very good effect. Thus, where descriptions permit it, the typology seems applicable and useful. It is worth noting, nonetheless, that compressed gangs have not been described despite their ubiquitousness and are probably the forms from which the Rochester, Denver, and Seattle longitudinal data are taken (see Thornberry and Porter, 2001, on gangs in traditional and emergent gang cities).

Two recent applications of the typology offer further support. Scott (2000) presented the typology to officials in 887 Illinois police agencies. Returns were received from 88% of these. Seventy-four percent of the street gangs in these jurisdictions fit within the typology[6] without further analysis. Similarly, the National Youth Gang Center (2000b) analyzed data from a nationally representative sample of police jurisdictions. This sample of 265 agencies placed 74% of their gangs within the typology, in this case with neotraditional types accounting for 39% of the total and compressed following closely with 35%. In neither study were the 26% nonfitting gangs further analyzed, but our experience with our own 201 respondents suggests that some number of the nonfitters might well have fallen into the typology as well. In any case, these two applications of the typology provide evidence for its utility.

The second validation comes from views of street gangs in Europe. Perhaps the most famous of the European studies is James Patrick's 1973 ethnography, *A Glasgow Gang Observed*, in which the traditional structure is well illustrated. Klein's more recent review of reports and observations (Klein, 1996) found traditional gangs reported in Kazan, Berlin, and Brussels; specialty (drug) gangs in Manchester, Berlin (skinheads), and Stockholm; compressed gangs in Stockholm, Zurich, Frankfurt, and Stuttgart; and neotraditional gangs in Berlin. None of the cities visited reported gangs not fitting the typology, although various cities of course, reported not having street gangs of any sort.

An additional opportunity is provided by Weitekamp (2001) in his review of reports on European gangs in a compendium of gang reports by various European authors in 1998 and 1999. This reading of these reports yields traditional gangs in Kazan; neotraditional gangs in Manchester; compressed gangs in Manchester, Copenhagen, Frankfurt, Oslo, and Paris; and specialty gangs in the Hague and Rotterdam. Descriptions not yielding data for placement in the typology came from Bremen and Slovenia. This review, like those above, is an after-the-fact exercise and has to be considered more as illustration than as proof. Nonetheless the fact that the exercise "works" provides further confidence in the utility of the structural typology, far more so it seems to us than in the case with the earlier behavioral and structural typologies offered in the gang literature.

Gang Transformations

Simple logic tells one that gangs come and go; note the different years of onset in Table 5.3 and the periods of duration in Table 5.1. Without the self-regeneration capacities of age-graded subgroups within traditional and neotraditional gangs, the others must die out, be replaced by new gangs, or continue in name only but with new members. The stability of "ganging" probably lies more in the characteristics of the particular community than in the particular group of young people who comprise the gang (Valdez and Sifaneck, 2004).

Additionally, gangs may be transformed from one type to another. Drug gangs are often spin-off cliques of other, larger forms. Traditional gangs by definition must have been of another type to start with; several age-graded subgroups can seldom emerge simultaneously. Further, we have descriptions from Taylor (1990) for Detroit, DiChiara for New Haven (1997), and Salagaev (2001) for Kazan of the transformation of smaller, territorial gangs into large, pseudocorporate criminal gangs. Bjorgo (1999) has provided descriptions of evolutions into and out of racist gangs in Scandinavia. Additionally, Weisel's findings from gang members' own reports in San Diego and Chicago were that her gangs "reflected patterns of consolidation (primarily through merger with, or acquisition of, smaller gangs), reorganization, and the splintering of larger gangs into spin off gangs" (2002: 48).

We note all this to remind the reader that the gangs used by our respondents in reporting to us, which yielded our structural typology, were taken at one slice of time. The typology is hopefully more stable than the particular gangs subsumed within it at the time the research was done. We were able to look at this stability issue by returning to our 59 police experts about four years after the phase I interviews. Fifty-three of the original 59 were still in place and able to report the status of their earlier best-known gangs. Of the 53 gangs, 10 were inactive or had been disbanded, leaving 43 or 81% stability—more than one might have expected given that only 14 had been of the traditional form. More interesting, perhaps, is the lower stability of form, where only 18 of 43 remained constant, at least as seen by our respondents.

- Of 14 original traditional gangs—all of them still active—8 were still reported to be true to form while 6 now were described as neotraditional, compressed, or collective forms.
- Of 8 neotraditionals, only 1 remained so, while 3 reportedly had progressed to traditional gangs and 2 each had become compressed and collective.
- Of 8 still-active compressed gangs, 5 remained in that form, and 3 had changed.
- Of 8 collective gangs, only 1 retained that most-elusive, unstructured form while 7 had moved to the other four categories. This suggests that the collective form is the most transitional of all.

- Finally, of 5 specialty gangs still in existence—4 were not—3 retained their form while 2 had "advanced" to traditional gangs.

While it would be nice to have a larger study of gang transformation over different periods of time, these data strike us as useful. The traditional and compressed gangs, by report of our police gang experts, are the most stable. The neotraditional and collective types, which we had originally thought to be transitional in nature, turned out indeed to be just that; 2 remained in class, while 14 changed to another form. Specialty gangs were most likely to disband, perhaps because they are most easily subjected to police suppression and undercover efforts. Only 2 gangs of the four other types transitioned into specialty gangs. Both had been collective gangs. Fleisher's description of his collective gang in Kansas City, the Fremont Hustlers, describes them as heavily involved in drug sales, as is common in specialty gangs.

How much gang transformation and of what type takes place? These data suggest that there is a good deal of instability, with traditional and compressed gangs being the most constant in form. Of the changes reported, transformations from one form to another were far more common than gang dissolution—25 cases compared to 10. The typology, we note, still works. Our respondents had little trouble reporting the necessary data, and we were able to recreate the typology with the dimensional data provided. But change was clearly evident, and gang researchers would be well advised to study both gang form *and* transformations, especially if translations to policy and practice are undertaken.

One further note is in order. In the case of the 10 gangs that were reported inactive or disbanded after four years, it would be nice to know how permanent that situation is. Does this mean that 10 neighborhoods are now free of gangs? Or is it more likely that communities that once spawned gangs will do so again? We are inclined, unfortunately, to suspect the latter, but we know of no research on this topic. A census of ex-gang neighborhoods and reactivated gang neighborhoods could provide an interesting research window on the gang-community interface and the natural epidemiology of gang problems.

This shifting and varied nature of street gangs can also result in well-intentioned but misleading descriptions. In an OJJDP bulletin on "hybrid gangs" (Starbuck, Howell, and Lindquist, 2001), it is claimed that "traditional gangs" have been supplanted by hybrid gangs. These are loosely defined as

- mixed race or ethnicity
- individual memberships in more than one gang
- use of indicia (colors, tattoos, etc.) of more than one gang
- cooperation between rival gangs
- mergers of small gangs
- unclear conduct norms
- borrowing of traditional gang names (Bloods, Latin Kings, etc.)

Our impression from this article, which suffers from a lack of data on these issues, is that "hybrid" is a catchall term that probably captures, in uncounted ways, our four structures other than the traditional gang. The stereotyping that allows this traditional versus hybrid dichotomy does little to advance our understanding of gang structures. However, the emphasis given by the article's authors to the wide variations in gang patterns over time and location is most welcome and appropriate. We hope it will be attended to, even as the reification of "hybrid gangs" recedes in popular parlance.

Where are the girls? The perceptive reader will by now have noted that the five scenarios and accompanying data do not include any mention of female gangs and gang members. Police generally gather data on female gang members far less reliably than on males. Because our data were taken from gang cops, we could not properly represent female involvement. While almost all research confirms that street gangs are predominantly male, those studies that include attention to females consistently report female involvement greater than is reported in official statistics or assumed by the general public. A reasonable estimate of the level of female gang involvement would place it close to 25%—one in four members is a girl (Klein, 1971; Moore, 1991; Esbensen and Huizinga, 1993; J. Miller, 2001; Decker and Curry, 2000). Female membership, as noted earlier, is higher among younger members, as the girls tend to desist from gang activity earlier than do boys.

We are not alone in failing to include data on females in a typology; none of the studies cited earlier do so either. We can think of no more fruitful further research on our typology than an investigation of how male-female relationships tend to differ among the five gang structures. We can note, however, that studies of traditional gangs have generally reported a typical pattern of "auxiliary" female gangs (Klein, 1971; W. Miller, 1973; Campbell, 1984; Moore, 1991). The auxiliary female gang is one of three logical forms of female participation. These are, generally, independent or autonomous gangs (e.g., Brown, 1977; Campbell, 1984), integrated membership (J. Miller, 2001; Fleisher, 1998), and auxiliary (Klein, 1971, reported 8 of 24 subgroups within his traditional gangs to be female). An unpublished survey in three cities recently found integrated forms in 57%, auxiliary forms in 36%, and autonomous forms in 6% of reports from gang girls (Curry, Williams, and Koenemann, n.d.). Jody Miller's (2001) recent study of integrated female members in Columbus and St. Louis suggests that "integrated" must be taken with a grain of salt, as the girls' reports of equal status with the boys is belied by numerous behavioral differences indicating a gender hierarchy favoring the males. Fleisher's ethnography of the Fremont gang in Kansas City—a collective gang to judge by his description—suggests that the loose structure of that gang form may allow for greater independence of female behavior than is likely in the more-traditional structures. From these few reports and from the fact that so little information is available on gender makeup of various gang structures, we can do no better here than to assert again the importance of this issue for further investigative efforts.

A particularly insightful glimpse at the role played by female gang members is presented by Peterson et al. (2001). Although limited by its use of eighth graders only in 11 schools across the nation, this report includes data from 464 gang members of whom 37% are female.[7] The authors compare responses from members of all-male gangs, majority-male gangs, all- or majority-female gangs, and sex-balanced gangs. Perhaps surprisingly, they report somewhat lower levels of organization in all-male and majority-female gangs, with organization being measured by leadership, meetings, and group symbols. These groups report more prosocial and less delinquent behavior. Conversely, the sex-balanced gangs report somewhat higher levels of organization and greater delinquency. The authors suggest that sex-balanced gangs pose more "gender threat" for the males, leading to more acting out. Then, it is suggested, the females in these sex-balanced gangs have more viable criminal role models to emulate.

Implicit in these findings are some obvious policy implications. The roles of females in gangs, long overlooked by many researchers and almost all social and justice agencies, must be reassessed for their impacts on both female and male gang members. The gender balance within gangs needs to be noted by police and social interveners, since this balance relates to group organization and crime leadership. Finally, it is time for the police and courts to stop ignoring the existence of female gang members, because they are "less serious" or "just immature" and will grow out of it. Why would one ignore 25% of a social problem?

For researchers, the implication may be less clear with respect to our structural issues. We have come a long way from the days that female gang members were reported only to be weapons carriers and sex objects ("toys for boys") for male members. But most comments on female gang structures have not advanced beyond the trichotomy of member-auxiliary-autonomous forms. Indeed, it is not clear to us that our five structures apply very well to these forms of female gang membership. In their recent and very reasoned summary of female gang research, Moore and Hagedorn (2001) call for new research on a number of topics, but gang structure is not one of these—perhaps an unintended but meaningful omission.

Summary

In this research, we have developed a structural gang typology which has proven applicable in the vast majority of a random sample of cities with reported gang problems. We have learned that

- traditional gangs, those most subject to prior gang research, are not the most common or typical gang form;
- some of the ethnic differences described in the literature do not hold up well;
- drug gangs, so much the subject of public pronouncements and some criminological research, comprise a relatively small proportion of street gangs; and
- differences among gang types do not readily correspond to the characteristics of their cities or regions in the country.

We caution the reader, also, that the gang typology which emerged from our data is time limited. The data collection period of the early 1990s follows by relatively few years the major gang proliferation across the nation that took off in the 1980s. We may have captured a brief movement in a period of major gang evolutionary change. We know, for instance, that drug gangs have gained their prominence only since the mid- to late 1980s.

It is reasonable to suggest that the collective gang, having such an amorphous form, may be a product of this evolutionary phase and will soon become even less common than it is now. It is also reasonable to suggest that compressed gangs, now so common but with a relatively short history, will evolve over time into neotraditional and traditional forms if they continue to exist. This is logical, since current members will grow older, and the gangs can only regenerate themselves via recruitment of new, presumably younger replacements. This could well result in the age-related cliques that typify the traditional gang.

Revisiting this issue in 5–10 years, using the same research methods, would seem very much in order to solidify our understanding of gang structures. Perhaps by that time, a sufficient number of police departments will have developed gang rosters and crime statistics appropriate to establishing valid relationships between gang structures and gang crime patterns.

The last point to be made here refers to an issue discussed earlier: the problem with finding a single, acceptable definition of street gangs. In addition to the consensus definition in the introduction, we believe that the five street gang structures provide an acceptable *operational* definition: a street gang is any durable, street-oriented youth group whose own identity includes involvement in illegal activity *and* is substantially described by the data in Tables 5.1, 5.2, and 5.3 or by the gang scenarios presented in this section. Such an operational definition is not as easily carried around in the head as would be the consensus nominal definition alone. Yet it would seem that most groups defined as street gangs do fit within the five structural descriptions. For now, the typology contributes to the definitional need.

The Importance of Group Processes

Street gangs generally are alike, and yet there is much difference among them. It is in finding and demonstrating the balance between likeness and difference that some of the "art" of gang research resides.

We opened this book by defining gangs in a few phrases that suggested their existence as a single class of groups, distinguishable from other classes of groups. Yet, in this chapter, we have distinguished among five forms of street gangs. Can we have it both ways: gangs are different and alike? We can, because they are.

Gang *structures* differ, depending on such variables as size, duration, age range, and the like. But these differences are trumped, covered over, by group *processes*. It is their peculiar nature as *groups* that make gangs alike despite their different structures. There is in this a strong policy message, we believe. To state it overgenerously, differences in structure provide clues for different strategies of gang control, whereas similarities in processes provide warnings of control strategies to be avoided. We will return to these policy differences in part III of the book; for now, we need to spell out some of the important group processes to be found in most street gangs, whatever their structural form. If it is the structures that suggest how gang controllers might act, it is the processes that determine how the gang members will react. The controllers send the messages; the members distort the messages to their own group purposes. In the street gang, normal group processes tend to be greatly exaggerated, making gangs a qualitatively different phenomenon. As one of our colleagues put it, "When street socialization takes over, a remarkably similar street orientation and culture emerges for each group, irrespective of ethnic traditions, and, with only slightly greater variation, regardless of gender."[8]

It is in the study of group processes that social psychologists have influenced gang research. Gang leadership, one of these processes, may well be the most-recognized concern among members of the public, who are understandably much influenced by media and police reports. Yet among gang scholars, few have found gang leadership to be a stable or predictable facet of gang activity. The exceptions, such as Yablonsky writing in the 1950s and 1960s and Sanchez-Jankowski writing in the 1990s, have built structural gang typologies on the bases of their reported observations of leadership patterns. Yet other scholars have been unable to find these reported patterns, and neither Yablonsky nor Sanchez-Jankowski produced objective data to buttress their assertions.

Most gang scholars (see summaries in Klein 1971, 1995a) have found leadership to be functional, shifting, unstable, and shared among many gang members. It often depends less on physical strength or criminal prowess than on verbal skills, opportunism, social capacities, and—in the case of traditional gangs—various age levels. Except in specialty gangs, leadership is usually not the hierarchical, command-oriented positional concept stressed by popularizers of gang matters. Forget *West Side Story*: think more in terms of playground politics where different goals and types of skills lead to impermanent levels of influence.

In most recent street gangs, leadership and influence are often so diffuse that attempts at gang control through the targeted arrest of "leaders" may most directly lead to the emergence of new leadership. Americans are admirers of leadership and tend to seek it out as the principal explanation of group movement. But as in politics, business, and the professions, it is more often the system than the person that dictates the principal action as well as the resistance to change. And so it is with street gangs, driven more by the group and its context than by charismatic leaders. Gangs may huddle, but there are few quarterbacks calling signals for them (e.g., Klein, 1971, 1995a; Short and Strodtbeck, 1965; Moore, 1991; Decker, 2000; Vigil, 2002).

Klein (1971: 95–96) quotes several of his influential gang members in response to his inquiries about leadership:

> Nobody speaks for an area. I don't give a damn who he is. Nobody. Or for a gang.

> We got no leaders, man. Everybody's a leader, and nobody can talk for nobody else.

> Y'understand, I can't talk for them other dudes. I'm saying it for me.

Decker and Van Winkle provide similar denials of leadership from their interviews in St. Louis and then conceptualize the issue as follows:

> Leadership within the gang has a situational character that is dynamic. Few gangs have a single identifiable individual who occupies the role as leader for an extended period of time. In part, this reflects the fact that subgroups within the gang more effectively set priorities and direct behavior than does the gang as a whole. Because allegiance to a small number of friends is stronger than that to the gang, the ability of a leader to control gang members is diminished. But the values of the street also prohibit a leader from effectively assuming control of gang members. The autonomy from authority so highly prized on the street inhibits effective leadership. (1996: 275)

Some clarity on the issue is achieved by shifting research focus toward members' levels of commitment to their gangs and to the internal, informal friendship cliques that underlie gang structures. Gang structures and functions come together as we look at clique structures, commitment to the gang, and how these both foster and limit gang cohesiveness. We preface these remarks by offering the reader our very strong opinion that levels of gang cohesiveness correlate directly with levels of gang crime and with gang responses to our efforts at gang control. Greater cohesion leads to greater crime involvement and greater resistance to gang control. This, more than anywhere, is where we derive the title of this book: *Street Gang Patterns and Policies.*

Consider first the simple logic of clique formation: can 20 young people, or 50, or hundreds of them affiliate with each other over time without forming smaller units based on friendship, or common residence, or school attendance, or shared interests, or similarities in age, gender, or ethnicity? The obvious answer is no: such cliques, however ephemeral, will form. Even in the amorphous collective gang, cliques will form. Fleisher illustrates this in his conversation with the girls in the Fremont Hustlers gang in Kansas City. His report deserves extensive quotation:

> "Membership" in the Fremont Hustlers is a peculiar idea. Wendy, Cara, and Cheri listed 72 males and females on the Fremont Hustlers membership roster; however, Fremont kids don't refer to one another as members, nor do they think of themselves as having "joined a gang."
>
> "Member," "membership," "join," and "gang" are static notions which fit neither the natural flow of Fremont social life nor the perceptions of Fremont kids. Even the question, Are you a member of the Fremont Hustlers? doesn't match these kids' sense of social logic. The question Do you hang out on Fremont? makes sense to them, but this question didn't bring me closer to understanding the kids' meaning for "joining a gang" and "gang membership." Fremont kids' perceptions of these issues are more complex than I had imagined. (1998: 39)

> Kids' vocabulary helps to describe how they perceive Fremont's social arrangements. Generally speaking, Fremont kids differentiate themselves into one category defined by "time" and another by "tightness." *Tightness* refers to the intensity of the relationship. Kids who hang out together much of the time are said to be tight, and kids who are tight "do shit" (commit crimes, use drugs) together. (1998: 40)

Fleisher then offers a listing of the cliques in the Fremont Hustlers, as reported by his most frequent informant, Cara:

> "Bloods": 3 members
> "Used to visit a lot": 5 members, including 2 sisters
> "Grew up on Fremont": 5 members, brothers

"In prison": 7 members, including 3 crime partners
"La Familia": 8 members, including 3 cousins
"Hang together (A)": 7 members
"Hang together (B)": 10 members, including 2 brothers and 3 cousins
"Hang out (tight)": 9 members, including 2 sisters and their step-sister, a brother and sister, and several cousins
"Hardly come around": 7 members, including one set of 2 brothers and another of 3
"Southside": 5 members, including a set of twins

This is not an elegant statement of clique structures, but it does illustrate the informant's sense for different bases underlying the cliques, and it also reveals the familial tightness that can set severe limits on attempts to reduce gang cohesiveness.

Fleisher has also developed clique structures among themselves and their friends reported by 74 female members across three large and four small gangs. A diagram of the cliques is shown in Figure 5.1,[9] where social

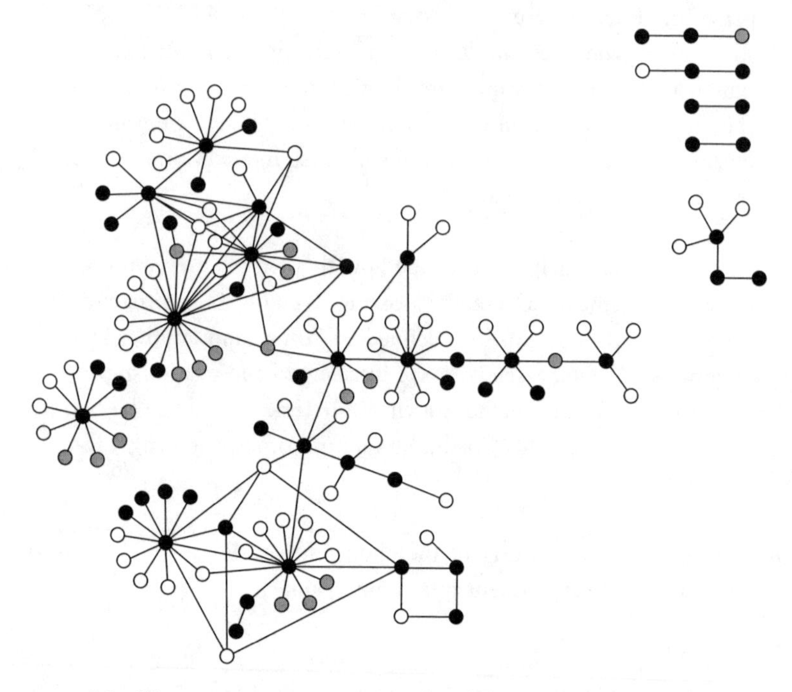

FIGURE 5.1. Clique structures across seven female gangs. Reported by Mark Fleisher.

networks are variously based on social friendships, monetary connections, and criminal connections. The shadings of gray, too complex to describe here, are based on the several gang affiliations and on the females' nominations of "friends, close friends, and best friends." As can be seen, the internal cliquing in a gang can become very complex: group processes are not simple. One ignores them at peril.

Klein's (1971) report on the Latins gang in East Los Angeles noted that over 50% of the members were siblings and first cousins. Klein's depiction of the several cliques within the Latins gang and the 21 cliques within four large black gangs joins with Fleisher's as some of the very few research attempts to ferret out the internal structures of gangs in the United States. They were joined recently by Lien's report (2005a) of the clique structures in three immigrant gangs in Oslo, Norway. Two of the gangs have crossovers of friends or siblings, while the third is fully independent of the other two. Most important in the depictions is the several bases of the nine cliques indicated within the cores of the three gangs. There include familial connections—brothers and cousins, including a family of seven brothers—crime partners, and common village backgrounds in the country of origin. Lien also shows a number of nongang peers, reminding us that gang members often have friends and relatives outside their groups. Finally, Lien's data reveal that cohesiveness as expected is stronger within cliques than across cliques.

This last point, about cohesiveness and clique structures, takes us back to Klein's data (1971), which are still the most detailed available on clique structures, cohesiveness, and commitment to the gang. In 4 large, traditional black gangs, he described 21 subgroups based either on age or gender; 7 of the 21 were female auxiliary gang structures. He cites similar data from W. Miller's analysis of 2 white gangs showing 8 male and 4 female subgroups. In all cases, the traditional groups averaged about 200 members but, because of the numerous subgroups, seemed to have only moderate levels of cohesiveness overall. The tightness is in the cliques or subgroups, not in the overall gang structure, a finding confirmed by Decker and Curry (2000) among St. Louis gangs.

Klein provided a particularly close look at the clique structure of 112 male members of the Latins over a six-month period of direct street observations and recording who was seen with whom and how often. If we define a clique as consisting of at least 3 members, then his data include six cliques, ranging in size from 3 to 26 (and the largest clique could in turn be broken further into three smaller groups based separately on school attendance, residential proximity, and criminal orientation).

Thanks to an independent assessment of which of the 112 were core and which were fringe members of the Latins, Klein was able to relate commitment to the gang to location in these cliques.

Of 59 core members of the Latins, 38, or 64%, were clique members during the six-month observation period. Of 53 fringe members, only 14, or 26%, were clique members. This also means that 60 members, over half the total, did not participate in gang activities sufficiently to be noted as a clique member. Clearly, the data illustrate the loose structure of such a traditional gang, more so than the neotraditional, compressed, collective, and specialty gangs. Traditional gangs are too large and too segmented to constitute the stereotypical organizational structure usually attributed to them. They are large and complex, but not well organized.

Beyond the clique structures, the distinction between male core and fringe members turned out in Klein's analysis to be of major importance. Core members, as nominated by gang workers, were up to two and a half times more active in formal gang activities. They had 70% more arrests. They were more violent, and their delinquent careers started earlier and lasted longer. It is, of course, the core members who are more often seen by police and local residents as active gang members, and thus they contribute disproportionately to general impressions of the "typical" gang member. Klein's further analysis of the core-fringe distinction provides an additional window onto what leads to core status. Surprisingly, it is not the usual demographic profile expected. Core members did not differ importantly from fringe members with respect to residential origin, family structure, family education, or family income. Even intelligence test scores were essentially the same for both groups.

However, a factor analysis of a mass of variables taken from probation records and gang worker reports did reveal two principal factors differentiating core from fringe members.[10] The first of these, labeled the "deficient-aggressive" factor, consisted of the following 12 variables (listed in order of the factor loadings):

- lower school performance
- lower judged intelligence
- lower impulse control
- more likely to get others in trouble
- higher recorded delinquency
- more often truant
- lower desire for rehabilitation
- more psycho- or sociopathic

- needs more help
- more dependent on group
- fewer outside interests
- more willing to fight

Boys scoring higher in this factor were significantly more likely to be core rather than fringe members. Individual deficiencies and aggressiveness constitute a route to core gang status. School help, personal counseling, and anger management seem to emerge as reasonable intervention modalities to reduce the drive toward core membership and the consequent greater involvement in criminal pursuits.

The second factor, labeled "group involvement," seems even more definitional of core membership, although it accounts for only 13% of the variance as compared to the 34% associated with the first factor. The variables, listed according to their factor scores, were

- more often participates in spontaneous activities
- more clique involvement
- greater total contribution to the group
- greater desire to lead
- more acceptance by core members

One can move to core membership as a function of individual deficiencies and aggressiveness as described by the first factor *or* as a function of the second, far more socially oriented group involvement factor, or both. Conversely, fringe members are gang affiliated through lower placement on either or both factors. Fringe members face less need for gang affiliation to compensate for individual problems or to satisfy peer group connections. The contrast clearly suggests that individual intervention with fringe members will be more effective. Their ties to the gang and therefore their resistance to intervention are lower than is the case with their core peers. Decades ago, Yablonsky (1963) suggested thinking of the gang as an analogy to an artichoke; one can peel off the outer leaves (fringe) in order to concentrate on the heart (core). The analogy seems appropriate and was confirmed by Klein's intervention with the Latins, where fringe members were the easiest to affect, and core members were both more pivotal and more difficult.

When people think of gangs as being highly cohesive, they are really responding to the core membership only, yet core membership may well be in the minority. It is the core membership that is tight, self-reinforcing, and the most resistant to intervention and control. It is to this core that Vigil refers in his description:

> Learning to back each other up during times of trouble cements the bonds between youths in a gang, creating a type of fictional kinship network. The development of this emotion-charged network is a core aspect of gang life. The gang begins as an alternative control system but over time becomes rooted as a competing, sometimes dominant socialization institution. (Vigil, 2002: 24)

For those readers whose attention is focused on the crime issues in gangs and who may find these group process matters a bit tangential, we hasten to point out that, in fact, data suggest there is a *direct* tie from gang cohesiveness to gang delinquency. We illustrate this by reference to three studies undertaken in the 1960s. The first of these is Klein's (1971) early 1960s research on the impact of an intervention program on four large African-American gangs in south-central Los Angeles. The second is Klein's (1971) late 1960s follow-up with an intensive intervention on a large Mexican-American gang in East Los Angeles. The third is Jansyn's 1966 report on group changes in a Chicago gang, also in the 1960s. Each project relates changes in cohesiveness and crime levels. More recent studies with similar care for objective data analysis of this topic unfortunately do not exist to our knowledge.

The first of these studies evaluated a four-year intervention with the use of gang workers; heavy group programming via weekly gang meetings, many outings, social and sports activities; special education, employment, and court interventions; and consistent clashes between program workers and the police. Data analysis on almost 600 male gang members revealed consistent indications that higher levels of programming led to higher levels of gang cohesiveness, while lower levels of programming were associated with lower levels of cohesiveness. Further analyses yielded the following:

- As gang cohesiveness increased, so did overall levels of recorded delinquency. When cohesiveness decreased, so did delinquency levels. These relationships held up in each of the four large groups, even though the reasons for the changes in cohesiveness varied among them.
- Some criminal offenses are more commonly committed with

companions, while others are more commonly committed alone or with only a few companions. High-companion offenses should be more affected by gang cohesiveness than low-companion offenses. As gang cohesiveness increased in response to the intervention program, analysis revealed that typically higher-companion offenses did indeed increase, while there was no such change in lower-companion offenses. This was not related to the measured seriousness of the offenses involved. The same effect on higher-companion offenses was revealed in a separate analysis of W. Miller's Roxbury gang project in Boston (1962).

- Since gang cohesiveness is generally thought to be a function of territorially based rivalries with opposing gangs, one would expect intergang incidents to be related to cohesiveness. Analysis of such violent incidents between gangs revealed their occurrence to be significantly more common among the more-cohesive gangs. Retaliation and "paybacks" were more common among the more-cohesive groups. In a revealing incident, the public stabbing death of a member of a less-cohesive gang yielded no attempt at retaliation, and "there was practically no discussion of it" (Klein, 1971: 116).

The second study reported by Klein (1971: part III) involved his very intensive attempt to test the cohesion-delinquency hypothesis in the field. The notion was to reduce as many sources of cohesiveness as possible in a traditional Mexican-American gang with a 30-year history in the community. The first test was to achieve cohesiveness reduction and the second to measure any consequent reduction in gang crime. Klein's team reduced and then eliminated all formal gatherings (meetings, outings, sports activities, etc.). Then, various alternative activities were offered: individual tutoring, individual counseling, individual mentoring, and most particularly job seeking. Over a period of 18 months, more than 100 jobs were procured, engaging 45 of the gang members. Equally important was the targeting of individuals for more and less attention strictly on the basis of their relationships to the gang in terms of their contribution to gang cohesiveness.

Depending on the measure employed, gang cohesiveness over the project period was reduced by a low of 11% and a high of 40%, most of this in the first six months and sustained thereafter. Recruitment of new members ceased altogether after the first year. Thus the first test, cohesiveness reduction, was well accomplished (even in the face of sibling and cousin relationships accounting for more than half of the gang membership).

As to the second test, delinquency reduction, the number of recorded offenses attributed to gang members was reduced by 35%, again mostly during the first six months when cohesiveness was most notably reduced. Overall nongang juvenile arrest rates reported by the two police stations serving the area showed no overall change during the period, suggesting more strongly that the observed gang delinquency reduction was project related. However, in contrast to the first four-year study, these changes were less related to accumulated individual changes in delinquency rates and more directly to the reduced size of the gang as cohesiveness and recruitment were reduced.

The third study is perhaps less convincing because it involved only one small gang in Chicago and was reported over a one-year period, which might therefore be subject to a simple seasonal interpretation. However, we are skeptical of its seasonal pattern and more inclined to accept the view of the author, Leon Jansyn (1966). It is important because Jansyn offers the other side of the coin in the cohesiveness-delinquency nexus. What he observed was a natural decline in gang cohesiveness to the point that the gang culture and image were threatened. It was at that low point that pivotal members of the gang became especially active and threatening, serving thereby to create an increase in gang cohesiveness. This interpretation fits well with the Short and Strodtbeck (1965) depiction of gang leadership reassertion after a fallow period and with the Decker and Van Winkle (1996) hypothesis about the cohesion-building function of threat.[11] Thus while higher cohesion yields higher delinquency, decreasing cohesion may reach an ebb that also calls forth an increase in delinquency—especially of a violent or dramatic nature. In either case, policy initiatives to reduce gang delinquency *must* take group processes such as cohesiveness into account, both to promote positive ends and to avoid unanticipated, negative consequences.

Osgood and Anderson, considering group-amplified delinquency generally, offer a routine activities theory orientation to the crime-amplification process that seems quite relevant:

> [O]pportunities for deviant behavior are especially prevalent when adolescents come together. There are two ways that a high average rate of unstructured socializing among a group of youth could increase opportunities for offending for all of them. Both of these

> processes are foreshadowed by Felson and Gottfredson's (1984) discussion of concentration effects that would arise with increases in the proportion of unsupervised youth.
>
> One reason to expect a contextual effect of unstructured socializing is that a higher mean-level of unstructured socializing may increase the pool of potential companions. In other words, it may be easier to find co-offenders when many adolescents spend lots of time hanging out. Ease of finding companions should both raise individual rates of unstructured socializing (feeding into the individual-level causal process) and increase the average number of companions. A larger number of companions could increase opportunities for deviance both by heightening the interactional processes among adolescents that support delinquency (see Dishion, Spracklen, Andrews, and Patterson, 1996) and by discouraging adults from attempting to exercise control over their behavior (Sampson and Groves, 1989). In both cases, a contextual effect is produced in that the average rate of unstructured socializing affects the delinquency of everyone in the group.
>
> Second, a high rate of unstructured socializing in a population would raise the rate of encounters among groups of adolescents. In this circumstance, there would be more chances of coming across rivals who are targets for assault or theft, of running into someone who has drugs or stolen goods for sale, or of learning about an unchaperoned party where trouble is likely. These patterns would produce context effects because the general level of unstructured socializing affects the number of opportunities for deviance available to everyone. (2004: 522–523)

This discussion brings us to a pivotal point in our understanding of street gangs, one that combines two elements of our definitional stance. The very last phrase in the consensus nominal definition introduced in the introduction to this book reads "whose involvement in illegal activity is part of their group identity." Crime and group identity are not merely fellow travelers in the gang world: they are mutual reinforcers. As a group becomes more gang-like, with an increasing orientation to illegality or to intergroup rivalries, it recognizes this in itself. Even the police, school officials, and family members note and comment on the process. The gang reaches a tipping point beyond which its identity becomes entwined with its community. It is no longer just a play group, a team, a peer group, a rowdy crowd—it is a *street gang*. It is the advancement into a delinquent or criminal or retaliatory mentality that brings the gang into its self-realization.

Lien notes the same process in her Oslo gangs: "we should examine in greater detail crime situations and their consequences in producing a specific mentality among gang members and a specific form of social bonds between members" (2002: 69). Later in the same work, Lien amplifies the point:

> Criminal thinking occurs as an after effect of crime, and it then develops and matures and becomes more and more motivating, the more that it is perpetrated. Finally, it may reach a point of no return that alters the whole structure of thinking and motivation. This is a tipping point theory of mind based on the aggregate outcome of a series of behavior[s] that needs to be interpreted and justified. (2002: 91)

Joan Moore, in her foreword to Vigil's 2002 book, *A Rainbow of Gangs*, makes much the same point about the function of illegal behavior in gang unity or cohesion. She notes:

> However, there is an additional factor in the gang that makes street socialization particularly powerful. Actual delinquency—breaking the law—gives gang members an additional reason to keep their activities secret. Each gang cohort develops a deep commitment to secrecy and to the protection of its members from all adults, not just the police, and from outsiders in general. A sense of loyalty becomes a permanent value. . . . This implies that the gang commands a much heavier commitment on the part of its members than does the ordinary clique of adolescent friends. (xii)

Moore and Vigil in an earlier collaboration (1989) provided an addendum to this tipping-point nature of the crime-cohesion connection. They referred to an "oppositional culture" that develops in the gang. The oppositional culture sets the gang up against society's institutions—the police, schools, discriminatory employers, and the like—such that each rejection of the gang merely reinforces its cohesiveness and its dependence upon itself. The war on gangs justifies the warring gang. Lien's observation of her Oslo gangs yields much the same conclusions. But she goes further in noting that part of the process includes the gang members' coming to view themselves as the victims of oppression, the unfair targets of racism, inequality, and suppression: "a reaction formation takes place turning the offender [gang member] into both a victim and a good guy" (2002: 82). She adds later, "He develops ideas of compassion, love, and sacrifice in relation to his friends, and he explains his acts through a construction of himself as a victim of society. The victimization point is necessary in order to justify the criminal act. He cannot be blamed, and the act is heroic rather than evil, and the victims get what they deserve" (2002: 89).

There is so much going on here:

- Crime and cohesiveness build upon each other.
- Gangs develop "group esteem" in place of self-esteem (Vigil, 1988).
- Territoriality serves to separate in-group from out-group, reinforcing all of the "specialness" of one's gang.
- When a member of his territory is attacked, there is a "demand character" to the event that calls for a payback; if the attack is with firearms, in particular, the demand is at its highest.

The dynamics of these group processes can become almost totally resistant to efforts at intervention. Indeed, any intervention may send a message that is contorted by the gang to reinforce its own status. Whether in the form of gang worker assignment, or special program activities for gang members, or suppression by police gang units, or enhanced court sanctions for convicted gang members, control attempts reinforce gang status and amplify the oppositional culture. These are *not* positive outcomes; let the intervener beware.

Given the foregoing, there is little surprise in the gang ethnographers' understanding for many years or the results of the Rochester, Seattle, and most recently the Montreal and Edinburgh longitudinal research projects about crime amplification we noted in chapter 2. The process of joining a street gang ipso facto results in a major increase in the member's level of illegal activity and especially of violent activity. When the member leaves the gang, the activity level recedes: the group processes lose their potential. All of this points to a bleak feature for any intervention into the ongoing processes of street gangs. It does, however reinforce some alternative emphases to which we will return in chapter 8, namely, early prevention on the one hand (before group processes work their magic) and reinforced gang desistance on the other (as group processes are waning).

One other positive note is also worth mentioning. The group processes we have emphasized are not monolithic. They do not apply equally to all gangs, nor equally to the five gang structures we have discussed, nor equally to all members of a gang. There is great diversity across gangs and across gang members. Group norms are not single standards, but ranges of expectations and behavior with various levels of fragility. We don't all come to equally slow or stop points at the red light. We don't all support our favorite sports teams with equal fervor. And we don't all blame each other when we feel neglected or oppressed.

Within any gang, and among many gangs, there are variations in the holds that group processes maintain on resistance to change and control, broadly conceived. There *is* room for intervention, even successful intervention, if we are willing to diagnose the situation carefully before we act. One can contrast, notes criminologist LaMar Empey (1967), a "strategy of activity" with a "strategy of search" or, as one wag stated it at the extreme, "Don't just do something; stand there."

Six

COMMUNITY CONTEXTS

The individual experiences and group dynamics discussed in chapters 4 and 5 occur in the broader context of the communities in which youths live, go to school, hang out with their friends, and interact with shopkeepers, community service providers, clergy, and other adults in their neighborhoods. What are the community features that help us to understand the emergence and persistence of gangs and the nature of gang activity? Some communities provide fertile soil for the growth of gangs; others clearly do not. Were we to craft a wildly successful gang intervention, such an effort would be doomed were it not to confront the elements in the surrounding community that foster and reinforce gang activity. It is just this inattention to the community factors that spawn gangs that, we argue in chapter 8, comes back to haunt those well-meaning and sincere attempts at gang control. It is as if the community context is taken as a given, as an unalterable element in the panoply of gang risk. To attempt gang prevention or intervention without attending to community dynamics seems foolhardy. Yet this is precisely the approach of failed program after failed program. There are of course, exceptions to this pattern, and we've described several in chapter 3. But by and large, programs have not integrated effective community interventions with individual and group strategies. In this chapter, we review the current state of knowledge about the community characteristics that foster gang development. In doing so, we recognize several key issues and limitations within this relatively undeveloped but growing body of literature.

Issues in Community Gang Research

First, despite the emphasis we place on community context in this chapter, it is critical to recognize that even in the most gang-torn communities, most youths don't join gangs. Even among those youths who do join, there is a wide variation in commitment to the gang and to those gang activities of most concern to gang practitioners and policy makers: crime and violence. Thus, the individual (including family, school, and peer) risk factors we described in chapter 4 and the group dynamics discussed in chapter 5 are likely to be more powerful in explaining gang participation within a given neighborhood. These individual and group characteristics provide important guidance to intervention on an *individual* or *group* level. While not addressing gang membership specifically, a recent multilevel analysis of contextual effects on self-reported serious juvenile offending in Germany concludes that "adolescents actively and individually shape the relevance of their neighborhood contexts" (Oberwittler, 2004: 228). Pending the type of multilevel analyses that could explain the variance in gang activity in relation to community versus other levels, we contend that community variation also provides an important vector of gang control.

Second, youths' experiences of their neighborhoods—the few blocks that surround their homes—are nested in an expanding array of geographic contexts: several neighborhoods comprise a community, several communities a city, or county. In research and popular writing, *neighborhood* and *community* are often used interchangeably, as are *community* and *city* and other geopolitical entities. Both conceptual and methodological challenges lie beneath the sloppy terminology.

There is much variation among U.S. cities regarding the definition of neighborhood. Chicago, St. Louis, and some eastern cities seem to have well-defined and articulated neighborhood boundaries recognized by all: Los Angeles does not. A recent transplant from Los Angeles to the southern California community of Irvine, 50 miles south, would note the well-defined neighborhood boundaries of that latter city, as crafted by developers and city planners. Each new section of development is marked by signs (if not walls and gates) attesting to its individual character, be it Sienna or Chambord, following the ground rules set by the early developments of Woodbridge and Oak Creek. In 1993, the Los Angeles Police Department embarked on a process to redesign its basic car-patrolling areas to reflect such "natural communities," defined on the basis of common characteristics or interests, such as culture, lifestyle, language, religion, and demographic similarity (Greene, 1998). One can imagine officers grappling with the challenge of defining a community within the polyglot of demographic changes and identities that characterize Los Angeles. The culmination of this exercise was a basic car grid that rarely bisected extant reporting district or census tract boundaries.

Like public agencies, researchers must confront the challenge of defining communities. In practice, researchers usually must accede to the existing geographic boundaries devised for some purpose other than representing the subjective entities of neighborhoods: census tracts or block groups, police reporting districts or divisions, city and county boundaries, or SMSAs (standard metropolitan statistical areas). These are artificial devices and a poor proxy for representing the ambiguous and abstract construct of *community*, the context of common interests and characteristics that defines the parameters of individual agency and behavior. Scholars of neighborhood effects argue that this strategy is a major limitation to understanding the social processes related to problem behavior among young people (Sampson, Morenoff, and Gannon-Rowley, 2002).

These difficulties are aggravated in gang research and particularly for our specific goals in this book. While recognizing the contributions of ethnographic researchers who describe the nature of the communities in which the individual gangs studied are embedded, our goal here is the search for general patterns that might inform gang programs and policy. One could piece together the neighborhood descriptions of Ruth Horowitz's study of the Lions on 32nd Street in Chicago and John Hagedorn's founders of Milwaukee gangs with Mark Fleisher's environs of the Fremont Hustlers in Kansas City and Diego Vigil's four ethnic gang communities in Los Angeles, among others. A systematic review of these selected areas would likely produce a picture of severe economic disadvantage, resource deprivation, and deteriorated physical environments. While such descriptions point to elements we'd like to measure in a broad sample of communities, these individual studies don't yield sufficient variation in types of communities studied to capture the more-generalized patterns.

In order to do that, we need a comprehensive data bank with community characteristics and gang information. If we are flexible about the meaning of the unit defined as a "community," our choices of sources yielding area-level data are promising. We have U.S. Census data in various forms (city, block group), official crime data from the Uniform Crime

Reports (city or county, often available in smaller units) or individual police agencies, and other government-sponsored data series. Far more elusive is systematically reported, reliable information about gang prevalence and activity. The National Youth Gang Center's annual survey series is the only nationally representative, systematic data source available. The National Youth Gang Survey (NYGS) is far from perfect for our purposes, however, since it is limited to police respondents reporting on gang matters without benefit of a systematic definition of *gang*, over a relatively brief time series (beginning in 1996). Moreover, the NYGS covers large geographic units of cities or counties, rather than neighborhoods or communities. Studies that are limited to broad, city-level characteristics could be supplemented by other research that captures a range of neighborhood-level characteristics within individual cities, but gang research on this scale has not yet been conducted.

Finally, the aspects of communities that are substantively important to capture are a matter of considerable debate. Here, theory is critical, and the gang arena is a leg up because early theorists emphasized community features as important components in explaining delinquent groups and gangs. Social disorganization, strain, opportunity, and subcultural deviance theory all have promoted attention to aggregated features of communities. Theories less explicitly focused on gang or delinquent groups—routine activities, control, interactional, and underclass theory, for example—also influenced gang research. This diversity of theoretical orientations has provided a rich grab bag of community aspects thought to influence gang emergence and persistence, as well as individual-level gang participation. Theory and research have not yet melded into one overarching explanatory framework but, for our purposes, offer some direction for community intervention.

The pertinent research on community factors generally falls within two broad categories: structural conditions and community processes. We also will consider three other community features. The racial or ethnic composition of communities is an important aspect of gang research. Second, variation in gang patterns between rural and urban communities has only recently received attention by researchers. Finally, we close our review of the community contexts relevant to gangs with a community-level construct that uses the period of onset of gang problems as a means of categorizing communities: the emergent versus chronic distinction (Spergel and Curry, 1993).

Structural Conditions

In their review of the recent research literature on neighborhood effects related to problem behaviors and health-related outcomes, Sampson et al. (2002) confirm the associations among neighborhood economic and social disadvantage—concentration of poverty, racial isolation, single-parent families, and rates of home ownership and residential stability—with crime, adolescent delinquency, and other indicators of social malaise. Given the consistent finding of a relationship between structural disadvantage and crime, is there a case to be made for the pernicious effect of disadvantage on gangs or gang crime beyond that which we observe for crime in general? This is an important issue for the discussion of the development of gang control policies, since as we've seen in chapter 3, gang targeting often gets co-opted to the more-general outcome indicators of crime or delinquency reduction.

City size is probably the most commonly considered structural variable in studies of gang emergence. Dating back to the early surveys of gang prevalence (W. Miller, 1982; Needle and Stapleton, 1983), researchers have observed the positive relationship between city population size and reported gang presence. The advent of more-sophisticated and thorough survey operations, culminating in the current annual surveys conducted by the National Youth Gang Center, haven't changed this conclusion: there is a direct, linear relationship between the number of people living in a place and the probability that that place has street gangs. As we have seen in chapter 1, many small towns and cities have generated gangs, but all large U.S. cities have them. However, population size, in and of itself, tells us very little about the community context that fosters gang emergence. Therefore, we limit the discussion that follows to those studies that consider community features in addition to population size.

Pamela Jackson (1991) attempted the first national analysis of the effects of the transformation from a manufacturing-based to a service-based economy on the emergence of gangs. This is a key application of W. J. Wilson's (1987) underclass theory to the gang setting. In the wake of Wilson's notion that economic restructuring with the consequent loss of manufacturing jobs led to the increased segregation of minorities in inner cities, several gang researchers argued that economic *decline* and *changes* in economic opportunity, not just economic deprivation, promoted gang proliferation (Hagedorn, 1988; Fagan, 1996; Klein, 1995a). Jackson drew on U.S. Census data for 1970 and 1980 and UCR data on index offenses reported to the police in 1980 to predict the impact of structural disadvantage and economic transformation on the existence of gangs in a representative sample of 51 U.S. cities. In an earlier study, other researchers had surveyed gang control and youth services personnel regarding the existence of gangs in these cities in 1981 (Needle and Stapleton, 1983), and Jackson used these gang prevalence data for her analyses. Looking at each variable independently, Jackson found that gangs were more likely to be present in cities characterized by large populations, density, large proportions of Hispanic residents (although percentage of black residents was negatively related), declines in population size, and declines in the number of jobs in wholesale, retail, and manufacturing trades, but not, importantly, characterized by poverty or serious crime rates. Subsequent multivariate analyses of 15 demographic, economic, and crime measures identified only the percentage change in wholesale and retail positions and the proportion of the population aged 15 to 24 years to be significant in explaining gang presence. Although this study did not address neighborhood variations, it suggests that the types of economic transitions important to underclass theory may be more important to understanding gang emergence than poverty, ethnic distribution, or overall crime.

A decade later, two researchers built on the foundation laid by Jackson's work. Wells and Weisheit (2001) used the NYGS data from 1996 to 1998 to study the influence of a broad range of structural factors on gang emergence and persistence. These scholars are primarily interested in gangs in rural locations, but in contrasting metropolitan to nonmetropolitan areas, they provide data that can be compared to the earlier work by Jackson. Wells and Weisheit report on the associations among 21 variables and metropolitan areas' gang status (stable nongang, transitory gang, and chronic gang), as derived from the reports of 1,333 NYGS law enforcement agency respondents. Taken individually, 16 structural indicators were significantly related to urban area gang status. Many of these confirm the findings from Jackson's analysis, but contrasting results on two economic dimensions are noteworthy. Three indicators of economic deprivation in the Wells and Weisheit study were predictive of gangs. Also, while increases in unemployment rate were positively related to gangs, change in the proportion of service jobs was not, and declines in manufacturing jobs fostered less, not more, gang presence. The authors note that these findings contradict the expectations advanced by advocates of economic decline and deindustrialization as major factors in gang emergence (Wells and Weisheit, 2001: 811). Both studies find the higher proportion of Hispanics in the population to be predictive of gangs. However, black residents were negatively correlated with gangs in the Jackson study, but unrelated to gangs in the Wells and Weisheit analysis. Wells and Weisheit do not report multivariate analyses of the metropolitan area data nor do they include crime rates. The variables they studied are related to one another, making it impossible to determine the unique structural features associated with gang status. Their findings point to economic deprivation and social instability in a region as important structural elements in explaining gang presence.

Other researchers have investigated the role of structural characteristics in explaining the variation in gang activity between neighborhoods within the same city. Rosenfeld, Bray, and Egley (1999) sought to identify the specific features of neighborhoods that promote what they termed the "social facilitation" of gang violence. They classified 707 homicides that occurred in St. Louis between 1980 and 1995 within the gang crime distinctions we discussed earlier in chapter 2: gang-motivated, gang-affiliated, and nongang youth homicides, with suspects between the ages of 10 and 24 years. They constructed composite measures of neighborhood disadvantage (primarily poverty, public assistance income, and female-headed households with children) and neighborhood instability (owner-occupied housing and residential stability of five years or more) for 588 census block groups. They found no differences in the measures of neighborhood context for the three types of homicides, concluding, "*both* gang and nongang youth homicides are concentrated in disadvantaged areas with moderate levels of instability" (1999: 505).

Curry and Spergel (1988) find differential effects of poverty and ethnicity in their investigation of gang homicides and juvenile arrests for serious crimes in Chicago's 75 community areas. In this study, the distribution of poverty, but not minority populations, explained the delinquency rate. Poverty also explained the gang homicide rate, but the relationship held only for certain ethnic communities. They found that poverty was positively related to gang homicides in black and white neighborhoods, but not in Hispanic neighborhoods. Controlling for poverty, the percentage of Hispanic residents was positively related to gang homicides. We will refer back to these findings on ethnic variations later in this chapter but observe the following policy implications of this research. Curry and Spergel have offered a community-level analysis that provides only mixed support for a poverty explanation of gang homicide. Their study suggests that interventions that address economic disadvantage may be an appropriate measure to reduce serious juvenile offending, but their effect on gang violence should vary by other community characteristics, in this case, ethnic composition.

This interpretation of the implications of community structure research resonates with Klein's review of prior research relevant to his model for explaining the onset and maintenance of gangs. "Thus it may turn out, although we're grasping at straws with the current data, that the underclass hypothesis will be more pertinent to black gang situations" (1995a: 204). Nevertheless, he proposes a series of underclass variables (i.e., industrial shift, education system failure, minority segregation, and outmigration of the middle class) that form the preconditions for gang emergence in a community, given the activation of a host of more-proximal community factors: a sufficient number of minority youths, the absence of appropriate jobs, the absence of acceptable alternative activities, concentrated minority populations, a comparatively high crime rate, and the absence of community and informal controls (1995a: 198, Figure 7-1).

The Jackson and Wells and Weisheit studies on gang emergence in cities highlight economic transitions or disadvantage, ethnic composition, and social instability. The St. Louis study suggests that these community descriptors are less useful in explaining differential patterns of gang and nongang violence, while the Chicago study finds important interactions between poverty and ethnicity. Studies of the characteristics of youth who join gangs help to elucidate the role of structural factors. Thornberry and colleagues (2003) argue that structural characteristics contribute only indirectly to whether or not a youth participates in a gang. According to their interactional theory, structural disadvantage reduces important social bonds to family and school, which promote antisocial learning environments, such as social networks of delinquent friends, and norms supportive of crime. Gang membership is fostered more immediately by high levels of stress and early involvement in violence that is promoted by these enhanced antisocial influences.

Analysis of the interview series of Rochester youth conducted by Thornberry and his colleagues generally confirms this theory. The impact of being African American or Hispanic, or having poorly educated parents, on joining a gang is due primarily to the way these conditions influence school performance and social learning environments. Family structure—whether a youth lived with two biological parents—retained a persistent direct effect on gang membership, even when social bonds, learning environments, and early involvement in violent behavior were considered. Interestingly, community disorganization—in this study, the parents' views of crime, deterioration, and disorder in their neighborhoods—had no effect on whether youth joined gangs.

Taken together, these studies of community structure reveal several important contexts for the development of gangs: poverty, economic transitions, ethnic and age composition of the population, and social stability. As Sampson and his colleagues observed, while some studies reveal mediating effects of community process variables on the relationship between structural factors and crime, "concentrated poverty and structural characteristics still matter" (2002: 465). Public policies that reduce economic and social disadvantage should net improvements in gang prevalence and violence, at least under some conditions. As we learned from the St. Louis study, effective economic policy should help both gang and nongang lethal violence. The Chicago study suggests that fewer benefits of antipoverty programs would accrue in Hispanic communities. Moreover, the toll of structural disadvantage on individual gang membership seems to weave a path through social bonds and adolescent peer environments. These attachments to primary social institutions—family, school, and friends—may be more amenable to manipulation than community structural conditions.

Community Processes

Alberta Gordon lives in a Chicago neighborhood studied by Mary Pattillo. Gordon describes how social relationships among community residents can be activated to exert informal social control with neighborhood youths:

> It was a respect and extended family [kind of thing]. So there are a lot of young people that I do know that call me Mama G. And I have no problem in telling them that they're wrong about doing something. And no problem in going to their parents because I know their parents. . . . [And I] have told their parents in return, if [my son] Michael is doing something and you know it's wrong, correct him and then let me know so that I can deal with it. (Pattillo, 1998: 762)

Mama G.'s willingness to call neighborhood youth on the carpet for misdeeds, and her expectations that her neighbors will do the same, illustrates the concept of neighborhood collective efficacy introduced by Sampson, Raudenbush, and Earls (1997) in an influential article in *Science*. Collective efficacy is a process whereby the social cohesion, or mutual trust, among neighbors forms the foundation for a mutual expectation that neighbors will intervene to confront incipient crime problems, especially those often committed by youth. Sampson et al.'s study of Chicago neighborhoods uncovered lower levels of crime and violence in communities with more collective efficacy, effects that withstood the competing influence of the structural variables of social instability and disadvantage. The structural aspects of community conditions provide a backdrop for the community processes that may affect more directly the nature of gang activity in a neighborhood.

Community processes are the social relationships among neighborhood residents, the informal and formal social ties that bind them to one another and to neighborhood social institutions like schools, churches, community groups, local political agencies, and public services. Bursik and Grasmick (1993) categorize these networks of social relationships and their implications for social control as private (relationships among friends), parochial (casual relationships among neighbors that link to local groups or associations), and public (the activation of ties to secure goods and services, especially police services, that are allocated by agencies located outside the neighborhood). These ties form the social capital that allows neighborhood adults to exert influence over youths, but these social relationships can be eroded by broad economic or political dislocations. For example, Fagan (1996) cites the loss of intergenerational job networks generated by the decline in manufacturing jobs as a catalyst for the disruption of effective social control and socialization from the private and parochial sectors. Gangs quickly replaced the waning influence of community adults as the dominant force of informal social control and socialization. This dynamic is echoed in the descriptions of diverse ethnic communities offered by Vigil (2002) that enumerate the social and economic marginalization of immigrant neighborhoods with attendant disruption of informal social control in family, school, and police authority. Like Fagan, Vigil locates gang persistence with the street socialization and development of street identities that react to, and further aggravate, the erosion of a community's mechanisms for informal social control.

The social ties and sources of informal social control discussed by Fagan and Vigil span the range of the private, parochial, and public spheres, but a missing element seems to be the social cohesion aspect of collective efficacy. Sampson et al.'s (2002) review of the neighborhood effects on crime literature finds that the relationship between social ties and crime is mediated by collective efficacy, not informal social control alone, but the combined effect of mutual trust among neighbors with shared expectations that neighbors will intervene on behalf of the neighborhood. Likewise, Bursik (2002) argues that the systemic model of neighborhoods and gang activity that he and Grasmick proposed must be reformulated to incorporate the salience of oppositional cultures. Such oppositional cultures represent competing social networks that promote values favorable to violence and gang activity, as well as informal "antisocial" control. Pattillo describes the pivotal role that a gang leader resident of a middle-class neighborhood played in crime control, as well as the reluctance of neighbors to use police resources due to thick kin and friendship ties among neighbors:

> One woman at a beat meeting complained of young men "gang-banging" (i.e., congregating) on her corner and of one man in particular who she thought was in charge. But, she said, "I didn't wanna give this young man's name [to the police] because his mama is such a sweet lady." (1998: 763)

Historically strained relationships with law enforcement further drive residents to call on alternative resources to respond to the dangers they perceive in their immediate environment. Anderson (1999) documents the "code of the street" as one such resource; the protection offered by an established gang is clearly another (Zatz and Portillos, 2000; Hagedorn, 1988; Vigil, 2002). Effective collective control of neighborhood crime problems rests on complex social relationships and shared values of informal intervention. In some neighborhoods, gangs are an intrinsic element of the social fabric and undermine the healthy community processes that support crime control.

An ecological study of characteristics associated with gang "set space"—the places that gang members spend most of their time—confirms the importance of informal social control. Tita, Cohen, and Engberg (2005) assessed measures of guardianship and abandonment, social disorganization, and economic deprivation and a composite indicator of underclass to identify the aspects of local areas (smaller than neighborhoods or census tracts) that attracted violent black gangs in Pittsburgh. Diminished social control, indicated by the absence of guardians and the physical abandonment of place, most consistently differentiated set space from non–set space areas. The underclass construct received some support, but poverty and unemployment were not related to set space, once other factors were controlled.

The appreciation of neighborhood processes is central to efforts to produce effective policies and programs for gang control. As we have seen in chapter 3, gang intervention programs often embrace a "comprehensive" formula, incorporating a melding of law enforcement and community efforts in their design, if not always fully in their execution. To these other program descriptions, here we can also add civil gang injunctions as particularly relevant to this discussion of community processes. A civil gang injunction is an order issued by a civil court judge, prohibiting identified members of a particular gang from engaging in a series of specified activities, including associating with one another, carrying pagers, making gang hand signs, signaling drug sales, and being in public after an established curfew. The gang is sued as a public nuisance, with evidence provided by law enforcement and, sometimes, community declarations. Violation of any of the provisions of the injunction can net targeted gang members a hefty fine and/or up to six months in jail. Spawned in the gang communities of southern California in the 1980s, gang injunctions have become increasingly popular with law enforcement, community residents, and public officials. Nationally, more than 100 police agencies reported use of injunctions in their jurisdictions, but further examination found that only one-fourth fully understood the term; the primary locus of injunction activity is in California (Maxson, 2004).

Injunction program documents and law enforcement practitioners frame this intervention within the tradition of community policing/prosecution. Injunctions are pitched as a strategy to engage community involvement with law enforcement and improve the quality of life in neighborhoods, presumably via the activation of social ties in the parochial and public spheres. A study of southern California injunction practitioners by Maxson, Hennigan, and Sloane (2003) and an expansion to a national sample by Maxson (2004) found few indicators of direct community participation in the selection of the targeted gang, in development of the evidence for the suit, or in its enforcement. However, there is some evidence that injunctions can reduce crime (Grogger, 2002).

A recent study by Maxson, Hennigan, and Sloane (2005) found relative improvements (i.e., reductions) in the visibility of gang members, gang intimidation, fear of gang confrontation, and fear of crime following the implementation of an injunction, though not in indicators of neighborhood efficacy, social cohesion, or informal social control. The positive findings were evident in the part of the injunction area that was most disordered; the less-disordered portion of the neighborhood experienced negative effects—more gang visibility and property victimization and less belief that the neighborhood could solve its own problems. The evaluation studies provide both caution and promise to injunction practitioners. The promising aspects derive from the strategy's apparent ability to effect, positively and relatively quickly, residents' views and experiences of the immediate threats presented by gang members. Over time and with vigilant attention to ongoing implementation, this immediate impact could evolve into increased collective efficacy and the buttressing of social control via expanded social linkages in the parochial and public spheres.

However, this optimistic outcome appears unlikely in the face of a lack of investment in the social fabric of communities. If we had seen resident groups form in the injunction area; if there were evidence of increased access to public resources; if new services for promoting social, educational, or vocational skills among youth had emerged in the injunction area, we might be more hopeful of long-term, salutary effects on this community. Years ago in Philadelphia, we were told of grandmothers canvassing their neighborhoods, carrying brooms in a unified symbolic gesture to sweep their streets of gang violence. Such expressions of collective efficacy could reflect a sea change in community regeneration following a targeted gang intervention. This injunction was largely a one-man show, and that man was the police, employing the new injunction penalties in a suppression operation. To do otherwise would have required law enforcement to engage community members in a process that promoted social ties, provided a forum for the development of mutual trust or social cohesion among neighbors, and reactivated the mechanisms for informal social control. Admittedly, this is a lot to ask of law enforcement, but community engagement is the sole parameter that distinguishes injunctions as an innovative strategy for improving gang neighborhoods from a run-of-the-mill gang suppression strategy.

Other Community Characteristics

Ethnicity

Ethnicity is one of the most widely discussed, and little studied, aspects of gangs. Conventional wisdom, and some research, considers black gangs to be more entrepreneurial and more instrumental in their gang activity (Skolnick, 1990). Law enforcement reports often depict Hispanic gangs as more expressive and more turf oriented. Asian gangs are routinely portrayed as the most organized and mobile, with stronger ties to adult organized crime groups (Chin, 1990). Most ethnographic gang studies are sited in just one ethnic community, and survey research rarely addresses the community contexts that might illuminate different ethnic patterns. In essence, there are very few gang studies that provide systematic comparative ethnic data on communities; we described in chapter 4 the few studies that have sufficient numbers of youth of different ethnic identities to compare patterns of risk or gang characteristics among ethnic groups in the same study location. The discussion of ethnic patterns below draws from those studies that provide comparative data on ethnicity as a dimension of the community context of gangs, but we recognize the varying community contexts within some ethnographic studies that include just one group. For example, Anderson's (1999) description of the street and decent codes of the streets of Philadelphia portrays these distinct orientations coexisting within the same community. Our own work in several southern California communities finds that youths living in the same neighborhoods report different levels of gang awareness and neighborhood danger.

The structural studies discussed above that include the proportion of particular ethnicities in the population unit studied suggest that the concentration of Hispanic residents, in particular, may be an important pattern. Gang homicide rates are highest in Chicago Hispanic communities, and poverty does not seem to influence levels of gang violence there (Curry and Spergel, 1988: Figure 2). Both the Jackson and the Wells and Weisheit studies found that the proportion of Hispanic residents in a city predicted to gang presence. These three studies fail to identify the features in communities with high proportions of Hispanic residents that foster gangs. Although Curry and Spergel contend that "gang violence stemming from the social disorganization of immigrant life overshadows the visible impact of poverty on gang violence rate" (1988: 396), their study does not include independent measures of social disorganization or immigration; these community-level processes are operationalized, "simply and grossly" (1988: 387), as the concentration of Hispanics in a community.

Two other studies provide comparative information about the ethnic character of communities relevant to this discussion of community contexts. Anthropologist Vigil (2002) investigated the patterns of immigration and processes of financial and social marginalization in four ethnic communities in Los Angeles: Mexican, Salvadoran, Vietnamese, and African American. This study reveals quite different immigration experiences among the four communities, yet an overarching similarity in the four ethnic groups of gang norms and behavior. Vigil argues that, despite different experiences, members of marginalized communities must adapt and adjust to the dominant culture, often in ways that erode prosocial bonds and the influence of social control institutions like the family, school, and law enforcement. For each group, this paves the way for the emergence of a street culture and street socialization that foster and perpetuate gangs.

Rather than identifying a unique aspect of a particular ethnic subculture that produces a unique gang form, this study reinforces the view that generic social processes derive from social inequality and marginalization, processes that affect many communities in predictable ways. Sanchez-Jankowski (1991), in his much-debated study of three ethnic gang communities, also concludes that particular minority ethnicity and race do not make much difference in gang characteristics. Neither study supports the notion of differential interventions for different ethnic communities. Our own work leads us, as well, to conclude that gang processes trump ethnicity. While programs should be sensitive to the unique cultural or ethnic experiences within communities, interventions might better address the processes of marginalization, weakened bonds, and depleted institutional control mechanisms in a generic way.

Rural Gang Communities

As a consequence of the patterns of gang proliferation described in chapter 1, researchers have begun to look more closely at gangs in rural communities. The differences in the natures of rural and urban communities could produce contrasting patterns of gang emergence, organizational structures, and activities—and such differences would suggest different approaches to gang prevention and intervention. We know little about gang-joining patterns and gang structures in rural areas, but the survey data gathered by the National Youth Gang Center has proved a useful starting point for exploring the prevalence and characteristics of rural gang communities.

The NYGS series for a large sample of rural counties reveals declining levels of gang prevalence. In 1996, 26% of rural counties reported gangs, a figure that dropped steadily to about 12% in each of the 2000–2002 surveys (Egley et al., 2004). Gang problems emerged later in rural counties: the majority (65%) of rural gang counties in 1996 said that gangs had surfaced no earlier than 1993 (Howell, Egley, and Gleason, 2002).

Wells and Weisheit (2001) combined NYGS data with other data sources to study gangs in rural or nonmetropolitan areas.[1] Thirty-seven percent of police agencies in their categorization of rural communities reported gangs in the 1996 survey (versus 66% in metropolitan areas). These prevalence estimates declined to 30% and 60%, respectively, in 1998. These researchers wanted to know which indicators of social and economic stability, economic deprivation, and population characteristics were associated with a persistent gang presence (22.6% of agencies), a transitory gang presence (20.4% of agencies reported gangs in one survey but not the other), or a persistent lack of gangs (57% of agencies) in rural areas. Economic factors (instability or deprivation) were not related to gang status, except for the surprising finding that rural communities experiencing economic growth were more likely to report gangs. Further, proximity to urban areas did not predict gangs in rural communities, challenging those who would argue that gang migration from urban areas "causes" rural gang problems (see chapter 1). The presence of gangs in rural areas was linked to the ecological indicators of social disorganization and with higher risk conditions in the population.

As we reported earlier in this chapter, these researchers also studied gangs in metropolitan areas. Their analysis of the two types of areas revealed similar effects of social stability and population composition. However, economic deprivation was important to understanding gang status in metropolitan areas, but unrelated to gang presence in rural areas. Thus, somewhat different models predict gang situations in the two types of areas. This research suggests that gang strategies that address economic disadvantage are less likely to be relevant in rural areas.

We have already noted the declining trend in gang prevalence in rural areas, and it appears that the transitory nature of gangs increases with the level of rurality. Weisheit and Wells (2004) find that just 14% of rural agencies reporting gangs in 1997 still had them in 2000, as compared to 58% of nonmetropolitan areas with an urban population of 20,000 or more. These researchers observe that gangs are hardly pervasive and persistent in rural areas,

> raising questions about the commonly held belief that once gangs have a foothold in the community it is rare for them to leave or disappear. Indeed, most rural gangs are so small and unstable that the loss of one or two members—through arrest, movement out of the area, or maturation—can easily mean the end of the gang. (2004: 4)

While still in its infancy, the available research on gangs in rural communities suggests caution in exporting programs developed in urban settings. More-recent gang onset, lower prevalence, the fluid nature of gang membership, and different community risk factors make many gang interventions inappropriate to rural communities. It is noteworthy that in telephone interviews with these law enforcement agencies, Weisheit and Wells report that "rural agencies appear to be ready to deal with gangs"

(2004: 6), and most frequently respond to gangs with suppression through strict enforcement, hardly a strategy customized for rural settings.

Onset of Gangs

A final community context that is increasingly studied in national surveys of gang cities is the time period when gangs first emerged. Spergel and Curry (1993) drew an analytic distinction based on the year of onset of gang problems. Working with data from their 1987 national survey of more than 100 cities, these scholars observed that the 45 gang cities in their sample (defined by the recognition of a gang problem and an organized response by law enforcement or services practitioners to it) fell roughly evenly into two categories. Chronic gang cities were those with a long history of serious gang problems, whereas emerging gang cities had confronted gang problems only since 1980. Emerging gang cities were often smaller and reported less-serious gang problems. Spergel and Curry determined that intervention strategies vary by these two types of communities. Although suppression strategies were used most often in both types, emerging gang cities more often employed community organization as a primary strategy, whereas chronic gang cities were more likely to use social intervention and, to a lesser extent, opportunities provision strategies.[2] This study is often recalled for Spergel and Curry's finding that the primary strategies used by communities to respond to gangs bear no observable relationship to the measured perceptions of the primary causes of gangs nor to the perceived effectiveness of the strategies used. Nevertheless, analysis of survey responses led Spergel and Curry to identify strategies with some promise of efficacy in the two community types: community organization in emerging gang cities and opportunities provision in chronic gang cities.

In our discussion of gang proliferation in chapter 1 and of community structural characteristics earlier in this chapter, we have seen that cities with larger populations are more likely to have gangs. The pattern of gang emergence, or gang onset, in U.S. cities is closely related to population size. Not only are larger cities more likely to have gangs, but gangs were more likely to surface in those cities earlier than in smaller cities. The different onset patterns by city size are readily observable in Figure 1.3. It is noteworthy that less than 20% of the largest cities and less than 10% of midsized (populations of 50,000–99,999) identified gang problems by the Spergel and Curry chronic gang city benchmark of 1980. As we approach the middle of the first decade of the twenty-first century, a city with a 20-year history of gang problems would seem to qualify as a chronic gang city. The precise temporal distinction that separates chronic from emergent gang cities has changed as we track gang problems over time, but as Spergel and Curry (1993) noted, the chronic-emergent distinction is important for understanding both the nature of gang problems and the appropriate attempts to control gangs. Whether we mark the dividing line in 1980, or 1985, or 1990, locales with chronic gang conditions seem to share some important considerations for gang intervention.

First, chronic gang cities are larger, have more gangs and gang members, and are more likely to have entrenched gang traditions than more recent gang cities. The sheer numbers suggest more varied gang structures and more diversity in gang activities, requiring a more-complex array of intervention strategies. Longer histories of gang rivalries, intergenerational transmission of gang values, and communities infused with gang cultures make some of the gangs in chronic gang cities far less vulnerable to intervention.

Second, the patterns of gang forms and activities seem to vary with the stage of onset of gang activity in a city. Writing in the mid-1990s, we observed that the specialty and compressed gang structures were far more common in emergent cities: about three-fourths of these gangs were located in cities with gang onset in 1985 and thereafter (Klein and Maxson, 1996: Figure 5). Conversely, about one-fourth of traditional gangs were located in cities that identified gang problems by 1970, and half were in cities with onset before 1985. Newer gang cities may have different constellations of gang structures that require different interventions than chronic gang cities.

A recent analysis of NYGS data suggests that characteristics of gang members in newer gang cities may be different as well. Howell, Moore, and Egley (2002) find distinct demographic and crime patterns in cities and counties reporting the onset of gangs during the 1990s. These jurisdictions report younger members, slightly more females, more Caucasians, and gangs with a racial/ethnic mixture. The police respondents in these localities also report far lower levels of gang involvement in violent crimes, including homicide, assault, robbery, and use of firearms, as well as in property and drug trafficking offenses.

Third is the pattern of gang persistence related to the onset of gang problems we described in chapter 1. Egley et al. (2004) found that 82% of cities with variable gang problems (that is, reports of gang problems in only one year of the survey and no gang problems in the other survey years, 1996–2001) had a year of gang onset during the 1990s. Variable gang problems typified half of the small cities (populations up to 50,000) and none of the cities with population of 100,000 or more.

Taken together, studies that address the onset of gangs in a community suggest that different approaches to intervention in chronic and emergent gang cities may be required. The types of gangs, characteristics of gang members, and gang activity in more-recent onset cities call for innovative strategies, and yet we also note that the perceived gang problems in smaller cities and rural areas can also disappear as quickly as they emerge. Thus, the warnings about misdirected and ineffective gang programs that we offered in chapter 3 may be particularly important for emergent gang cities. Gang intervention can backfire and perhaps disturb the natural processes of extinction already occurring in many places.

The research on other community contexts also proved relevant to program development. Economic disadvantage and instability seem to place communities at risk for gangs and gang violence in urban but not rural areas. However, we have noted discordant findings as to the effects of poverty and economic decline on gang emergence in urban areas and also differential effects by race and ethnicity. Community dynamics, social disorganization, and in particular collective efficacy may have more direct influences on gang development. Finally, it appears that the dimensions of community contexts we've discussed may well be overshadowed by more-compelling or immediate aspects of adolescents' environment and experiences in their families, schools, and peer social networks. As we observe in chapter 8, this is indeed where a lot of the intervention action is sited.

Our final chapters present a framework for understanding the array of program efforts to control gangs and for identifying notable gaps in program activity. This exercise makes clear the opportunity for practitioners to integrate more fully important features of the community context in gang programs.

Part III

Multiple goals for gang control policies need to be clearly articulated. These can then be related in an organized fashion to individual-, group-, and community-level gang data as they relate to prevention, intervention, and suppression programs. This combination of goals, data, and strategies provides a wide assortment of gang control options from which policy makers can choose.

Seven

MULTIPLE GOALS FOR GANG CONTROL PROGRAMS AND POLICIES

As we move to the final part of this book, we move away from the firm ground of gang data to the more-speculative arena of gang control goals (chapter 7) and gang programs and policies (chapter 8). The end point for those primarily concerned with policy issues is chapter 8, which portrays options for gang control. In parts I and II, we have already achieved our goal of providing the reader with pertinent modern empirical data about street gangs.

What sorts of things do we know that have implications for gang control? Consider the chapters in part I. We know that gangs have become far more than a big-city problem. They can be hatched in moderate-sized cities, small towns, even Indian reservations. This fact alone forces us to think broadly about what are the socioeconomic and community factors that spawn street gangs.

We know also that street gang crime is highly varied in its composition, that it is a function both of what individual members bring to the group and what the group contributes above and beyond individual propensities. And we know that violence and drug sales, while prominent features of law enforcement and public images of gang behavior, actually comprise a relatively small portion of what gang members bring to the table.

We also know, unfortunately, that major modern attempts at gang control have largely failed to achieve their ends. This is for a number of reasons: reliance on inadequate conventional wisdoms, failure to incorporate gang data into program designs, failure to implement effectively the very designs proposed to yield gang control, and a disjuncture between what is proposed and what should yield reductions in gang activity.

In part II, we have reviewed data that the authors see as pivotal to understanding gangs, their members, and their community contexts. We know that gang members are of many types, defying easy stereotypes. We know that a number of factors—far fewer than the number predictive of delinquency involvement generally—predict who is more and who is less likely to join gangs, although these predictions are not yet particularly strong. We know that these factors—risk factors—derive from individual, family, peer, school, and community domains. We are thus required to think broadly about programs that might reduce the risks of gang joining. We also are learning for the first time that genuine protective factors are few and far between. Risk reduction seems more promising than protection enhancement.

We know that gangs (like communities and members) manifest much variety, and yet there are some dependable types of gang structures that allow us to find patterns in the variety. These structures can provide cues to different approaches to gang control. We know, as well, that certain processes common to all groups can be exacerbated within gangs, that gangs can twist and distort prosocial group processes in such a way as to increase gang cohesiveness and crime while at the same time defeating well-intentioned efforts at gang intervention and suppression. We may be able to think through how better to manipulate these group processes, and we can now clearly suggest what will have deleterious effects on our efforts—and therefore what not to do.

With respect to gang neighborhoods and communities, we have suggested that most gang control programs do little to involve community factors in these programs. This is both surprising, as the community issues are obvious, and understandable—mucking about in community change is terribly complex and frustrating. We have suggested that the relevant literature finds structural factors—race, poverty, age distributions, and the like—to be important but mostly as they are mediated by more proximal factors: family, friends, schools.

With respect to community processes, we noted that neighborhood collective efficacy, types of local social control, and contrasting or oppositional cultures seem directly related to the emergence and stability of street gangs and the criminal activity and violence in which they participate. Finally, we noted that the movement to employ antigang injunctions holds some promise but is severely limited by the disjuncture between the rhetoric of community involvement and the absence of genuine community involvement in most instances.

Given all of this, all of the information in parts I and II, is there still time to get better at street gang control, or are we by now at the stage of too little, too late? Suppose we were back in the 1940s or 1950s, when gangs were found in a number of major cities but were not spread around the country as they are now. Further, suppose that gang crime were relatively minor and that even gang violence were committed without commonly resorting to sophisticated firearms. And suppose, in addition, we could reasonably predict an expansion of gang numbers and gang violence in the absence of coordinated knowledge for policy options to treat gang problems.

This is where we stood in the 1950s in this country, before we lost control. And this is approximately the situation now in Europe, where we have identified gang problems in at least 50 major cities in 20 countries. It was the Eurogang program that led to the gang definition we use in this book, as described in the introduction: "any durable, street-oriented youth group whose involvement in illegal activity is part of its group identity."

In some ways, it was the current status of street gangs in Europe and the developments of the Eurogang program that led to the structure of this book and its emphasis on data-oriented options for gang control. Following the second Eurogang workshop, located in Oslo, we were invited to give a talk entitled "Strategies for Street Gang Control" for the combined audience of several state ministries. The talk was based on the facts that (1) data about gangs in Europe were minimal and scattered about with little coordination in gathering them, (2) goals for gang control were as yet ill defined, and (3) the problem had not yet gotten out of control.

Yet across many cities and many countries, there were common elements which held promise for generic gang knowledge and, perhaps, for generic approaches to gang control. As we prepared a paradigm of the interplay between data and control strategies for the Norwegian situation, it became clear that roughly the same paradigm should apply to the United States. Indeed, we have become quite convinced of this, and we will expand and demonstrate the paradigm in chapter 8. Implicit in this decision is our belief that it *still* remains true of the United States that gang data remain relatively uncoordinated and that goals for gang control remain ill defined. The principal difference between the European and

U.S. gang situation is that the problem in the United States *is* out of control (as illustrated in all three chapters of part I). Now we must prepare the way to the paradigm.

Six Selected Goals for Gang Control

1. Individual-level goals for gang control are several. They need not (or perhaps cannot) be tackled or achieved simultaneously. For example, practitioners might be most interested in *preventing gang joining* (or at least delaying it). We know from data presented in this book that the result of joining a street gang is to increase greatly one's delinquency and to create "disorder in the life course" (Thornberry et al., 2003), such as school dropout, early pregnancy and parenthood, and unstable employment. The risk factors for gang joining can be found among five domains: individual characteristics, family variables, peer relations, school involvement, and community characteristics. These leave plenty of room for preventive programs of interest to a wide range of practitioners. For example, we know from research in Seattle (Hill et al., 1999) that of 65 variables tested, 25 tested at ages 10–12 predicted significantly to gang membership at between ages 13 and 18. The Seattle and Rochester data (Thornberry et al., 2003) also reveal that the larger the number of risk factors and the larger the number of the five domains in which they fall, the greater is the risk for gang joining.

A second individual-level goal is *encouraging gang desistance*. This involves a different kind of targeting—not risk factors, but variables capable of overcoming the group processes that reinforce gang membership. Data on such variables have not been well documented because we have seen so few examples of successful gang intervention programs. Reducing sources of gang cohesiveness has shown some promise (Klein, 1971), and we know that over time most gang members become former gang members. They mature out, probably as a function of involvements and changes such as stable sexual partnerships, meaningful employment, wearying of the stresses and danger of gang violence, and—in fewer cases—incarceration in correctional institutions.

In a review of the gang desistance literature, Decker and Lauritsen (2002) cite Sanchez-Jankowski on the diversity of routes out of the gang and Vigil on the difficulty of leaving the gang because of the concern for rejecting one's peers and friends. However, Decker and Lauritsen found that most of the research on desistance was merely descriptive: "We found no research designed to assess systematically the conditions under which members choose to leave the gang" (2002: 54).

Their own interviews with St. Louis gang members reveal, for a number of members, that "a combination of maturational reform, aging, and proximity to violence produced the motivation for leaving the gang" (2002: 58). They emphasize the confrontation with violence, such as personal victimization or a friend's victimization. "The trick, then, is to intervene immediately following acts of violence, when gang members are separated from their gang" (2002: 67), as in emergency room, police station, or family settings. However, these processes can be clarified, so here is an area where coordinated action and research within projects might yield great benefit.

A third individual-level goal is *crime reduction* during gang membership. By this we mean individual reduction above and beyond that attributable to the consequences of gang (as a unit) dissolution or disruption. One might accept gang membership as a given or accept the inevitability of gang formation in certain neighborhoods, yet still attempt to reduce the criminal involvement of individual gang members. This could take the form of less delinquency and crime, or less serious delinquency and crime (e.g., violence reduction). If anyone has empirically demonstrated the capacity to achieve this goal, we are not aware of it. Even the substantial reduction (35%) reported by Klein (1971) for the Latins gang was the result of gang dissolution, not a reduction of the average delinquency involvement of the remaining members.

2. Group-level goals for gang change similarly come in several forms. We alluded above to *gang reduction and dissolution*, perhaps the most obvious goal in gang-involved cities. Elsewhere (Klein, 1995a: 198–199), we have suggested several structural factors that serve to maintain or reinforce gang existence. These include (a) oppositional structures and institutions, such as the police, school officials, and some forms of gang intervention programs; (b) rival groups (usually other street gangs); and (c) shared perceptions of barriers to improving one's life opportunities. Programs aimed at reducing such gang maintenance factors certainly should be within our intervention repertoire. Particularly important is *intergang violence reduction*. Gang rivalries are the source of much of the most-extreme gang violence, far more, for instance, than that often attributed to drug distribution disputes (Block and Block, 1995). Attempts at rivalry reduction, conflict mediation, and gang truces have a long history. The L.A. Bridges' corollary, Bridges II, funded various agencies to

engage in conflict resolution between warring gangs. Positive anecdotal reports on the success of this and similar adventures are unfortunately matched by a total absence of valid empirical demonstrations of success in intergang violence reduction.

Another group-level goal is as simply stated as it is difficult to conceive or achieve: *prevention of gang formation*. In Klein (1995a), we suggested two broad categories of structural factors that predict to gang formation in a formerly gang-free community and one cultural factor. All three categories might seem well beyond our control if we are faint-hearted about altering the local manifestations of broad societal conditions.

The first category was labeled *underclass* variables, after Wilson (1987) and first adapted to the gang situation by Hagedorn (1988). They set the stage for gang formation and include (a) the industrial shift away from the inner city to locations no longer available to inner-city youth, (b) failures in urban education systems, (c) minority segregation, and (d) the outmigration of the urban middle class and its informal systems of local social control.

The second category of gang-spawning factors was labeled *onset* variables, proximal realities that on their own or as by-products of the underclass factors seem to lead most directly to gang formation. Included are the number of youths and young adults aged 10–30, the absence of jobs, high crime or delinquency levels, concentration of minority (or marginalized) residents, the absence of opportunities for alternate activities, and the absence of effective social controls.

These two categories have to do with social structure. The third, somewhat more ephemeral, we refer to as the "diffusion of street gang culture" (Klein, 1995a: 205–208). Not all cities are sufficiently encumbered by the underclass and onset factors that one might expect the spontaneous generation of street gangs. It's as if the urban genetics predispose a community to gang formation, but require an environmental trigger to see the genes "expressed" in imitation of gangs. Most gang cities became so only in the late 1980s or early 1990s (Klein, 1995a; National Youth Gang Center, 1999). We believe, as do many of our agency informants across the country, that this trigger was the media-produced image of gang culture (accompanied in some cases by the migration of gang members from places like Los Angeles and Chicago to smaller, vulnerable locations).

There is a form of social mimicry in this: young people see gang members portrayed in print, radio, television, and movie media and are further bombarded by the merchandising of "gang clothes" and styles of communications. Millions of nongang youth know what it is to look like, walk like, talk like, and act like media images of gang members. Some of their sports heroes manifest the styles as well. Members of local groups, street clubs and teams, rap and break-dancing groups (see Hagedorn, 1988), and play groups (see even Thrasher, 1927), and many nongroup loners as well, can try on gang life. Many will find it an ill fit. Others will be further attracted by the excitement, the group support, the sense of rebellion exuded by street gangs. They will be hooked. Of a number of youths who started to hang around Klein's Latins, about half soon disappeared, but half slowly assumed membership in the gang during the first few months of the project. Gangbanging should be seen as an *option*—it is available in many settings but requires a willingness to become involved.

One other group-level goal should be mentioned, especially in view of our description of the five gang structures in chapter 5. This is the *prevention of gang regeneration.* Traditional gangs, it will be recalled, exist for as many as 20 years or more—in some Chicago and Los Angeles cases, for more than 50 years—and regenerate themselves by adding successive cliques of younger members. Neotraditional gangs show the same but less-consistent pattern of self-regeneration. Thus a reasonable goal for gang control in these two types of gang structure would be to interrupt this process. We have seen "natural" interruptions due to political forces in Chicago, as the Blackstone Rangers became the Black P Stone Nation and then the El Rukns, perhaps different traditional gangs but perhaps merely new versions of a continuing process. In Los Angeles, several traditional black gangs in south-central Los Angeles[1] were effectively disrupted by the civil disorders of the late 1960s, only to reemerge in similar form a few years later with the names Crips and Bloods. The same communities spawned the gangs of both eras. Klein's (1971) successful cessation of the regeneration in the Latins gang through an intensive intervention program was followed two years after the program's completion by the reemergence of the gang in the same location, where it continues to exist 30 years later.

Such experiences with traditional gangs do not make one sanguine about the likelihood of achieving the goal of interrupting gang regeneration. However, most gangs are not of the traditional type, and it may well be that the progression of neotraditional and compressed gangs into the traditional form could be prevented. Recall from chapter 5 that, after four years, a number of the gangs other than traditional ones had "progressed" to the traditional form.

3. Community-level goals for gang control are based on the notion that it is communities that spawn street gangs. Gang control may be

achieved by mitigating community factors that help to yield gangs or by strengthening community capacities to exercise social control of gangs. In either case, it is clear that leaving gang control to the police and courts cannot begin to suffice. Getting the police involved in gang control is easy, while getting neighborhoods and communities involved is very difficult. Our discussion in chapter 6 suggested several community-level goals as most worth pursuing. The first is finding ways to increase community efficacy in line with the suggestions of Sampson et al. (1997). The second is attempting to develop the several types of local control enumerated by Bursik and Grasmick (1993). A third would be to seek a better understanding of the processes by which local habits and cultures either permit or even encourage the rhetoric of violence that so permeates gang members' thinking. Elijah Anderson's work (1999) is a good example of such an attempt, describing the "code of the street" in Philadelphia.

4. Choosing and clarifying the Spergel strategies—prevention, intervention, and suppression—are themselves major goals to be achieved in gang control policy. The specifics of the approach are fully explicated in Spergel's major book (1995). Because the approach is part of the paradigm to be presented in chapter 8, we need to suggest here how prevention, intervention, and suppression goals might relate to the individual-, group-, and community-change goals for street gang control.[2]

Prevention at the individual level is designed to keep youth from joining gangs. Two general options are available. One is to mount programs for the general youth population, as was done in the G.R.E.A.T. program discussed in chapter 3. The most obvious problem here is that most youths will not become gang involved in any case, so such programs are bound to be inefficient even if effective. The second option is to aim programs at youth judged to be most at risk of gang joining. In chapter 3, both L.A. Bridges and the Illinois program claimed this goal, but their failure to come to grips with what puts a youth at risk of gang involvement defeated their purpose. The data on risk factors presented in chapter 4 should be helpful on this score.

Still, the current knowledge of such gang risk factors is at a rudimentary level. Data from our own cross-sectional analyses in California, combined with findings from the longitudinal studies in Rochester and Denver, show that most delinquency predictors are not gang predictors and that only three individual-level variables attain significance in differentiating gang from nongang youth. These are (a) youth with already forming delinquent self-concepts, (b) youth who have been subjected to a set of critical events in their lives, and (c) youth with access to few if any helpful adults outside the family.[3] The goal of individual-level prevention for now remains difficult to achieve if it is based on empirical data (as we insist it must).

Prevention at the group level also represents a problem of targeting, in this case targeting nongang groups (rather than individuals) that are likely to be transformed into street gangs. There are many more non-troublesome youth groups than there are gangs. Targeting them all with prevention strategies seems inefficient at best. There is, as with individuals, always an iatrogenic issue as well. Few youth groups might be said to be at risk of becoming street gangs, but there is nothing but unverified anecdotal evidence to suggest which groups these might be. Thrasher (1927) mentions various candidate types of groups, starting with young play groups. Hagedorn (1988) identifies some break-dancing groups that formed rivalries and then progressed to gang forms. Los Angeles–area enforcement officials have documented some tagger crews that moved from that status to "tag bangers" and thereafter to street gangs, but which tagger crews are susceptible to such a progression is unknown. New research by Maxson and Whitlock (2003) in Los Angeles middle schools shows surprising similarities between tagger crews and gangs, but few such similarities with the newer phenomenon of "party crews." Since gangs form in part out of responses to the reactions of those around them, one would want to think preventively about youth groups that produce antisocial behavior problems or community consternation or groups having distinct competitors or rivals. Still, the false positives in such predictions of gang formation will far outweigh the correct predictors.

Prevention at the community level assumes a relationship between community or neighborhood characteristics and gang formation. It may be beyond our capacities to alter significantly both economic disadvantage and residential instability, two global structural factors often associated with urban deviance.[4] Yet it may be an attainable goal to increase a neighborhood's capacity to exercise informal social control over troublesome youth and groups. In the inevitable absence of sufficient control by law enforcement, residents, local businesspeople, clergy, and agency officials might be better organized in prevention programs to forestall gang formation. This was one of the principal goals of the long-established but poorly evaluated Chicago area projects.

Moving to the intervention level of strategies necessarily narrows the focus of one's goals. Intervention involves affecting individuals, groups, and communities already stereotyped with the gang label. Individual-level goals can be to remove members from their gangs, or to reduce their levels of participation, or to reduce their criminal involvement while in the gangs. Past approaches have included individual counseling, provision of outreach or gang workers, and opening up alternative opportunities to gang members. A crucial element here is to learn *how* to target *which* members for *which* type of intervention. Factors such as gang members' age, gender, and commitment to the gang are critical. Some members are more amenable to change than are others. Some, at various stages of their gang existence, are simply beyond our reach.[5]

Group-level intervention is harder to conceive. Goals may include reducing external pressures for gang maintenance, transforming gang-related values into more-acceptable prosocial values (social service and political involvement are two strategies often attempted), or reducing conflict and tensions between rival gangs. Klein's project with the Latins was an attempt to reduce the cohesiveness of the gang as a unit to test whether or not success in achieving that goal directly would lead to achieving indirectly the goal of reducing individual-level criminal behavior. This illustrates the possibility for tackling one goal through manipulating another.

But, as we emphasized in chapter 5, group processes in the gang present unique and difficult challenges beyond the same processes in other groups. Group-level intervention must overcome those very potent processes, an approach that may be counterintuitive or run counter to some potent conventional wisdoms among intervention practitioners that one should not "break up" a naturally occurring group. Treatment of deviant youths in group settings—on the street, in correctional facilities, in schools, and in mental health settings—has been a common practice for hundreds of years, pitting the convenience of the group setting against the peer contagion that is inherent in that setting. One intensive review of such peer-group intervention points clearly to an imbalance of negative iatrogenic effects over ameliorative effects (Dishion, McCord, and Poulin, 1999). Group-level interventions should be undertaken with severe caution and close, data-based monitoring of effects.

Community-level goals for gang intervention, like individual- and group-level goals, are far more narrowly targeted than prevention goals. They focus on already-involved gang communities, more than likely communities or neighborhoods with traditional forms of gangs. These are areas where an almost symbiotic relationship may have developed between the gang and some constituencies of the community. The goal of intervening in such situations must be stated in long-term language, with long-term commitments from programs and their supporters.

Suppression, whether at the individual, group, or community level, is a qualitatively different approach from the others. By suppression, Spergel and others mean not ordinary law enforcement but something more intense. Terms like "crack down," "harass," and "intimidate" come to mind. Elements of the L.A. Plan described in chapter 3 provide examples, wherein police, prosecution, and correctional agencies developed gang units to provide special emphasis on gang activities. Civil abatement and special antigang legislation provide other examples.

Suppression approaches are generally more narrowly defined and focused than prevention or intervention. In most instances—though this need not be the case—they are self-inclusive. They do not reach out to engage collaborations from prevention and intervention practitioners. Suppression programs have a tendency to be ideological more than conceptual.

At the individual level, suppression aims to arrest, prosecute, and incarcerate gang members as formal operations. Often this involves cracking down on gang "leaders" with the mistaken conventional wisdom that it will result in group dissolution. More informally, the goal is to deter gang members from associating with each other and committing arrestable crimes. The reduction of individual acts of crime is the unifying goal.

At the group level, suppression goals call for gang size reduction and the interruption of gang-level crime: intergang violence and drug sales for the benefit of the gang are examples. Individual criminal acts are rephrased as being "for the benefit of the gang" or "in furtherance of gang goals." Such goals have recently led to enforcement and legislative definitions of what constitutes a street gang, or a "criminal street gang," so that the group unit is given the same targetable legitimacy as the individual gang member. Such legislation, along with antigang civil injunctions, are examples of group targeting.

Suppression goals at the community level are almost off the chart in modern American society, as they call forth charges of racism or class-based discrimination. This is sometimes seen in the use of broad street sweeps, where large task forces of police and others literally target a neighborhood or community to "retake" it from the gangs. Operation Hammer, used by the Los Angeles Police Department, employed 1,000 officers a night to sweep the black gang-involved neighborhoods of, first, south-central L.A. and, later, other areas, reaching for mass arrests of suspects. Few convictions resulted from Operation Hammer, but community resentment flourished. The operation clearly signaled the distinction between mere deterrence and outright suppression.

The preceding discussion of prevention, intervention, and suppression goals makes manifest how complex it can be to think through the many goals of gang control approaches. For the authors, however, these matters get even more complex because of our conviction that gang control programming has not proven to be enough. Such programming has not advanced our understanding of gang control sufficiently to recommend specific programs for specific settings. If gang control efforts are to become more useful, we must specify fifth and sixth goals.

5. This next goal is to maximize the use of data, both local and generic. Three of the programs described in chapter 3 failed on this score, while the G.R.E.A.T., Spergel Model, and SafeFutures programs did respond to this goal. Given the general theme of this book, using data to develop policy options, this is the goal we find most important as well as unfortunately the least often achieved.

Pivotal to achieving the goal of gathering and employing valid gang data is the need to settle on useful definitions of street gangs. We addressed this question quite extensively in the introduction to this volume. The consensus Eurogang definition of a street gang seems quite robust: a durable, street-oriented youth group whose involvement in illegal activity is part of its group identity. Since its formation, that definition has been employed to good effect in a number of new studies of street gangs in Europe (Decker and Weerman, 2005). It properly identifies those gangs and also seems to differentiate them from nontroublesome youth groups on the one hand and from prison, motorcycle, and terrorist gangs on the other. With it, we have some optimism about formulating broad generalizations about street gangs and about finding policy options that can apply broadly.

With that concern settled for now, our question is about what kinds of data we want people to bring forth in order to formulate appropriate gang control policies and programs. We suggest two broad categories of data, each with a pivotal qualification. The first is gathering together *generic* data on street gangs, as these might apply to local situations. This is what we have done in part II of this volume. Those sorts of data patterns should be explicitly used in program formulations. The qualifications on which we would insist is that these must be *previously verified* data patterns; this is not the place to allow entry of unverified intuitions, insights, and personal experiences (e.g., the street expertise of the gang worker or the gang cop; see Klein, 2004).

The second category is *local* data, those that describe the communities and the gangs at which a program is targeted. The Spergel projects and SafeFutures programs provide extensive guidelines for determining which local data are most essential. The qualification is that these data must be *verifiable* to the extent that most participants in the gang control program can agree upon them. What gang workers tell us about their gangs may be suspect as will be the crime descriptions provided by the police. Social agencies' descriptions of community situations similarly need verification, as do the complaints of local youths themselves. This means not only that local data must be gathered, but also that they must be shared, critiqued, and perhaps reconsidered as different actors respond to them. Social agency, police, school, and resident viewpoints affect the data they present. All can stand scrutiny and an honest attempt to assess their validity.

It is, of course, the responsibility of program administrators and their funders to determine which local data are most pertinent, but they must not do so arbitrarily, as is the usual practice. They might be faced with a cafeteria of data choices and asked to justify explicitly the utility of each form of local data. Such a cafeteria of choices might include the following:

- Number of gangs in the area, their structural types, their arrest patterns over at least three years, their ethnic, age, and gender compositions.
- Capacity (and criteria used) to identify gang-prone youth and gang-spawning areas.
- Community responses to gangs in the past: police approaches, agency programs, school policies, etc., including any indications of success or barriers to success.
- Available resources. Prior efforts suggest that the explicit willingness of agencies to participate is critical, including willingness to adjust their policies and practices to fit the needs of gang programming.
- Explicit capacities and intentions to provide continuity, following the initial funding support period. Most gang control programs should plan on at least 10-year continuity, enough to outlast most gangs.

Aside from the specifics of the fifth goal—the planned collection of program-relevant data (generic and local)—the description given here makes clear the seriousness of the efforts we are encouraging. Funding entities and community agencies should not be in the business of coordinated gang control programming unless they are willing to undertake the preliminary data-gathering steps outlined here. Of course, police can continue their own efforts, schools can do what they do, social agencies can continue their in-house and outreach programming, but let's not call these serious gang control programs because they won't be able to assess or diagnose their successes and failures in a publicly (to say nothing of scientifically) verifiable fashion. Gang control habits are not the kinds of programs needed at this point; they don't use the knowledge available nor do they convince us of their value in gang reduction.

6. If the above sounds harsh, it is because we share with many of our criminological colleagues and many public policy agents the belief that we have been spinning our wheels in the muds of gang control. It's time to move to four-wheel drive. People running gang control programs need to be able to steer toward clear goals and adjust to barriers encountered along the way. Thus our sixth and final goal is for gang control programs to position themselves *ahead of time* to obtain independent evaluation of both program process and program outcome. Gangs, gang members, and gang-spawning communities can be highly resistant to change; one must assume *no* change in the absence of proof to the contrary. We are of course discouraged by the twin facts that most gang control efforts have gone unevaluated and that those with adequate evaluations have not provided formulas for success.

When we fail, we need to know why. Process evaluations are critical to understanding what went wrong and what may be improved. The G.R.E.A.T., Spergel Model, and SafeFutures reports are available as models of process evaluations. Therefore we concentrate our thoughts here on outcome evaluation and in particular on the various kinds of data that might be pertinent—another cafeteria of choices. We can portray this cafeteria of outcome measures in two ways, by a simple listing or by a heuristic categorical paradigm. We will do both.

A fairly obvious listing of outcomes to be considered might look like this:

- Decreases and changes in crime patterns: violence, intergang incidents, weapons carrying, drug use, drug sales, general crime,[6] and reduced gang size
- Increased individuation (peer resistance, decreased gang affiliation of individual members)
- Proportionately fewer youths joining gangs
- Increased life skills, preparation, and access to opportunities such as schools, jobs, etc.
- Improved informal social control by community residents and businesses, greater community efficacy, lower fear of crime

7.1. *Program Goals and Measures*

	Individual Goals	Group Goals	Community Goals
patterns	violence, drug use and sales, general crime	intergang incidents, territoriality, group cohesiveness, gang size	injunctions, "hanging around," resident fear, witness intimidation, graffiti
uation		peer resistance, group activities, alternative activities	participation in neighborhood, school activities
lls	school progress, jobs, family relations		voluntarism
al social			parent groups, police support, "safe passage" programs, greater community efficacy, lower fear of crime
zational	increased use of schools, parks by gang members	lower stigmatization, stereotyping of gangs	interorganizational cooperation, info sharing, access for gang members
on pre-	improved early identification, needs assessments		community awareness, condemnation of gangs, support groups

- Organizational change: agencies being more responsive to gang members; more adaptation to gang control, such as police gang units, antigang legislation and abatements, providing street workers
- Better focus on prevention; improved targeting of gang-prone youths

It is also feasible to develop a paradigm of outcomes and measures, based on individual, group, and community levels of change. For illustration, we present one such model in Table 7.1 (but others are rather easily imagined; the point is to be explicit and systematic about it).

Does it seem like a lot to consider? It does to us. But displays like this serve to emphasize just how complex thinking about aspects of gang control can be. We are no longer satisfied with simplistic approaches to goal setting, programming, or assessing outcomes. The best way to face complexity is just that—face it.

Eight

A MODEL FOR POLICY CHOICES

Logically, in light of all we've presented in the prior seven chapters, this might seem the time to prescribe the solution. We should now reveal the secrets to success in gang control. But prescriptions are based on tested trials that have proven to be successful. We are reluctant to take pills that have disputed value. We are wary of side effects, and rightly so.

Well, the world of gang control can provide few guidelines for success, only continuing approaches that "feel right," those that conform to conventional wisdoms. We noted it in the mid-1990s, and it remains true now: "The saddest message of all is simply this; little that has been done can be demonstrated to be useful. Thus, the clues for the future have less to do with what might work, than with avoiding in the future what has not worked" (Klein, Maxson, and Miller, 1995: 249). The existence of street gangs in thousands of jurisdictions does not suggest that we are ready to prescribe. The continuing federal, state, and local initiation of new and many retread programs does not suggest that we are ready to prescribe. Even the spokespersons for the major federal programs admit the problem. Wyrick and Howell note, "Although thousands of programs have been implemented . . . , the ongoing difficulties with youth gangs make one lesson very clear: there are no quick fixes or easy solutions for the problems that youth gangs create or the problems that create youth gangs" (2004: 21). And so, the suggestion is that we stop, step back, and consider where we want to go and why—in light of what we have learned about gangs to date. And so, in this chapter, we do not prescribe, we do not tell the reader what program to mount nor how to mount it.

Instead, we offer options and make the operating assumption that caring and intelligent practitioners in the gang world can come to some wise decisions—wiser, at least, than has generally been the case in the past. It will certainly aid this enterprise to keep in mind our consensus definition: any durable, street-oriented youth group whose involvement in illegal activity is part of its group identity. This allows us to set aside prison gangs, motorcycle gangs, terrorist groups, and adult crime groups or cartels. It also allows us to omit the vast majority of youth groups and cliques that only occasionally involve themselves in criminal activity, even groups like party crews and tagger crews. The definition allows us to concentrate on street gangs as *qualitatively* different groups.

Finally, let us undertake this enterprise without the all-too-common equating of gangs with racial, ethnic, or national characteristics. In gangs, group process trumps ethnicity, and social marginality is the most common factor that yields these groups. Commonly, but not uniformly, gang formation is spawned in communities or subsections of communities with poverty, discrimination, inadequate resources, and low community efficacy and where official (police, court, school, etc.) hostility is felt. But these are the contexts; the proximal common factor seems to be social marginality, and the resultant glue is the set of group processes that connects gang-prone youth together.

We are going to organize our discussion by reference to three considerations. The first is the handy categorization emanating from Spergel's (1995) work: *prevention*, *intervention*, and *suppression*. The second is the material in chapters 4, 5, and 6 in which we have selected four concerns to be considered in program development. At the individual level (see chapter 4), we combine these into the category of *targeting* the appropriate youths. We add to this *group processes* and *group structures* (chapter 5) and *community context* (chapter 6). Finally, we set these factors into the framework of two goals: *individual change* and *group-level change*. When we align these against each other, we get the complex paradigm for organizing gang control programs illustrated in Table 8.1.

While Table 8.1 may at first blush seem overly complex, it is in fact a logical depiction of the material we have discussed in prior pages. It consists of the following:

1. The two halves, upper and lower, recognize the fact that one can seek control of individual gang members or of gangs as

TABLE 8.1. *Gang Control Options: Strategies and Issues for Individual and Group Change*

Individual Changes

	Targeting	Group Process	Gang Structures	Community Co
Prevention				
Intervention				
Suppression				

Group Changes

	Targeting	Group Process	Gang Structures	Community Co
Prevention				
Intervention				
Suppression				

whole units. Strategies for change may be developed for both individual *and* group goals, but most programs concentrate on only one of these.

2. Along the left-hand side in each case, we list Spergel's distinction, now popular across the nation, among prevention, intervention, and suppression. It is the case here that gang control efforts may fall into two of these strategies or even three (though rarely). However, the majority of them stress only one of the three. Broadly conceived, the prevention programs are aimed at youths prior to their possible entry into street gangs (L.A. Bridges, G.R.E.A.T., and the Illinois programs described in chapter 3 are examples). These targeted youths are sometimes at low risk and sometimes at higher risk of gang joining. Intervention programs are aimed at youths already in gangs in order to wean them away or reduce their involvement. Suppression programs are directly targeted at gang members whose illegal activities can subject them to street enforcement, arrest, and incarceration. Generally, suppression refers to enforcement actions that go beyond the usual practices of police, courts, and corrections. Finally, as Table 8.1 suggests, these three strategies can be applied to achieve either individual *or* group change—or even both.

3. Across the top of both halves of Table 8.1, we have listed the four issues that were stressed in part II of this book. *Targeting* refers to the specific types of youth or groups a program hopes to affect. In the prevention strategy, this means attempting early identification of youths, groups, or communities that can reasonably be expected to become gang involved. The more broadly the targets are defined, the less efficient the program becomes (yielding too many false positives). This is why knowledge of gang-joining predictions (see the consistently supported constructs in chapter 4) becomes crucial to prevention in the individual sector and why an appreciation of crime patterns (chapter 2) can help one to focus on the more problem-producing youths, groups, and communities. The issue of targeting, whether for prevention, intervention, or suppression, is really one of *correct* targeting. This requires knowledge about gangs generally and local gangs specifically. As noted in chapter 7 on goals, one should both have *generic* data in mind and gather specific *local* data prior to designing a gang control program.

Group process refers to the material covered in chapter 5. It reminds us that *gangs are groups*, and the better programs will be those that use what is known about group processes and about the peculiarities of *gang* group processes in particular. All three strategies—prevention, intervention, and suppression—will be substantially weakened if group processes are ignored. It must be remembered that street gangs form an "oppositional" culture (Moore and Vigil, 1989) in which members often turn our well-meaning control efforts upside down. That is, many prevention, intervention, and suppression activities become reinterpreted by gang members as disrespect for the gang or attacks on the gang. This reinterpretation merely solidifies the bonds of membership and may even lead to increased gang joining by susceptible local youths. This kind of group process is one of the reasons we stress that the street gang is qualitatively different from other youth groups; it feeds off its opposition, even when that opposition is meant to be helpful. As noted by Lien (2005b) and others, the involvement in and commitment to criminal acts in the gang are central to this process, because these are the acts leading to the opposition even while they are reinforcing gang cohesion.[1]

Gang structures refers primarily to the five types described in the earlier portion of chapter 5. The differences, for instance, between traditional gangs and specialty gangs are very important. They tend to display different kinds of members and are, as noted earlier, likely to yield different responses to various control strategies. To confuse the two, or to be unaware of the differences, can lead in some cases to ineffective programming and in others to programs that make matters far worse.

Finally, *community context* reflects the issues raised in chapter 6. Communities are both the proximal source of street gangs as well, we believe, as an essential source of gang control mechanisms. To target gang members or gangs without attention to the local sources of their emergence and maintenance must yield time-limited effects even in successful programs. Beyond this, failing to enroll and strengthen community assets cuts one off from a host of mechanisms that can support and—most important—sustain programs that have positive impacts. In a well-reasoned statement about using community assets, Venkatesh describes three community-based interventions in Chicago. In the absence of effective law enforcement approaches to street gang control, each of the three was an attempt "to resolve gang conflicts and to gain a measure of control over the neighborhood youth gang. As such, they highlight the tremendous potential of local community social organizations to serve as a foundation for street gang social policy design and implementation" (1999a: 16).

Unfortunately—and typically—none of the three interventions received any form of independent evaluation. The uniqueness of the Chicago gang situation and its community context makes one wary of quick generalizations to other settings, in any case.

Table 8.1 serves several functions for us. First, it helps to tie together issues raised in prior chapters—strategies, goals, and research results critical to dealing with street gangs. Second, it allows a program planner to see how his or her interests in gang control might fit into a larger scheme and how to begin thinking through the bases for a program's development. Third, it allows us to place past programs into a scheme that demonstrates where gang control efforts in the past have concentrated their energies. It is this third function that engages us next. We will place past programs into the scheme in order to assess what have been the options chosen in the past and what sorts of gaps have existed.

Table 8.2 provides the necessary data for this assessment. The combination of three strategies, four gang data issues, and individual-versus group-change goals yields a total of 24 cells, which we have labeled boxes 1 through 24. Within each box, we have entered numbers designating almost 60 gang control projects or programs with which the authors have

TABLE 8.2. *Gang Control Programs: Strategies and Issues for Individual and Group Changes*

Individual Changes

	Targeting	Group Process	Gang Structures	Community Context	
Prevention	[**Box 1**] 6, 7, 12, 13, 14, 15, 16, 18, 21, 27, 29, 30, 37, 38, 40, 46, 47, 49, 54	[**Box 2**] 6, 38	[**Box 3**]	[**Box 4**] 4, 12, 13, 14, 23, 27, 38, 39, 43, 57	$\Sigma = 31$
Intervention	[**Box 5**] 3, 7, 13, 14, 17, 25, 32, 44, 47, 50, 56, 58	[**Box 6**] 4, 55	[**Box 7**]	[**Box 8**] 13, 14, 38, 43, 53, 57	$\Sigma = 20$
Suppression	[**Box 9**] 1, 2, 8, 9, 10, 11, 13, 14, 15, 19, 20, 21, 26, 28, 31, 33, 34, 36, 41, 44, 48, 51, 52, 56	[**Box 10**] 1	[**Box 11**]	[**Box 12**] 13, 14, 37	$\Sigma = 28$
	$\Sigma = 55$	$\Sigma = 5$	$\Sigma = 0$	$\Sigma = 19$	$\Sigma\Sigma =$ **79**

Group Changes

	Targeting	Group Process	Gang Structures	Community Context	
Prevention	[**Box 13**] 13, 14	[**Box 14**]	[**Box 15**]	[**Box 16**] 13, 14	$\Sigma = 4$
Intervention	[**Box 17**] 13, 14, 45	[**Box 18**] 45, 55	[**Box 19**]	[**Box 20**] 13, 14, 53	$\Sigma = 8$
Suppression	[**Box 21**] 1, 8, 10, 11, 13, 14, 16, 22, 42	[**Box 22**] 1	[**Box 23**]	[**Box 24**] 13, 14	$\Sigma = 12$
	$\Sigma = 14$	$\Sigma = 3$	$\Sigma = 0$	$\Sigma = 7$	$\Sigma\Sigma =$ **24**

become familiar from personal experience, from descriptions in the gang literature, and from media reports. These 58 efforts are listed at the end of the chapter. Before proceeding, the reader might want to review this list briefly to get a sense of the numbered entries in Table 8.2. It should be kept in mind that some of these are specific programs, while others may be better classed as strategies. The distinction between programs and projects, on the one hand, and strategies, on the other, can be a bit arbitrary. We deliberately include both in our listing.

A number of the programs on the list will be self-evident from their titles. Others are described in chapter 3 of this book. Some, less obvious, are described briefly here and exemplify the variety of options that exist. Where available, we note the existence of an evaluation of the program.

1. Operation Ceasefire, often called the Boston Gun Project, is a suppression project that targets both individual gang members and gangs as units and is thus concerned with both individual change and group change. Further, it is one of the very few projects to use information on group processes in gangs. In Table 8.2, it is listed in four boxes, 9, 10, 21 and 22, indicating a broader spread than is the case for most projects. It uses deterrence theory to crack down on gun crimes in particular, warning and demonstrating to gangs that there are severe penalties for firearms use. This spread over several of our boxes, along with the deliberate application of the tenets of deterrence theory, mark the Boston Gun Project as unusual. There is some controversy over the program's effectiveness and replicability in other geographic areas.

3. Homeboy Industries appears only in box 5, targeting individual gang members for intervention via job training and placement. Organized by Father Gregory Boyle, the gang-specific employment has included a bakery and clothing accessories manufacturing (caps, T-shirts, and the like) as one of several interventions within Father Boyle's district in the Boyle Heights area of Los Angeles. No independent evaluation of the program exists.

12. The Youth Gang Drug Prevention Program was established by the U.S. Department of Health and Human Services. Multiple projects were funded nationwide, targeting individuals for both prevention and intervention. The five-year program emphasized coordinated agency programs in peer counseling, family education, mentoring, crisis intervention, restitution, and recreation. An independent evaluation documented reductions in delinquency and drug use, but no impact on gang involvement.

17. The El Monte Boys' Club initiated a project in which gang members arrested by the local police were referred for jobs by the police, with

the collaboration of Boys' Club staff. Placed in our box 5, this individually targeted intervention program was, in its day, unusual for the willingness of the police department to collaborate in what others might have labeled a social work approach. No independent assessment of the program has been reported.

22. CLEAR (Community Law Enforcement and Recovery) is a multi-agency program in Los Angeles bringing together representatives of the police, sheriff, city attorney, district attorney, and probation department. Located in our box 21, it is a suppression-oriented task-force approach targeting specific gangs as units. Community engagement is also listed as a component, but this aspect is poorly documented. Primary aims are to increase arrest and conviction rates in selected "hot" gang activity areas through coordinated enforcement agency activities. An early independent assessment suggests positive implementations in the first target area and a gang violence reduction level that may be related but may also be a regression effect. Expansion of the program to other target areas has not yielded any independent assessments as yet.

25. The Gang Violence Bridging Project falls into our box 5, intervention targeted at individual gang members. They are enrolled in a state college degree program with a curriculum tailored to their gang backgrounds and, in many cases, continuing gang status. Conflict resolution, remedial education, social skills, and close mentoring are designed to smooth the passage from homeboy to community contributor. No independent assessment has been provided.

32. The Orange County (California) 8% Project provides intensive "wrap-around" services of multiple sorts for first-time probationers who have been identified as the most-likely recidivists. Some of these juveniles are gang members, but the program, which we locate in box 5, was not designed specifically for gang members. Early assessments were encouraging but did not relate specifically to gang members or gang activity. Nonetheless, as in the Illinois program described in chapter 3, some jurisdictions have touted the 8% program as a gang intervention procedure.

34. T.A.R.G.E.T. (Tri-Agency Resources Gang Enforcement Team) is a task force program in Orange County, California, fitting into our box 9. It involves local police departments, the district attorney, and to a lesser extent the probation department. The most likely core gang member recidivists were targeted for intensive surveillance by interagency teams, leading to higher levels of arrest, custody, and convictions. A contracted, semi-independent evaluation suggested a major reduction in gang crime among affected members but did not assess the spread of effect, if any,

to other members (i.e., effective incapacitation but unknown levels of general deterrence).

49. The Paramount program in southeast Los Angeles was pure prevention, targeted at all pupils in the early primary grades of a gang-involved city. It fits into our box 1 and in some sense may be looked at as a primary-grade version of G.R.E.A.T., without the police instructors. The curriculum involved lessons in cartoon form, rather than didactic lectures, about gang and nongang behavior and attitudes. We know of no independent research evaluation.

56. The Reno (Nevada) Community Policing Project is located in our boxes 5 and 9, a combined intervention and suppression program targeted primarily at less-committed gang members but also emphasizing community awareness by special police teams. In this sense, the program has elements of Spergel's community organization strategy. No impact assessment was provided.

58. Amer-I-Can, in our box 5, is an intervention program targeted at known gang members by Jim Brown, the Hall of Fame football great. Working on participants' self-esteem and on good communication and positive goal setting, Brown was typical of charismatic mentors convinced of the need and the value of transforming young toughs into activists for their own cause. No assessments of Amer-I-Can or similar operations are known to exist.

As one reviews these program examples, those covered in chapter 3, and the overall listing of 58 programs, it is important to recall that most of these have not been independently assessed to determine their effectiveness. We don't wish to throw out the baby with the bathwater. Some of these efforts may well be worthwhile; we simply don't have the data to suggest how many, or which.

Additionally, we can note that poor or inadequate implementation of program goals have been common experiences. The ideas behind a worthwhile program cannot be assessed if the ideas are not well and consistently implemented; the programs come not to represent their original interests. A colleague of ours, frustrated by a string of poor implementations, introduced us to his new mantra: M I L T F P 4 1. This stands for "Make It Like the Frigging Picture, for Once."

With these caveats in mind, we invite the reader to look again at Table 8.2. Note that there is a summary number at the end of each row and column. For example, among individual change programs there are 31 entries for prevention and 55 that emphasize individual targeting. These summary numbers for rows and columns reflect, among other things, that the almost 60 programs yield a total of 103 placements in the boxes; some programs appear twice, and some are spread even further. These placements provide grist for our mill:

1. Sixty-two percent of all the programs appear in only one box. Thus, the majority are narrow in scope and narrow in the gang issues they address. This, we believe, does not bode well for the likelihood for affecting much change in the complex world of street gangs.
2. This leaves only 38% that appear in at least two boxes. Only two programs (1 and 38) appear in four boxes, while only the Spergel Model projects (13) and SafeFutures (14) are genuinely comprehensive (occurring in half of the boxes). Gang control programs for the most part are narrowly conceived, narrowly implemented.
3. There is a good distribution across prevention (34%), intervention (27%), and suppression (39%) approaches; i.e., there is balance *across* programs although not within programs. Suppression is slightly favored.
4. Clearly, targeting programs at individual change (53%) and gang unit change (14%) tells where programs concentrate their understanding of gang issues. Two-thirds of all the entries fall under this first column. Relatively little attention is given to the community context of gangs (25%) and almost none (8%) to group processes and group structure. In some ways, we are most struck by this last finding: *people attempting to control gang problems largely ignore the fact that gangs are groups.* The need for our chapter 5 is manifest.
5. Finally, as suggested by Spergel's original survey in the mid-1990s, the most popular approach is suppression. A narrow police view of gang control programming dominates in an arena crying out for alternative perspectives and in an arena devoid of valid demonstrations of suppression effectiveness.

If suppression wins the day, if the targeting of individual gang members is four times as common as the targeting of groups, if the community context is underrepresented and issues of group process and structure all but totally ignored, and if individual change goals are three times as common as group change goals, then there is ample room to try new approaches. In chapter 7, we discussed individual-, group-, and community-level goals, but now we learn that group and community goals are often ignored in gang control programming. This may be nothing more than a reflection of our society's emphasis on individual enterprise and accountability.

We stand in stark contrast to some other areas of the world in this respect. In the Far East, most notably China and Japan, accountability to one's group—family, peer group, organization, or work group—is paramount. Social change is oriented to the manipulation of the individual's accountability to his or her group affiliations. In Western Europe, individual responsibility tends to be located in community structures, with an attendant greater use of social welfare approaches to problems of deviant behavior. Gangs in the Far East are cast as group problems and in Europe as social welfare and immigration problems.

Yet in America, although gangs are groups spawned in describable community contexts, we respond to them much more as requiring individual change efforts. Whether we are correct in doing this or not, we certainly are inefficient. How many individuals must we change—through prevention, intervention, suppression—to effect an acceptable level of gang control? How much more efficient might it be to achieve group-level goals or community-level goals?

Thoughts like these force us—or should force us—to reconsider just what it is we wish to achieve in gang control. Further, the analysis of the patterns revealed in Table 8.2 suggests that we have indulged in an unbalanced fashion in programs rooted in our individually oriented assumptions about human behavior and change. This chapter and chapter 7 on program goals remind us that we can expand our assumptions and look more toward achieving group-level and community-level goals. For example, the material we have presented on the five gang structures implies that some types of gangs may be more susceptible to different control approaches.

Traditional gangs, and neotraditional as well, are usually of only moderate cohesiveness overall, but may contain subgroups with higher cohesiveness. Suppression efforts are likely to yield *increased* cohesiveness because they reinforce the group identity that is so important to the members. Suppression of specific "leaders" (usually police-defined, seriously involved core members) will yield short-term disruption at best because gang leadership is quite ephemeral and usually limited to age peers. The influence of older leaders on younger members is usually slight, and incarcerated leaders will soon be replaced in function in any case.

Core members of traditional and neotraditional gangs in the middle age ranges are likely to be beyond our capacity to affect: their ties are too strong. However, early prevention and intervention projects can wean away potential and new recruits, while job opportunities and persistent life-skills counseling may reinforce the tendency for older members to decrease their gang commitments (see Decker and Van Winkle, 1996). In sum, while suppression can be counterproductive, emphasis on alternative opportunities provision with carefully targeted new joiners and older leavers can be helpful. We emphasize *careful* targeting.

By way of contrast, specialty gangs tend to be smaller, more cohesive, tightly led in a hierarchical fashion, and more characterized by codes of loyalty and silence. These descriptors are needed by a gang that is essentially business oriented. Drug distribution gangs (street gangs, not adult cartels) are more susceptible to suppression efforts, since any disruption of the hierarchy, market territory, or sources of supply will disrupt the business and diffuse their criminal enterprise (see Padilla, 1992). The control efforts we recommended above for traditional and neotraditional gangs are targeted at individuals. The control efforts aimed at drug gangs and the like should be aimed as well at the gang as a *unit*: the unit can be disrupted. Drug-bust operations, stings, and civil abatement make sense here, while they will prove counterproductive with the other gang types.

This comparison of approaches to control in two contrasting types of street gangs provides another lesson. Street gangs don't come with banners proclaiming their location in the gang typology. The type of gang is determined with data. Before choosing an appropriate strategy for gang control, one needs the requisite data to determine the gang type: size of the gang, its duration, any subgroupings, age range, territoriality, and criminal versatility or specialization. These were the data that produced the typology presented in chapter 5, and these are the data needed before one decides on an approach to gang control. Data collection before selecting control options is a critical part of our approach, one of our principal goals, and part of our preaching.

Without implying any endorsement of specific options among the 60 or so found in Table 8.2, and without suggesting which goals are "best," let's look at a few more examples. We hope in doing so to lure the reader into thinking carefully about how goals, strategies, and data concerns can shape choices among gang control options.

Example 1. The G.R.E.A.T. program (see chapter 3) has become extremely popular, even being imported to Europe. It is a prevention program targeted at individuals, with no acknowledgment of gang processes or structure and no attention to community context. It showed a small significant impact on youths' values, attitudes, and perceptions, but none whatsoever on gang joining or gang activity. In addition, it aimed at all children in the schools given the program, rather than concentrating the resources on those who might be more vulnerable to gang recruitment. It seems reasonable, if one were to choose the G.R.E.A.T. option, to consider several modifications. One would be to use the data on early identification of gang joining—the risk factors of chapter 4. Another would be to select schools in communities according to their current gang involvement; again, data collection is required. Yet another modification would be to reanalyze what is known about life skills and possible G.R.E.A.T. curriculum content that are most *directly* related to gang joining and resistance. G.R.E.A.T.'s success in affecting intervening variables suggests that theorizing about this relationship to *street gangs* (not general delinquency) might bridge the gap more successfully in the future.

Example 2. Operation Hammer (see chapter 3) was a somewhat extreme but not isolated example of gang suppression. Such suppression programs are loosely (but not carefully) based on a deterrence theory that emphasizes the quickness and severity of punishment. Certainty of punishment, a third prong of deterrence theory, is seldom achieved by such suppression operations. Equally important, perhaps, is that such programs send the message to gang members that their behaviors are unacceptable, but they offer no alternatives. If suppression goals were combined with intervention goals, they might prove to be more effective. For example, the El Monte Boys' Club program, number 17 in our list of options, had police cooperate with a social agency to connect arrested gang members with job opportunities in the community. Getting and retaining jobs represents an alternative to gang activity, especially if closely monitored by experienced youth counselors. This cross-strategy combination of goals might offer a synergistic effect.

Example 3. Operation Hardcore, described in chapter 3, was—and is—a special prosecutor's unit designed to maximize the conviction rate for seriously criminal gang members. Its goal is suppression, its rationale is deterrence, and its strategies are limited to prosecutorial activities and heightened collaboration with the police. It aims at "special deterrence," meaning the targeting of individual felons without attention to explicit attempts to send the message to other gang members.

We can contrast this with Operation Ceasefire, the much-publicized Boston Gun Project. This latter program seems more promising, despite some controversy about its outcome, for several reasons. First, it undertook explicit procedures to produce general as well as special deterrence, thus expressing a far broader goal. Second, it engaged not only the local criminal justice agencies but also local community agencies. Third, it placed major emphasis on relevant data collection prior to launching the program. Included in these data were gun locations, gun sources inside and outside of the community, and information about the most-active and pivotal street gangs involved in gun-related serious violence. Fourth, although given less emphasis, there was some offering of alternative activities through social services, drug rehab, and the like.

The contrast between Hardcore and Ceasefire is one between ideology pursued vigorously and theory pursued equally vigorously but the latter with careful planning, data collection, and broader goals. Hardcore achieved high levels of convictions for serious offenders. Ceasefire may have saved lives by reducing access to the guns that threatened them. We offer this contrast to highlight options, but clearly we do not find all options to be of equal value in controlling street gang activity.

Example 4. Antigang injunctions and civil abatements were described in chapter 6. Their goals are both individual- and group-level suppression. While based in community settings, and nominally justified by the collection of information on community victimizations by gang members, community-level issues and involvements tend to be only superficially engaged. This is a gang control option that could easily be expanded into a more-comprehensive operation. The main barrier, we suspect, is the disinclination of police and prosecutors to engage community elements in lasting, collaborative relationships where enforcement is merely one element of the control process.

Initial injunction and abatement crackdowns could be systematically connected to community-level prevention by the formation of community groups—block clubs, parents' group, local businesspeople's groups—to develop informal social control to complement the formal enforcement activities. The CLEAR project, number 22 in our list, gave lip service to this process but did not truly engage in it.

Example 5. Detached worker programs, number 55 on our list, were popularized during the 1950s and 1960s and can still be found today. The use of detached workers or outreach gang workers is a pivotal component of the Spergel Model. This book has not covered detached worker programs because their heyday was many decades ago, but a comparison of two models can be instructive for our current purposes.

Three of these projects—one in Boston (W. Miller, 1962), one in Chicago (Carney et al., 1969), and one in Los Angeles (Klein, 1971: parts I and II)—were similar attempts to use group processes in an intensive effort at gang intervention. Each gathered voluminous data on the intervention process, some of which revealed that the interventions either had no positive effect on gang activity or actually increased it. A fourth project (Klein, 1971: part III) used data from the other three to mount an intervention explicitly engaging group processes to reduce gang cohesiveness and thereby reduce gang crime. This time, the outcome was positive.

Comparing the first three projects to the fourth yields several lessons. Using prior data to formulate a program with explicit goals and outcome measures makes it far easier to understand program outcomes. In these cases, it was the role of group cohesiveness that emerged as a pivotal issue. In addition, all four projects demonstrated the value of conceptually designed interventions that did not simply rely on conventional wisdom. Third, the contrast between the failed projects and the more-successful one suggests that the use of outreach workers can be of positive support in bridging between gangs and communities, but their use must be carefully guided and monitored so as not to have boomerang effects.

Example 6. Comprehensive gang control programs, such as those based on the Spergel Model (see chapter 3), deserve special attention because so much time, money, and federal commitment have been expended on them. If the results to date are equivocal, it is not from lack of effort. Corrective actions might yet support the use of such broad programs. First, however, various issues of implementation must be resolved. The model itself needs careful scrutiny to see how goals and strategies can be more tightly related and—the evaluator's nightmare—how different components of a comprehensive program can be disaggregated to reveal the strengths and weaknesses of each. This latter is as monumental a task in statistics as program implementation is in manipulating the gang context.

In his address to the Norwegian ministries in 1999, Decker suggested that the complexities of truly comprehensive gang control programs may be too great to overcome and that we should settle for more-limited attempts. In part, his comments derived from his frustrating role as evaluator of the SafeFutures program. For our part, we are not yet ready to accept this conclusion. We have learned enough about the Spergel Model and its implementation problems to retain it as an option. However, it remains an option with uneven validation of positive outcomes, despite its widespread promulgation by the U.S. Department of Justice. Its future use must be preceded by careful analysis of its past use.

As promised, we have not prescribed options, preferring to lay them out in a way that preventers, interveners, and suppressors can make some rational choices. Nonetheless, we are not without some viewpoints; we have suggestions to offer of various sorts. We conclude this exercise by offering these suggestions. As difficult as gang control has proven to be, we are inclined toward optimism if these suggestions lead to relevant actions.

1. Control efforts *must* begin with careful, conceptually derived goals whose achievement can be empirically measured. The time for conventional wisdoms and anecdotal evidence is long past.
2. Far more attention must be paid to gang structures, group processes, and community contexts. An overemphasis on individual goals and targeting cannot yield widespread change.
3. Chosen control options must be clearly articulated in relation to goals, gang issues, and measurable outcomes.
4. The role of carefully collected data prior to, during, and following program implementation must be given greater priority. Gang control programs in the absence of information will teach us little.
5. Many available options, although they have been poorly articulated, poorly implemented, or inadequately evaluated, may yet prove to be useful. The listing of options in this chapter should be revisited and then reconsidered for careful, tested applications. Throughout this book, we have spoken of program failures in implementation as well as outcome. This is, perhaps, an oversimplification. In revisiting past options that may yet hold promise, we suggest considering them in at least four ways. First is the matter of their design. This means the degree to which the strategies (such as prevention, intervention, and suppression) have been thought through *and* the degree to which issues of targeting, gang processes, gang structures, and community contexts have been well articulated. Second is the issue of implementation: have the past programs truly implemented the design underlying them? That is, has program integrity been high enough that program results really tell us about the value of what was implemented? Third, we must assess the quality of an evaluation of the program. If it has been inadequate, then there is little to justify *repeating* the effort; we should start as if the program were a new entity. Fourth, one

must consider carefully any demonstrated program results, positive as well as negative. Given program integrity and evaluation quality, are there reliable outcomes that justify choosing a program as a legitimate option? Anecdotal evidence should not suffice. Testimonials as to areas of success or failure should not suffice. Ideally, one should look for demonstrable changes in such things as gang joining, gang size, gang activity, crime and victimization rates, community response, and so on. The test should be clear—and clearly passed.

6. Finally, we want to offer a tentative response to the query most often presented to us by policy makers and by media representatives who think we should follow our negative conclusions about gang control with the "solutions" to the problem: "Dr. Klein, Dr. Maxson, just what should be done about gangs?" We have settled on a very broad response to the query, one which locates the problem in a context but merely throws the question back to one of available options. There are three broad approaches one can take to the widespread problem of street gang existence:
   - First, one can target individual youths—and, in fact, many individual youths—in hopes of affecting their gang membership and activity. As seen in Table 8.2, this is what we have done for the most part. It is not affecting the size of the problem.
   - Second, one can acknowledge that street gangs exist because of the social marginalization of many groups in our society. The combined effects of racism, poverty, inadequate social resources, and barriers to equal opportunities yield a host of social problems, street gangs being one of these. Therefore, thorough change in the very structure of our society—its institutions, its basic values, and its imbalance of power relationships—must be undertaken. Whatever the truth of this statement, it's not about to happen. The "revolution" ain't coming, as those in control of this society don't want it.
   - Third, one can locate the more proximal risks of gang development, and many of its control options as well, in the local community. This community may be defined as a block, or a neighborhood, or an ethnic enclave, or a legal jurisdiction. *Communities spawn gangs* and have the potential, at least, to prevent or control them. This is where we would put our

> money—a great deal of money. The overall goal would be *local social control*—by community members, in their community, of their own problems. Call it social efficacy, or community empowerment, or social organization, long-term effective control must reside where the gangs emerge. There is just one hitch to this powerful suggestion: as a society and as academic and political professionals, we have not yet learned how to bring about long-term, local social control in communities that have already lost it.

How might we combine this local control approach with some of the options covered in the preceding pages? There is a place here for a thoughtful state-level or federal program of action-research (to borrow an old term). Conceptually, many would agree that a broad, comprehensive approach to gang control must eventually emerge. For this to happen, a long-term ambitious strategy is needed. We suggest several steps.

- First, undertake a review of all of the options to select those most appropriate, conceptually, to having some effect on bringing about local social control.
- Second, locate these in the paradigm presented in Tables 8.1 and 8.2 and select those that will, together, yield a comprehensive pattern.
- Third, implement and test a few of these at a time. Continue an iterative process like this, over time, until a pattern of useful programs emerges and becomes, thereby, a comprehensive strategy.

How long would this take? Years and years is the answer. But then, we said that a long-term, ambitious strategy is needed. We are in our present situation, after all, despite not just years but *decades* of uncoordinated, inadequately conceptualized gang control programming and policy. If we don't do something truly major—and we can't transform our society—we condemn ourselves to more decades of street gang dominance.

We could, of course, do nothing, and let nature take its course. But this book is about doing something. Part I revealed the need, part II presented the issues based on many years of accumulated gang knowledge, and part III has spoken to goals and options. We opt for *something*, no matter how complex, over nothing, the easiest route.

Past Gang Control Projects and Programs

1. Operation Ceasefire (Boston)
2. Chicago Police Unite
3. Homeboy Industries
4. L.A. Bridges II
5. Chicago Area Projects
6. Gang Resistance, Education, and Training (G.R.E.A.T.)
7. Boys' and Girls' Clubs gang programs
8. Police gang units
9. Gang curfews
10. Antigang legislation
11. Antigang civil abatement and injunctions
12. DHHS drug-based gang prevention projects
13. Comprehensive community-wide program (Spergel Model)
14. SafeFutures
15. COPS Antigang Initiative
16. DHHS Family and Youth Service Bureau (FYSB) for girls
17. El Monte Boys' Club job referrals
18. Jeopardy program
19. Operation Hammer
20. Hardcore prosecution
21. Gun interdiction programs
22. Community Law Enforcement and Recovery (CLEAR; Los Angeles)
23. Graffiti removal projects
24. Gang victims' services
25. Gang Violence Bridging Project (Los Angeles)
26. Cicero (Illinois) injunction
27. L.A. Bridges I
28. Antigang probation and parole units
29. Truancy programs
30. Mentoring programs
31. Gang boot camps
32. 8% Project (Orange County, California)
33. Convicted gang member registration
34. Tri-Agency Resources Gang Enforcement Team program (T.A.R.G.E.T.; Orange County, California)
35. Gang truces, dispute resolution, crisis intervention
36. Gang roster sharing and databases
37. Ex-gang counselors

38. Individual community activists
39. Preteen programs in high-risk areas
40. Ex-gang testimonials (e.g., "Tookie" Williams)
41. Core member street harassment
42. Federal-local enforcement task forces
43. Community-led surveillance (DADS, Gang Moms, etc.)
44. Gang parents' groups
45. CIN/CYGS (Community Intervention Network, Philadelphia/ Community Youth Gang Services, Los Angeles): outreach gang surveillance
46. Youth centers (narrow to comprehensive)
47. Grassroots shelters (e.g., House of Umoja)
48. School gang surveillance programs
49. Paramount (California) schools program (cartoons and beyond)
50. Job Corps
51. RICO statutes
52. Antiloitering ordinances (e.g., Chicago)
53. Gang empowerment projects (political)
54. School prevention programs
55. Detached (gang) workers
56. Reno community policing program
57. Community empowerment and community policing (e.g., Boyle Heights)
58. Amer-I-Can program

Selected Citations for Gang Control Options (see bibliography for full references)

1. Operation Ceasefire: Kennedy, 1997, 1998: Kennedy, Braga, Piehl, and Waring, 2001
2. Chicago Police Unite: www.jointogether.org
3. Homeboy Industries: Fremon, 1995; Ripston, 1997; Tyson, 2004
5. Chicago Area Projects: Kobrin, 1959
6. G.R.E.A.T.: Esbensen, 2001
7. Boys' and Girls' Clubs: Feyerherm, Pope, and Lovell, 1992
8. Police gang units: Katz, 2001
10. Antigang legislation: Klein, 1995a; Pawloski and Brown, 1998; Institute for Law and Justice, 1993
11. Antigang civil abatement and injunctions: Bishop, 2001; Pyle, 1995; Maxson et al., 2005
12. DHHS drug-based gang prevention projects: M. Cohen et al., 1995

15. COPS Antigang Initiative: Fearn et al., 2001
19. Project Hammer: Klein, 1995a
20. Hardcore prosecution: Dahmann, 1982
22. CLEAR: Lyons, 1998
23. Graffiti removal projects: Thereux, 1995
24. Gang victims' services: Allen, 1998
25. Gang Violence Bridging Project: Sahagun, 1999
26. Cicero injunction: Slater, 1999
27. L.A. Bridges: Klein, 1997
34. T.A.R.G.E.T.: Kent, 1994; Kent and Smith, 1996; Valdez, 2000
37. Ex-gang counselors: Krikorian, 1998
40. Ex-gang testimonials: Willworth, 1996; Mehren, 1996
42. Federal-local enforcement task forces: General Accounting Office, 1996
54. School prevention programs: Gottfredson and Gottfredson, 1999, 2001
55. Detached workers: Spergel, 1966; Klein, 1971
56. Reno community policing program: Weston, 1993
58. Amer-I-Can program: J. Katz, 1995

Notes

Introduction

1. *Operational* definitions are a different matter. In Eurogang program youth surveys and in the multinational second International Self-Report Delinquency Program (ISRD II), the following sequence of questions is used to establish gang affiliation. Number 1 is a funneling question, numbers 2 through 6 operationalize the consensus definition, and number 7 is a self-admission report that can be evaluated by reference to the first six questions.

1. Some people have a certain group of friends that they spend time with, doing things together or just hanging out. Do you have a group of friends like that?

   __No

   __Yes

2. Which one of the following best describes the ages of people in your group?

   __Under twelve

   __Twelve to fifteen

   __Sixteen to eighteen

   __Nineteen to twenty-five

   __Over twenty-five

3. Does this group spend a lot of time together in public places like the park, the street, shopping areas, or the neighborhood?

   __No

   __Yes

4. How long has this group existed?

   __Less than three months

   __Three months but less than one year

   __One to four years

   __Five to ten years

__Eleven to twenty years
__More than twenty years

5. Is doing illegal things accepted by or okay for your group?
   __No
   __Yes
6. Do people in your group actually do illegal things together?
   __No
   __Yes
7. Do you consider your group of friends to be a gang?
   __No
   __Yes

2. At the same time, it is reasonable to assume that there is a counterbalancing undercount of members (not of gangs) because younger members don't enter into police files until they are detected and recorded (while older members may be retained in the files well after they cease gang activity).

3. This rather wordy definition never sat well with police officials. Said one in direct response, "I'll tell you what a gang is: it's a group of thugs. They're hoodlums, they're crooks and criminals."

4. We leave aside the silliness of the phrase "three or more persons"; gangs don't come in groups of three. This is simply linguistic gimmickry for the sake of the legislation.

Chapter 1

1. As we are interested here in the proportion of a population that reports gang membership, we limit this review to studies that achieved a response rate of at least 70%. Excluded, for example, is the Sheley and Wright (1995) study. They report gang prevalence rates for populations in 10 inner-city high schools and 6 juvenile correctional facilities, but response rates were just 10% (schools) and 41% (inmates).

2. Occasionally, studies identify a category of youths who do not claim membership but report behavior that indicates some gang involvement, such as hanging out with gang members, wearing gang colors, and throwing gang signs (Eitle, Gunkel, and Van Gundy, 2004; Katz, Webb, and Decker, 2005; Curry, 2000; Curry, Decker, and Egley, 2002). Because these youths deny gang membership, we exclude these "gang associates" from the gang prevalence rates we consider but acknowledge the continuum of gang involvement and group identification.

3. We alert the reader to studies that ask about membership in such a way that membership in nongang delinquent groups might be included by notations in the following tables.

4. It is likely that the highest gang prevalence figure reported in Table 1.1—

37% in the Montreal sample (Gatti et al., 2005)—results from an item that combines nongang delinquent group participation with gang membership.

5. In some cases, studies that report demographic distributions within gangs have been converted to the marginal sample parameters, or researchers provided us with the correct percentages.

6. Interestingly, Esbensen and his colleagues (Esbensen, Winfree, He, and Taylor, 2001) report that core gang members in their sample have similar personal characteristics (i.e., age, race, sex) as other gang members, yet differ in attitudes and crime profiles (see chapter 4 for further discussion of core-fringe patterns).

7. Following Miller's studies in the 1970s, the five national surveys included telephone interviews with police in a random sample of 78 cities with populations of more than 100,000 in 1988 by Needle and Stapleton (1983); a survey of law enforcement in a selective sample of 101 cities in 1988 by Spergel and Curry (1990); a mail survey to police in more than 1,100 cities, all with populations of more than 100,000, plus a selective sample of more than 900 smaller cities by Maxson, Woods, and Klein (1996); a mail survey to police in 122 cities, all with populations of more than 200,000, plus a selective sample of other places in 1992 by Curry, Ball, and Fox (1994); and a mail survey to police in all cities with populations of more than 150,000 and a random sample of 284 cities with populations between 25,000 and 150,000 in 1993 by Curry, Ball, and Decker (1996). Egley et al. (2004) provide a brief summary of the major findings from each of these surveys.

8. See Egley et al. (2004) for precise sample numbers for the NYGS. In the 1996–2001 surveys, random samples were selected in rural counties and cities with populations between 2,500 and 24,999; all larger cities and suburban counties were enumerated. Reflecting the 2000 U.S. Census, the sample was reconfigured so that, beginning with the 2002 NYGS, cities with populations between 2,500 and 49,999 were randomly selected, as were rural counties. All cities with at least 50,000 in population and all suburban counties were surveyed. We thank Arlen Egley of the National Youth Gang Center for providing additional clarification on the NYGS design and data for this chapter.

9. The exception is Vermont, although anecdotal reports would include it as well.

10. Age and race/ethnic discrepancies are difficult to compare because our earlier discussion used relative prevalence in the population as the comparison, while the NYGS gathers demographics as a proportion of all gang members. Many self-report studies report demographics this way as well, but can't provide an exact comparison to police records because studies that follow youth throughout adolescence and into adulthood (the best contrast to police files) take place in just one city, and studies with more-comprehensive geographic representation capture a limited age range.

11. W. Miller identified 13 cities that had gang problems in the 1970s but not the 1990s (2001: 18, Table 7). With the exception of Charleston, South Carolina,

all are smaller cities, with populations ranging from 5,000 to 52,000. Five of the 13 are regularly surveyed in the NYGS. Charleston persistently reports no gangs; only Manteca, California, reports gang problems now. Huff (forthcoming) argues that some midwestern cities have seen gangs ebb and flow. For example, St. Louis saw gangs reemerge in the 1950s after dying out in the early twentieth century, and Milwaukee gangs desisted in the 1950s, only to emerge again in the 1980s.

12. A detailed summary of the methods and findings from these case studies are available in Maxson, Woods, and Klein (1995).

Chapter 2

1. For example, Curry, Ball, and Fox state in a research brief published by the National Institute of Justice, "Gang-related crime is above all a violent crime problem. Homicides and other violent crimes account for about half of all recorded gang-related crime incidents" (1994: 1).

Chapter 3

1. Following a major corruption scandal in one of the CRASH units, first revealed in 1999, these units were disbanded and replaced by units with a different name and an unclear mandate.

2. After many years of relative inactivity, the interagency task force was reconstituted at the turn of the twenty-first century. At a meeting on June 4, 2003, there were 43 attendees, 65% of whom were from law enforcement, corrections, and other criminal justice agencies.

3. Normally, the absence of evaluation reflects either disinterest or the conviction that one's program is effective and therefore requires no independent proof. In the case of injunction programs, Los Angeles enforcement agencies steadfastly declined independent evaluations, even though the money and personnel for them were readily available.

4. Compare this to D.A.R.E., where it is known that most adolescents at least experiment with drugs of one form or another.

5. The lead evaluator of the G.R.E.A.T. program was Finn-Aage Esbensen. Our description is derived from publications by Esbensen and his colleagues. Professor Esbensen reviewed a draft of this chapter and recommended only minor changes.

6. Esbensen does not agree that the results were presented in a rosy fashion, as we state. In a personal communication, he notes:

> The fact that there were any statistically significant program effects . . . with such a small dosage is in itself noteworthy. In light of this, we reported the findings in a manner that highlighted the modest positive

> findings while also acknowledging that most of the potential outcome measures did not achieve statistical significance. To call this "a far rosier picture" I believe, is simply inaccurate. But . . . we will simply have to agree to disagree on this point.

7. Attorney General Ryan later became his party's candidate for governor of Illinois.

8. We are indebted to Scott Decker at the University of Missouri at St. Louis for access to draft reports on the implementation of the Illinois program. This section of chapter 3 has been reviewed by Greg Scott, who at the time of the program's implementation was director of the Illinois Gang Prevention Center. His review includes agreement with our characterization of the program, saying, "I love this chapter" (personal communication).

9. An extension raised the final sum by 2002 to approximately $50 million.

10. This critique of L.A. Bridges is summarized from a far longer report to the ad hoc committee. It received no comment from all but a few officials, but those who did respond, we must report, did so in the strongest terms. One characterized the report as uninformed and incomplete, a "premature assessment" and "an irresponsible condemnation." Another referred to the author as a "pompous ass" (personal communication). All other comments, resulting from news and other coverage of the report, were supportive of the conclusions.

11. This section of the chapter has been reviewed by Professor Spergel at our request. A number of changes have been made to accommodate his concerns. Although he wants the name to be noted as the OJJDP Comprehensive Community-wide Gang Program Model, it is generally known as the Spergel Model, and we will refer to it as such.

12. The Spergel team included G. David Curry, Candace Kane, Kwai Ming Wa, and Rolando Sosa.

13. Known technically as the National Youth Gang Suppression and Intervention Program.

14. For the record, Spergel does not agree with this characterization, feeling that the model had been fully activated for some years, noting in his review to us, "there was adequate knowledge of the model and how it should be implemented, but alone, that was not sufficient" (personal communication).

15. Spergel disagrees with this depiction, but it does reflect the discussion of the advisory committee and OJJDP staff, both of which continually asked for a better statement until it was produced in December 1998.

16. Robert Nash Parker, *Project Bridge Local Evaluation, 1994 to 1999*, Presley Center, University of California, Riverside, 2002. This report shows an unclear understanding of the Spergel Model, yet another indication of the model's poor articulation. Spergel's findings, he notes, do not agree with those of Parker.

17. These are well set out on pp. 184–185 and in appendix C of Spergel, 1995.

18. The list is taken from OJJDP's request for proposals.

19. This was a complaint lodged by the advisory committee, but Spergel feels that targeting criteria were designed adequately and shared appropriately with the sites. One of his site evaluators, however, told us that "the gang problem throughout the study sites was a 'phantom' that could not be caught" (personal communication). The end result was some sites focusing on "at-risk kids" and not gang members.

20. We express our gratitude to Dr. Spergel for sharing these draft reports to OJJDP. They are voluminous, but for most readers the executive summaries will provide enough coverage of the Spergel Model application in the three sites.

21. Included as sources are interim evaluation reports provided by Scott Decker and his associates at the University of Missouri at St. Louis and Decker and Curry (2002b). Decker has reviewed this section of chapter 3 and found little that required change.

22. History demonstrates clearly that gang members can be very frustrating clients. You don't go into the gang control business if you can't tolerate their intransigence and learn to work around it.

Chapter 4

1. There are further details on our method that will be of interest to some readers. First, studies with multiple indicators of the same construct are more likely to generate inconclusive findings. We used some judgment in determining the overall direction of findings; for example, if just one of five indicators were significant, the study was coded as nonsignificant rather than inconclusive. Second, studies reporting nonsignificance are a subset because researchers often review bivariate results and select only significant variables to report or those with theoretical import to include in further analyses. Also, in Table 4.2, significant bivariate relationships not supported in multivariate analyses are shown as significant bivariate findings only. Third, most studies use logistic regression to distinguish gang from nongang groups. Some report coefficients and/or odds ratios, while others report only statistical significance. To be inclusive, we relied on statistical significance ($p < .05$) rather than assessing the effect size of coefficients, and we use the number of studies yielding similar results as our summary outcome. Finally, total sample outcomes are reported as available. Where findings are solely offered separately for males and females, only the male findings are included in Table 4.2. Sex differences in risk factors are considered later in the chapter.

2. Studies included in Table 4.1 but not in the earlier tables are those with purposive, rather than representative, sampling designs. The latter are important for determining gang prevalence, the focus of chapter 1. The former provide useful information on gang risk factors, and thus we include them here. Further details about the research designs of nonrepresentative sample studies are available in the publications cited.

3. Bjerregaard and Smith (1993) provided the first sex comparisons of risk factors in this current period, but used an early data set from the Rochester Youth Study. Therefore, we use Thornberry et al. (2003) to represent the most-thorough longitudinal analyses from this study.

4. Both Bjerregaard and Smith (1993) and Esbensen and Deschenes (1998) detect significant sex differences in the magnitude or direction of coefficients on a few variables. For example, Bjerregaard and Smith find that early engagement in sexual intercourse increases the probability of joining a gang by 34% for females, but just 17% for males.

5. We've argued that the reasons for gang joining vary by study location, so we've selected only those differences that are stable in the two sites. There were no cross-site reversals. Six items generated differences in one site but not the other. Get a reputation, a member forced him to join, excitement, and get what you don't get from home were higher in the gang group in one site only; to fill empty time and learn new skills were higher in the nongang group in one site only. Three reasons did not differentiate gang from nongang youth in either site: for support and loyalty, to avoid home, and to feel proud of a group.

Chapter 5

1. We start the modern period with Miller, despite his major role during the classical period, because his 1970s work was the first to make the attempt in more than one research site, a sine qua non of the comparative goal.

2. See also the rather strange ethnic "typology" presented to a national sample of prosecutors and reported by Johnson, Webster, and Connors (1995). It consisted of locally based African-American gangs; gangs based in the Los Angeles area (e.g., Crips and Bloods); gangs with origins in the Caribbean; Hispanic gangs; Asian gangs; motorcycle gangs; hate gangs (e.g., Ku Klux Klan, Aryan Nation); and others.

3. These materials were first reported by us in the *Journal of Gang Research* 3(1) (1995): 33–40, and are reproduced here with permission.

4. Other typologies mentioned earlier have *not* been cross-validated in independent studies. Attempts have been made in the case of the Cloward and Ohlin categories, but replication has generally failed.

5. This included 16 male and 8 female gangs.

6. Not surprisingly, given the dominance of Chicago's super-gangs, traditional gangs were reported to be most common in Illinois (about 30% of the cases reported). Next most common were compressed gangs at 24%.

7. This high percentage is a function of age; females drop out of gangs at an earlier age than do males.

8. Vigil is comparing Mexican-American, Salvadoran, black, and Vietnamese gangs (2002: 11). The most cogent argument for considering street gangs as var-

iants of adolescent groups generally is offered by several developmental psychologists, yet even they fail to appreciate the qualitatively different nature of the gang (see Cairns et al., 1997).

9. Personal communication from Professor Fleisher, used here with permission.

10. A full report of the factor analysis, including the factor loadings, can be found in Klein (1971: 70–76).

11. They note, "The key element [of gang violence] is the collective identification of threat, a process that unites the gang and overcomes the general lack of unity by increasing cohesion" (Decker and Van Winkle 1996: 261).

Chapter 6

1. These researchers used Economic Research Service data from the U.S. Department of Agriculture to designate *metropolitan areas* as "counties that contain a city of 50,000 or more people, along with less populated areas that are economically dependent on such a city, with a total area population of 100,000 or more" (Wells and Weisheit, 2001: 799). *Nonmetropolitan counties* are those not included within the metropolitan designation. The NYGS data for municipal and county agencies that responded to the 1996–1998 surveys were categorized according to this metropolitan-nonmetropolitan distinction and therefore do not match the rural county category adopted by the NYGS.

2. Descriptions of the Spergel Model intervention strategies appear in chapter 3.

Chapter 7

1. Recently renamed by public officials South Los Angeles to avoid the stigmatization of the prior associations with the "south-central" name.

2. The issues are made even more complex by including Spergel's five strategies, as spelled out in chapter 3 of this book. We do not include them here so that we can maintain our focus on goals.

3. Other variable domains are equally slim: the combined project findings yielded only two family, three peer, one school, and two neighborhood variables as significant predictors of joining street gangs.

4. For instance, see the recent work on "retaliatory homicide" by Kubrin and Weitzer (2003).

5. See Klein (1971) for the case of "Richard" who, during an 18-month period, went through 10 jobs, various education and drug services, and intensive counseling, ending with his conviction for murder.

6. We are enamored of one deterrence program and outcome from the past.

In the year 673 in England, St. Etheledra, queen of Northumbria, founded a religious community in Ely. She lived 12 years as the wife of King Egfrid, but is said to have remained pure and virginal throughout those years. Standing there now is the beautiful Ely Cathedral, home to a succession of famous bishops. But among these, to the likely shame of the mighty Etheledra, was Thomas de Lisle, bishop from 1345 to 1356. Bishop de Lisle headed a gang of local thugs who terrorized the countryside with a general cafeteria pattern of crime—arsons, kidnappings, extortions, thefts, and murder. It was only when the bishop assaulted King Edward's cousin, Lady de Wake, that gang control action was taken. De Lisle was stripped of his office and banished. Crime reportedly plummeted (Aberth, 1996).

Chapter 8

1. As Lien notes:

> [A] gang, then, operates as a moral unit and violent crime acts are given moral justifications in the narratives constructed by the gangs. As long as the acts are justified by this way of thinking it will be difficult to change it. All groups who set themselves apart from society, like gangs, other criminals, religious sects, and counter-cultural groups develop a sense of gemeinschaft, immunization techniques and a prickly suspicion that makes dialog with outsiders difficult and tense. Their scheme of thought could possibly be called an ideology. It has logic. It is beneficial to some and not others, it is immune to corrections and it has moral backing and justification. (2005b: 115–116)

Bibliography

Aberth, John. 1996. *Criminal churchmen in the age of Edward III: The case of Bishop Thomas de Lisle.* University Park: Pennsylvania State University Press.

Allen, Anjeanette M. 1998. *Victims of gang violence project.* New York: Victims Services.

Alonso, Alejandro A. 1999. Territoriality among African-American street gangs in Los Angeles. Master's thesis, Department of Geography, University of Southern California.

Anderson, Elijah. 1999. *Code of the street: Decency, violence and the moral life of the inner city.* New York: Norton.

Ball, Richard, and G. David Curry. 1995. The logic of definition in criminology: Purposes and methods for defining "gangs." *Criminology* 33(2): 225–245.

Battin, Sara R., Karl G. Hill, Robert D. Abbot, Richard F. Catalano, and J. David Hawkins. 1998. The contribution of gang membership to delinquency beyond delinquent friends. *Criminology* 36: 93–115.

Battin-Pearson, Sara R., Jie Guo, Karl G. Hill, Robert D. Abbot, and J. David Hawkins. 1998. *Early predictors of sustained adolescent gang membership.* Unpublished manuscript. Seattle: Social Development Research Group, University of Washington.

Battin-Pearson, Sara R., Terence P. Thornberry, J. David Hawkins, and Marvin D. Krohn. 1998. *Gang membership, delinquent peers, and delinquent behavior.* Washington, DC: Office of Juvenile Justice and Delinquency Prevention, NCJ 171119.

Bennett, Trevor, and Katy Holloway. 2004. Gang membership, drugs and crime in the UK. *British Journal of Criminology* 44(3): 305–323.

Bishop, Jule. 2001. Civil gang abatement: A community based policing tool of the office of the Los Angeles city attorney. In *The modern gang reader*, 2d ed., ed. Jody Miller, Cheryl L. Maxson, and Malcolm W. Klein, 320–329. Los Angeles: Roxbury.

Bjerregaard, Beth, and Alan J. Lizotte. 1995. Gun ownership and gang membership. *Journal of Criminal Law and Criminology* 86(1): 37–58.

Bjerregaard, Beth, and Carolyn Smith. 1993. Gender differences in gang participation, delinquency and substance use. *Journal of Quantitative Criminology* 4: 329–55.

Bjorgo, Tore. 1997. *Racist and right wing violence in Scandinavia.* Oslo: Tano Aschehoug.

Bjorgo, Tore. 1999. *Falling apart: Process of disintegration and disengagement in gangs.* Oslo: Norwegian Institute of International Affairs.

Block, Carolyn Rebecca, and Richard Block. 1995. Street gang crime in Chicago. In *The modern gang reader*, ed. Malcolm W. Klein, Cheryl L. Maxson, and Jody Miller, 202–210. Los Angeles: Roxbury.

Bolland, John M., and Holli R. Drummond. 1999. *Causes and consequences of gang affiliation.* Presentation at American Society of Criminology annual conference. Institute for Social Science Research, University of Alabama.

Boyle, Patrick. 2001. A DAREing rescue. *Youth Today* 10(4): 16–19.

Bradshaw, Paul. 2005. Terrors and young teams: Youth gangs and delinquency in Edinburgh. In *European street gangs and troublesome youth groups*, ed. Scott H. Decker and Frank M. Weerman, 193–218. Walnut Creek, CA: AltaMira.

Braga, Anthony A., David M. Kennedy, and George E. Tita. 2002. New approaches to the strategic prevention of gang and gang-involved violence. In *Gangs in America*, 3d ed., ed. C. Ronald Huff, 271–285. Thousand Oaks, CA: Sage.

Brown, William K. 1977. Black female gangs in Philadelphia. *International Journal of Offender Therapy and Comparative Criminology* 21: 221–228.

Bursik, Robert J. 2002. The systemic model of gang behavior: A reconsideration. In *Gangs in America*, 3d ed., ed. C. Ronald Huff, 71–82. Thousand Oaks, CA: Sage.

Bursik, Robert J., Jr., and Harold Grasmick. 1993. *Neighborhoods and crime: The dimensions of effective community control.* New York: Lexington.

Cairns, Robert B., Tom W. Cadwallader, David Estell, and Holly J. Neckerman. 1997. Groups to gangs: Developmental and criminological perspectives and relevance for prevention. In *Handbook of antisocial behavior*, ed. Dana M. Stoff, James Brieling, and Jack D. Maser, 194–204. New York: Wiley.

Campbell, Anne. 1984. *The girls in the gang: A report from New York City.* Oxford: Basil Blackwell.

Caplan, Nathan. 1968. Treatment intervention and reciprocal interaction effects. *Journal of Social Issues* 24(1): 63–88.

Carney, Frank, Hans W. Mattick, and John D. Callaway. 1969. *Action on the streets.* New York: Associated Press.

CBSNEWS.com. 2004. Gangs making smaller cities home. *CBS Evening News.* August 21. Downloaded August 25, 2004.

Chicago Crime Commission. 1995. *Gangs: Public enemy number one.* Chicago: Chicago Crime Commission.

Chin, Ko-Lin. 1990. Chinese gangs and extortion. In *Gangs in America*, ed. C. Ronald Huff, 129–145. Thousand Oaks, CA: Sage.

Chinn, Derrik. 2003. Gangs migrate to Columbus from bigger cities: Members traffic in drugs, guns. *Lantern*, June 4.

Clayton, Richard R., Anne M. Cattarello, and Bryan M. Johnstone. 1996. The effectiveness of Drug Awareness Resistance Education (Project D.A.R.E.): Five-year follow-up results. *Preventive Medicine* 25: 307–318.

Cloward, Richard A., and Lloyd E. Ohlin. 1960. *Delinquency and opportunity: A theory of delinquent gangs*. New York: Free Press.

Cogan, David. 1998. The gang's all there. *Los Angeles Magazine*, August.

Cohen, Albert K., and James F. Short, Jr. 1958. Research in delinquent subcultures. *Journal of Social Issues* 14: 20–37.

Cohen, Jacqueline, Daniel Cork, John Engberg, and George Tita. 1998. The role of drug markets and gangs in local homicide rates. *Homicide Studies* 2(3): 241–262.

Cohen, Marcia J., Katherine Williams, Alan L. Beckman, and Scott Crosse. 1995. Evaluation of the national youth gang drug prevention program. In *The modern street gang*, ed. Malcolm W. Klein, Cheryl L. Maxson, and Jody Miller, 266–275. Los Angeles: Roxbury.

Covey, Herbert C. 2003. *Street gangs throughout the world*. Springfield, IL: Thomas.

Covey, Herbert C., Scott Menard, and Robert J. Franzese. 1997. *Juvenile gangs*, 2d ed. Springfield, IL: Thomas.

Cox, Ruth P. 1996. An exploration of the demographic and social correlates of criminal behavior among adolescent males. *Journal of Adolescent Health* 19: 17–24.

Craig, Wendy M., Frank Vitaro, Claude Gagnon, and Richard E. Tremblay. 2002. The road to gang membership: Characteristics of male gang and nongang members from ages 10 to 14. *Social Development* 11(1): 53–68.

Curry, G. David. 1999. Race, ethnicity and gender issues in gangs: Reconciling police data. In *Problem-oriented policing: Crime-specific issues and making POP work*, vol. 2, ed. Corina Sole Brito and Tracy Allan, 63–89. Washington, DC: Police Executive Research Forum.

Curry, G. David. 2000. Self-reported gang involvement and officially recorded delinquency. *Criminology* 38(8): 1253–1274.

Curry, G. David, Richard A. Ball, and Scott H. Decker. 1996. Estimating the national scope of gang crime from law enforcement data. In *Gangs in America*, 2d ed., ed. C. Ronald Huff, 21–36. Thousand Oaks, CA: Sage.

Curry, G. David, Richard A. Ball, and R. J. Fox. 1994. *Gang crime and law enforcement recordkeeping*. Washington, DC: National Institute of Justice.

Curry, G. David, and Scott H. Decker. 1998. *Confronting gangs: Crime and community*. Los Angeles: Roxbury.

Curry, G. David, Scott H. Decker, and Arlen Egley, Jr. 2002. Gang involvement and delinquency in a middle school population. *Justice Quarterly* 19(2): 275–292.

Curry, G. David, and Irving A. Spergel. 1988. Gang homicide, delinquency and community. *Criminology* 26: 381–405.

Curry, G. David, and Irving A. Spergel. 1992. Gang involvement and delinquency among Hispanic and African-American adolescent males. *Journal of Research on Crime and Delinquency* 29(3): 273–291.

Curry, G. David, Katherine Williams, and Lynda Koenemann. (n.d.). *Structure, culture and delinquency in female gang involvement.* St. Louis: Department of Criminology, University of Missouri.

Dahmann, Judith. 1982. *An evaluation of Operation Hardcore: A prosecutorial response to violent gang criminality.* McLean, VA: Mitre Corporation.

Decker, Scott H. 1996. Collective and normative features of gang violence. *Justice Quarterly* 13(2): 243–264.

Decker, Scott H. 2000. Legitimating drug use: A note on the impact of gang membership and drug sales on the use of illicit drugs. *Justice Quarterly* 17(2): 393–410.

Decker, Scott H. 2001. The impact of organizational features on gang activities and relationships. In *The Eurogang paradox: Street gangs and youth groups in the U.S. and Europe*, ed. Malcolm W. Klein, Hans-Juergen Kerner, Cheryl L. Maxson, and Elmar G. M. Weitekamp, 21–39. Dordrecht: Kluwer Academic.

Decker, Scott H., ed. 2003. *Policing gangs and youth violence.* Belmont, CA: Wadsworth.

Decker, Scott H., and G. David Curry. 2000. Addressing key features of gang membership: Measuring the involvement of young members. *Journal of Criminal Justice* 28: 473–482.

Decker, Scott H., and G. David Curry. 2002a. Gangs, gang homicides, and gang loyalty: Organized crimes of disorganized criminals? *Journal of Criminal Justice* 30: 1–10.

Decker, Scott H., and G. David Curry. 2002b. I'm down for my organization: The rationality of responses to delinquency, youth crime, and gangs. In *Rational choice and criminal behavior*, ed. Alex R. Piquero and Stephen G. Tibbetts, 197–218. New York: Routledge.

Decker, Scott H., G. David Curry, Maria Weldele, Eric Baumer, Adam Bossler, Steve Schnelby, Natalie Voris, and H. Arlen Egley. 2002. *Safe future in St. Louis.* St. Louis: Department of Criminology and Criminal Justice, University of Missouri.

Decker, Scott H., and Janet L. Lauritsen. 2002. Leaving the gang. In *Gangs in America*, 3d ed., ed. C. Ronald Huff, 51–67. Thousand Oaks, CA: Sage.

Decker, Scott H., and Barrik Van Winkle. 1996. *Life in the gang: Family, friends, and violence.* Cambridge: Cambridge University Press.

Decker, Scott H., and Frank M. Weerman, eds. 2005. *European street gangs and troublesome youth groups.* Walnut Creek, CA: AltaMira.

DeFleur, Lois. 1967. Delinquent gangs in cross-cultural perspective: The case of Cordoba. *Journal of Research in Crime and Delinquency* 4: 132–141.

Deschenes, Elizabeth Piper, and Finn-Aage Esbensen. 1999. Violence and gangs:

Gender differences in perceptions and behavior. *Journal of Quantitative Criminology* 13(1): 63–96.

DiChiara, Albert. 1997. *We ain't no gang, we a family! Gangs as projects.* Paper presented at the 1997 meeting of the American Society of Criminology. Hartford, CT: University of Hartford, Department of Sociology.

Dishion, Thomas J., Joan McCord, and François Poulin. 1999. When interventions harm: Peer groups and problem behavior. *American Psychologist* 54(9): 755–764.

Dishion, Thomas J., Kathleen M. Spracklen, David W. Andrews, and Gerald R. Patterson. 1996. Deviancy training in male adolescent friendship. *Behavior Therapy* 27: 373–390.

Downes, David M. 1966. *The delinquent solution: A study in subcultural theory.* New York: Free Press.

Dukes, Richard L., Ruben O. Martinez, and Judith A. Stein. 1997. Precursors and consequences of membership in youth gangs. *Youth and Society* 29(2): 139–165.

Egley, Arlen, Jr. 2002. *National Youth Gang Survey trends from 1996 to 2000.* Washington, DC: U.S. Department of Justice, Office of Juvenile Justice and Delinquency Prevention.

Egley, Arlen, Jr. 2005. *Highlights of the 2002–2003 National Youth Gang Surveys.* Washington, DC: Office of Juvenile Justice and Delinquency Prevention.

Egley, Arlen, Jr., James C. Howell, and Aline K. Major. 2004. Recent patterns of gang problems in the United States: Results from the 1996–2002 National Youth Gang Survey. In *American youth gangs at the millennium*, ed. Finn-Aage Esbensen, Stephen G. Tibbetts, and Larry Gaines, 90–108. Long Grove, IL: Waveland.

Egley, Arlen, Jr., and Aline K. Major. 2004. *Highlights of the 2002 National Youth Gang Survey.* Washington, DC: U.S. Department of Justice, Office of Juvenile Justice and Delinquency Prevention.

Eitle, David, Steven Gunkel, and Karen Van Gundy. 2004. Cumulative exposure to stressful life events and male gang membership. *Journal of Criminal Justice* 32: 95–111.

Empey, LaMar T. 1967. *Alternatives to incarceration.* Washington, DC: Office of Juvenile Delinquency and Youth Development.

Ennett, Susan T., Nancy S. Tobler, Christopher L. Ringwalt, and Robert Flewelling. 1994. How effective is drug abuse resistance education? A meta-analysis of Project D.A.R.E. outcome evaluations. *American Journal of Public Health* 84(9): 1394–1401.

Esbensen, Finn-Aage. 2000. *Preventing adolescent gang involvement.* Washington, DC: Office of Juvenile Justice and Delinquency Prevention, NCJ 182210.

Esbensen, Finn-Aage. 2001. The national evaluation of the Gang Resistance Education and Training (G.R.E.A.T.) Program. In *The modern gang reader*, 2d ed., ed. Jody Miller, Cheryl L. Maxson, and Malcolm W. Klein, 289–302. Los Angeles: Roxbury.

Esbensen, Finn-Aage, and Elizabeth Piper Deschenes. 1998. A multisite examination of youth gang membership: Does gender matter? *Criminology* 36(4): 799–827.

Esbensen, Finn-Aage, Elizabeth Piper Deschenes, and L. Thomas Winfree. 1999. Differences between gang girls and gang boys: Results from a multisite survey. *Youth and Society* 31(1): 27–53.

Esbensen, Finn-Aage, and David Huizinga. 1993. Gangs, drugs, and delinquency in a survey of urban youth. *Criminology* 31(4): 565–587.

Esbensen, Finn-Aage, David Huizinga, and Anne W. Weiher. 1993. Gang and nongang youth: Differences in explanatory factors. *Journal of Contemporary Criminal Justice* 9(2): 94–116.

Esbensen, Finn-Aage, and Dana Peterson Lynskey. 2001. Youth gang members in a school survey. In *The Eurogang paradox: Street gangs and youth groups in the U.S. and Europe*, ed. Malcolm W. Klein, Hans-Juergen Kerner, Cheryl L. Maxson, and Elmer G. M. Weitekamp, 93–114. Dordrecht: Kluwer Academic.

Esbensen, Finn-Aage, and D. Wayne Osgood. 1998. *National evaluation of G.R.E.A.T.* Washington, DC: U.S. Department of Justice, National Institute of Justice.

Esbensen, Finn-Aage, and D. Wayne Osgood. 1999. Gang Resistance, Education, and Training (G.R.E.A.T.): Results from the national evaluation. *Journal of Research in Crime and Delinquency* 36: 194–225.

Esbensen, Finn-Aage, D. Wayne Osgood, Terrance J. Taylor, Dana Peterson, and Adrienne Freng. 2001. How great is G.R.E.A.T.? Results from the longitudinal quasi-experimental design. *Criminology and Public Policy* 1: 87–118.

Esbensen, Finn-Aage, Dana Peterson, Adrienne Freng, and Terrance J. Taylor. 2002. Initiation of drug use, drug sales, and violent offending among a sample of gang and nongang youth. In *Gangs in America*, 3d ed., ed. C. Ronald Huff. Thousand Oaks, CA: Sage.

Esbensen, Finn-Aage, and Frank M. Weerman. 2005. Youth gangs and troublesome youth groups in the United States and the Netherlands: A cross-national comparison. *European Journal of Criminology* 2(1): 5–37.

Esbensen, Finn-Aage, and L. Thomas Winfree, Jr. 1998. Race and gender differences between gang and non-gang youth: Results from a multisite survey. *Justice Quarterly* 15: 505–526.

Esbensen, Finn-Aage, L. Thomas Winfree, Jr., Ni He, and Terrance J. Taylor. 2001. Youth gangs and definitional issues: When is a gang a gang, and why does it matter? *Crime and Delinquency* 47: 105–130.

Fagan, Jeffrey. 1989. The social organization of drug use and dealing among urban gangs. *Criminology* 27: 633–669.

Fagan, Jeffrey. 1990. Social processes of delinquency and drug use among urban gangs. In *Gangs in America*, ed. C. Ronald Huff, 183–219. Thousand Oaks, CA: Sage.

Fagan, Jeffrey. 1996. Gangs, drugs, and neighborhood change. In *Gangs in America*, 2d ed., ed. C. Ronald Huff, 39–74. Thousand Oaks, CA: Sage.

Fearn, Noelle E., Scott H. Decker, and G. David Curry. 2001. Public policy responses to gangs: Evaluating the outcomes. In *The modern gang reader*, 2d ed., ed. Jody Miller, Cheryl L. Maxson, and Malcolm W. Klein, 330–343. Los Angeles: Roxbury.

Felson, Marcus, and Michael Gottfredson. 1984. Social indicators of adolescent activities near peers and parents. *Journal of Marriage and the Family* 46: 709–714.

Feyerherm, W., C. Pope, and R. Lovell. 1992. *Youth gang prevention and early intervention programs*. Unpublished final research report. Portland, OR: Portland State University.

Fleisher, Mark. 1998. *Dead end kids: Gang girls and the boys they know*. Madison: University of Wisconsin Press.

Fremon, Celeste. 1995. *Father Greg and the homeboys*. New York: Hyperion.

Freng, Adrienne, and L. Thomas Winfree. 2004. Exploring race and ethnic differences in a sample of middle school gang members. In *American youth gangs at the millennium*, ed. Finn-Aage Esbensen, Stephen G. Tibbetts, and Larry Gaines, 142–162. Long Grove, IL: Waveland.

Gatti, Uberto, Richard E. Tremblay, Frank Vitaro, and Pierre McDuff. (2005). Youth gangs, delinquency and drug use: A test of the selection, facilitation and enhancement hypotheses. *Journal of Child Psychology and Psychiatry* 46(11): 1178–1190.

General Accounting Office. 1996. *Violent crime: Federal law enforcement assistance in fighting Los Angeles gang violence*. Washington, DC: U.S. General Accounting Office.

Gibbs, John P. 1975. *Crime, punishment, and deterrence*. New York: Elsevier.

Gordon, Rachel A., Benjamin B. Lahey, Eriko Kawai, Rolf Loeber, Magda Stouthamer-Loeber, and David P. Farrington. 2004. Antisocial behavior and youth gang membership: Selection and socialization. *Criminology* 42(1): 55–87.

Gottfredson, Gary D., and Denise C. Gottfredson. 1999. *Survey of school-based gang prevention and intervention programs: Preliminary findings*. Ellicott City, MD: Gottfredson Associates.

Gottfredson, Gary D., and Denise C. Gottfredson. 2001. *Gang problems and gang programs in a national sample of schools: Summary*. Ellicott City, MD: Gottfredson Associates.

Greene, Jack C. 1998. The road to community policing in Los Angeles: A case study. In *Community policing: Contemporary readings*, ed. G. P. Alpert. and Alex Piquero, 123–158. Prospect Heights, IL: Waveland.

Greene, Jack R. 2003. Gangs, community policing, and problem solving. In *Policing gangs and youth violence*, ed. Scott H. Decker, 3–16. Belmont, CA: Wadsworth.

Grogger, Jeffrey. 2002. The effects of civil gang injunctions on reported violent crime: Evidence from Los Angeles County. *Journal of Law and Economics* 45(April): 69–90.

Hagedorn, John M. 1988. *People and folks: Gangs, crime, and the underclass in a rustbelt city*. Chicago: Lake View.

Hall, Gina Pedley, Terence P. Thornberry, and Alan J. Lizotte. Forthcoming. The gang facilitation effect and neighborhood risk: Do gangs have a stronger influence on delinquency in disadvantaged areas? In *Studying youth gangs*, ed. James F. Short, Jr., and Lorine A. Hughes. Walnut Creek: AltaMira.

Hamm, Mark S. 1993. *American skinheads: The criminology and control of hate crime*. Westport, CT: Praeger.

Harrell, Erika. 2005. *Violence by gang members, 1993–2003*. Washington, DC: U.S. Department of Justice, Bureau of Justice Statistics.

Hawkins, J. David, Todd Herrenkohl, David P. Farrington, Devon Brewer, Richard F. Catalano, and Tracy W. Harachi. 1998. A review of the predictors of youth violence. In *Serious and violent juvenile offenders: Risk factors and successful interventions*, ed. Rolf Loeber and David P. Farrington, 106–146. Thousand Oaks, CA: Sage.

Hill, Karl G., James C. Howell, J. David Hawkins, and Sara R. Battin-Pearson. 1999. Childhood risk factors for adolescent gang membership: Results from the Seattle Social Development Project. *Journal of Research in Crime and Delinquency* 36(August): 300–322.

Hill, Karl G., Christina Lui, and J. David Hawkins. 2001. *Early precursors of gang membership: A study of Seattle youth*. Washington, DC: Office of Juvenile Justice and Delinquency Prevention, NCJ 190106.

Horowitz, Ruth. 1990. Sociological perspectives on gangs: Conflicting definitions and concepts. In *Gangs in America*, ed. C. Ronald Huff, 37–54. Thousands Oaks, CA: Sage.

Howell, James C., Arlen Egley, Jr., and Debra K. Gleason. 2002. *Modern day youth gangs*. Washington, DC: Office of Juvenile Justice and Delinquency Prevention.

Howell, James C., John P. Moore, and Arlen Egley, Jr. 2002. The changing boundaries of youth gangs. In *Gangs in America*, 3d ed., ed. C. Ronald Huff, 33–18. Thousand Oaks, CA: Sage.

Huff, C. Ronald. 1989. Youth gangs and public policy. *Crime and Delinquency* 35: 524–537.

Huff, C. Ronald, ed. 1990. *Gangs in America*. Thousand Oaks, CA: Sage.

Huff, C. Ronald, ed. 1996. *Gangs in America*, 2d ed. Thousand Oaks, CA: Sage.

Huff, C. Ronald. 1998. *Comparing the criminal behavior of youth gangs and at-risk youths*. Washington, DC: U.S. Department of Justice.

Huff, C. Ronald, ed. 2002. *Gangs in America*, 3d ed. Thousand Oaks, CA: Sage.

Huff, C. Ronald. Forthcoming. Gangs. In *Encyclopedia of the Midwest*, ed. Richard Sisson, Christian Zacher, and Andrew Clayton. Bloomington: Indiana University Press.

Huizinga, David, and Karl F. Schumann. 2001. Gang membership in Bremen and Denver: Comparative longitudinal data. In *The Eurogang paradox: Street gangs and youth groups in the U.S. and Europe*, ed. Malcolm W. Klein, Hans-Juergen Kerner, Cheryl L. Maxson, and Elmar G. M. Weitekamp, 231–246. Dordrecht: Kluwer Academic.

Huizinga, David, Anne Wylie Weiher, Scott Menard, Rachele Espiritu, and Finn Esbensen. 1998. *Some not so boring findings from the Denver Youth Survey.* Unpublished manuscript. Boulder: Institute of Behavioral Science, University of Colorado.

Hunt, Geoffrey, and Karen A. Joe-Laidler. 2001. Situations of violence in the lives of girl gang members. *Health Care for Women International* 22: 363–384.

Hutson, H. Range, Deirdre Anglin, Demetrios N. Kyriacou, Joel Hart, and Kelvin Spears. 1995. The epidemic of gang-related homicides in Los Angeles County from 1979 through 1994. *Journal of the American Medical Association* 274(13): 1031–1036.

Hutson, H. Range, Deirdre Anglin, and Michael J. Pratts. 1994. Adolescents and children injured or killed in drive-by shootings in Los Angeles. *New England Journal of Medicine* 330(5): 324–327.

Institute for Law and Justice. 1993. *Gang prosecution legislative review.* Washington, DC: National Institute of Justice.

Jackson, Pamela Irving. 1991. Crime, youth gangs and urban transition: The social dislocation of postindustrial economic development. *Justice Quarterly* 8(3): 379–397.

Jackson, Robert L. 1997. Nationwide spread of LA gangs is alarming, FBI says. *Los Angeles Times*, April 27.

Jansyn, Leon, Jr. 1966. Solidarity and delinquency in a street corner group. *American Sociological Review* 31: 600–614.

Joe, Karen A., and Meda Chesney-Lind. 1995. Just every mother's angel: An analysis of gender and ethnic variations in youth gang membership. *Gender and Society* 9(4): 408–431.

Joe-Laidler, Karen A., and Geoffrey Hunt. 1997. Violence and social organization in female gangs. *Social Justice* 24(4): 148–169.

Johnson, Claire, Barbara Webster, and Edward Connors. 1995. *Prosecuting gangs: A national assessment.* Washington, DC: National Institute of Justice.

Johnstone, John W. C. 1981. Youth gangs and black suburbs. *Pacific Sociological Review* 24(3): 355–375.

Katz, Charles. 2001. The establishment of a police gang unit: An examination of organizational and environmental factors. *Criminology* 39(1): 37–73.

Katz, Charles M., Vincent J. Webb, and Todd A. Armstrong. 2003. Fear of gangs: A test of alternative theoretical models. *Justice Quarterly* 20(1): 95–130.

Katz, Charles M., Vincent J. Webb, and Scott H. Decker. 2005. Using the Arrestee Drug Abuse Monitoring (ADAM) program to further understand the relationship between drug use and gang membership. *Justice Quarterly* 22(1): 58–88.

Katz, Charles M., Vincent J. Webb, and Doug Schaefer. 2000. The validity of police gang intelligence lists: Examining differences in delinquency between documented gang members and non-documented delinquent youth. *Police Quarterly* 3(4): 413–437.

Katz, Jesse. 1995. Three years on the turf in gang land. *Los Angeles Times Magazine*, February 19.

Kennedy, David M. 1997. Pulling levers: Crime offenders, high-crime settings, and a theory of prevention. *Valparaiso Law Review* 31(2): 149–484.

Kennedy, David. M. 1998. Pulling levers: Getting deterrence right. *National Institute of Justice Journal* 236: 2–8.

Kennedy, David. M., Anthony A. Braga, Anne M. Piehl, and Elin J. Waring. 2001. *Reducing gun violence: The Boston Gun Project Operation Cease Fire.* Washington, DC: National Institute of Justice.

Kent, Douglas R. 1994. *Evaluating criminal justice programs designed to reduce crime by targeting repeat gang offenders.* Westminster, CA: Westminster Police Department.

Kent, Douglas R., and George T. Felkenes. 1998. *Cultural explanations for Vietnamese youth involvement in street gangs.* Final report submitted to the Office of Juvenile Justice and Delinquency Prevention, U.S. Department of Justice. Westminster, CA: City of Westminster Police Department.

Kent, Douglas R., and Peggy J. Smith. 1996. *Tri-Agency Resources Gang Enforcement Team: 1995 year-end report.* Westminster, CA: Westminster Police Department.

Klein, Malcolm W. 1971. *Street gangs and street workers.* Englewood Cliffs, NJ: Prentice-Hall.

Klein, Malcolm W. 1979. Deinstitutionalization and diversion of juvenile offenders: A litany of impediments. In *Crime and justice: An annual review of research*, ed. Noval Morris and Michael Tonry, 145–201. Chicago: University of Chicago Press.

Klein, Malcolm W. 1984. Offense specialization and versatility among juveniles. *British Journal of Criminology* 24: 185–194.

Klein, Malcolm W. 1995a. *The American street gang: Its nature, prevalence, and control.* New York: Oxford University Press.

Klein, Malcolm W. 1995b. Street gang cycles. In *Crime*, ed. James Q. Wilson and Joan Petersilia, 217–236. San Francisco: Institute for Contemporary Studies.

Klein, Malcolm W. 1996. Gangs in the United States and Europe. *European Journal on Criminal Policy and Research* 4(2): 63–80.

Klein, Malcolm W. 1997. *Guiding Los Angeles's response to street gangs: An S C 2 Project failure.* Los Angeles Social Science Research Institute: University of Southern California.

Klein, Malcolm W. 2002. Street gangs: A cross-national perspective. In *Gangs in America*, 3d ed., ed. C. Ronald Huff, 237–254. Thousand Oaks, CA: Sage.

Klein, Malcolm W. 2004. *Gang cop: The words and ways of officer Paco Domingo.* Walnut Creek, CA: AltaMira.

Klein, Malcolm W., Hans-Juergen Kerner, Cheryl L. Maxson, and Elmar G. M. Weitekamp, eds. 2001. *The Eurogang paradox: Street gangs and youth groups in the U.S. and Europe.* Dordrecht: Kluwer Academic.

Klein, Malcolm W., and Cheryl L. Maxson. 1996. *Gang structures, crime patterns, and police responses.* Final report to the National Institute of Justice. Los Angeles: University of Southern California.

Klein, Malcolm W., Cheryl L. Maxson, and Jody Miller, eds. 1995. *The modern gang reader.* Los Angeles: Roxbury.

Kobrin, Solomon. 1959. The Chicago Area Project: A 25-year assessment. *Annals of the American Academy of Political and Social Science* 322: 1–29.

Krikorian, Michael. 1998. Ex-gang members work to bring peace. *Los Angeles Times,* January 26.

Kubrin, Charis A., and Ronald Weitzer. 2003. Retaliatory homicide: Concentrated disadvantage and neighborhood culture. *Social Problems* 50(2): 157–180.

Lacourse, Eric, Daniel Nagin, Richard E. Tremblay, Frank Vitaro, and Michel Claes. 2003. Developmental trajectories of boys' delinquent group membership and facilitation of violent behaviors during adolescence. *Development and Psychopathology* 15: 183–197.

Lahey, Benjamin B., Rachel A. Gordon, Rolf Loeber, Magda Stouthamer-Loeber, and David P. Farrington. 1999. Boys who join gangs: A prospective study of predictors of first gang entry. *Journal of Abnormal Child Psychology* 27(4): 261–276.

Lane, Jodi. 2002. Fear of gang crime: A qualitative examination of the four perspectives. *Journal of Research in Crime and Delinquency* 39(4): 437–471.

Lane, Jodi, and James W. Meeker. 2003. Fear of gang crime: A look at three theoretical models. *Law and Society Review* 37(2): 425–456.

LeBlanc, Marc, and Nadine Lanctot. 1998. Social and psychological characteristics of gang members according to the gang structure and its subcultural and ethnic makeup. *Journal of Gang Research* 5: 15–28.

Levitt, Steven D., and Sudhir Venkatesh. 1999. *An economic analysis of a drug-selling gang's finances.* Chicago: Department of Economics, University of Chicago.

Lien, Inger-Lise. 2002. The pain of crime and gang mentality. Unpublished paper. Oslo: The Norwegian Institute of Urban and Regional Research.

Lien, Inger-Lise. 2005a. Criminal gangs and their connections. In *European street gangs and troublesome youth groups,* ed. Scott H. Decker and Frank M. Weerman, 31–50. Walnut Creek, CA: AltaMira.

Lien, Inger-Lise. 2005b. The role of crime acts in constituting the gang's mentality. In *European street gangs and troublesome youth groups,* ed. Scott H. Decker and Frank M. Weerman, 105–125. Walnut Creek, CA: Altamira.

Lizotte, Alan J., Marvin D. Krohn, James C. Howell, Kimberly Tobin, and Gregory J. Howard. 2000. Factors influencing gun carrying among young urban males over the adolescent-young adult life course. *Criminology* 38(30): 811–834.

Luna, Claire. 2004. Gang charges added in fatal knife attack. *Los Angeles Times*, December 28.

Lyons, Morgan. 1998. *A case study of the Los Angeles City and County anti-gang initiative: The Community Law Enforcement and Recovery (CLEAR) program.* Los Angeles: Lodestar Management/Research.

Maxson, Cheryl L. 1993. Investigating gang migration: Contextual issues for intervention. *Gang Journal* 1(2): 1–8.

Maxson, Cheryl L. 1995. *Street gangs and drug sales in two suburban cities.* Washington, DC: National Institute of Justice.

Maxson, Cheryl. 1998a. Gang homicide: A review and extension of the literature. In *Homicide studies: A sourcebook of social research*, ed. M. Dwayne Smith and Margaret A. Zahn, 197–220. Newbury Park, CA: Sage.

Maxson, Cheryl L. 1998b. *Gang members on the move.* Washington, DC: U.S. Department of Justice, Office of Juvenile Justice and Delinquency Prevention.

Maxson, Cheryl L. 2004. Civil gang injunctions: The ambiguous case of the national migration of a gang enforcement strategy. In *American youth gangs at the millennium*, ed. Finn-Aage Esbensen, Stephen G. Tibbetts, and Larry Gaines, 375–389. Long Grove, IL: Waveland.

Maxson, Cheryl L., G. David Curry, and James C. Howell. 2002. Youth gang homicides in the United States in the 1990s. In *Responding to gangs: Evaluation and research*, ed. Winifred L. Reed and Scott H. Decker, 107–137. Washington, DC: U.S. Department of Justice.

Maxson, Cheryl L., Margaret A. Gordon, and Malcolm W. Klein. 1985. Differences between gang and nongang homicides. *Criminology* 23(2): 209–222.

Maxson, Cheryl L., Karen Hennigan, and David C. Sloane. 2003. For the sake of the neighborhood? Civil gang injunctions as a gang intervention tool in southern California. In *Policing gangs and youth violence*, ed. Scott H. Decker, 239–266. Belmont, CA: Wadsworth.

Maxson, Cheryl L., Karen Hennigan, and David C. Sloane. 2005. It's getting crazy out there: Can a civil gang injunction change a community? *Criminology and Public Policy* 4(3): 501–530.

Maxson, Cheryl L., Karen Hennigan, David Sloane, and Kathy Kolnick. 2004. *Can civil gang injunctions change communities? A community assessment of the impact of civil gang injunctions.* Final report to the National Institute of Justice. Los Angeles: University of Southern California.

Maxson, Cheryl L., and Malcolm W. Klein. 1983. Gangs: Why we couldn't stay away. In *Evaluating juvenile justice*, ed. James R. Kluegel, 149–155. Thousand Oaks, CA: Sage.

Maxson, Cheryl L., and Malcolm W. Klein. 1995. Investigating gang structures. *Journal of Gang Research* 3(1): 33–40.

Maxson, Cheryl L., and Malcolm W. Klein. 1996. Defining gang homicide: An updated look at member and motive approaches. In *Gangs in America*, 2d ed., ed. C. Ronald Huff, 3–20. Thousand Oaks, CA: Sage.

Maxson, Cheryl L., and Malcolm W. Klein. 2002. "Play groups" no longer: Urban street gangs in the Los Angeles region. In *From Chicago to L.A.: Making sense of urban theory*, ed. Michael Dear, 239–266. Thousand Oaks, CA: Sage.

Maxson, Cheryl, Malcolm Klein, and Karen Sternheimer. 2000. *Homicide in Los Angeles: An analysis of the differential character of adolescent and other homicides.* Unpublished report to the National Institute of Justice. Los Angeles: University of Southern California.

Maxson, Cheryl L., Malcolm W. Klein, and Monica L. Whitlock. 1997. *Exploring youth violence risk and protective factors.* Proposal submitted to the National Institute of Justice, U.S. Department of Justice. Los Angeles: University of Southern California.

Maxson, Cheryl L., and Monica L. Whitlock. 2002. Joining the gang: Gender differences in risk factors for gang membership. In *Gangs in America*, 3d ed., ed. C. Ronald Huff, 19–35. Thousand Oaks, CA: Sage.

Maxson, Cheryl L., and Monica Whitlock. 2003. *School-based protection of youth at-risk for joining groups: Final report.* Los Angeles: Social Science Research Institute, University of Southern California.

Maxson, Cheryl L., Monica L. Whitlock, and Malcolm W. Klein. 1997. *Gang joining and resistance: Who can "just say no" to gangs?* Final report submitted to Administration for Children and Families, U.S. Department of Health and Human Services. Los Angeles: University of Southern California.

Maxson, Cheryl L., Monica L. Whitlock, and Malcolm W. Klein. 1998. Vulnerability to street gang membership: Implications for practice. *Social Service Review* 72(1): 70–91.

Maxson, Cheryl L., Kristi J. Woods, and Malcolm W. Klein. 1995. *Street gang migration in the United States.* Final report submitted to the National Institute of Justice, U.S. Department of Justice. Los Angeles: University of Southern California.

Maxson, Cheryl L., Kristi J. Woods, and Malcolm W. Klein. 1996. *Street gang migration: How big a threat?* Washington, DC: U.S. Department of Justice, Office of Juvenile Justice and Delinquency Prevention.

McGarrell, Edmond F., and Steven Chermak. 2003. Problem solving to reduce gang and drug-related violence in Indianapolis. In *Policing gangs and youth violence*, ed. Scott H. Decker, 77–101. Belmont, CA: Wadsworth.

Mehren, Elizabeth. 1996. Do not follow in my footsteps. *Los Angeles Times*, September 11.

Miethe, Terance D., and Richard C. McCorkle. 2002. Evaluating Nevada's antigang legislation and gang prosecution units. In *Responding to gangs: Evaluation and research*, ed. Winifred L. Reed and Scott H. Decker, 169–185. Washington, DC: National Institute of Justice.

Miller, Jody. 1998. Gender and victimization risk among young women in gangs. *Journal of Research in Crime and Delinquency* 35(4): 429–453.

Miller, Jody. 2001. *One of the guys: Girls, gangs, and gender.* New York: Oxford University Press.

Miller, Jody, and Rod K. Brunson. 2000. Gender dynamics in youth gangs: A comparison of males' and females' accounts. *Justice Quarterly* 17(3): 420–488.

Miller, Jody, and Scott H. Decker. 2001. Young women and gang violence: Gender, street offending, and violent victimization in gangs. *Justice Quarterly* 18(1): 115–140.

Miller, Jody, Cheryl L. Maxson, and Malcolm W. Klein, eds. 2001. *The modern gang reader*, 2d ed. Los Angeles: Roxbury.

Miller, Walter B. 1958. Inter-institutional conflict as a major impediment to delinquency prevention. *Human Organization* 17(3): 20–23.

Miller, Walter B. 1962. The impact of a "total community" delinquency control project. *Social Problems* 10(2): 168–191.

Miller, Walter B. 1973. Race, sex, and gangs: The Molls. *Society* 11(1): 32–35.

Miller, Walter B. 1975. *Violence by youth gangs and youth groups as a crime problem in major American cities.* Washington, DC: Office of Juvenile Justice and Delinquency Prevention.

Miller, Walter B. 1980. Gangs, groups, and serious youth crime. In *Critical issues in juvenile delinquency*, ed. David Shichor and Delos H. Kelly, 115–138. Lexington, MA: Heath.

Miller, Walter B. 1982. *Crime by youth gangs and groups in the United States.* Washington, DC: U.S. Department of Justice, Office of Juvenile Justice and Delinquency Prevention.

Miller, Walter B. 2001. *The growth of youth gang problems in the United States: 1970–98.* Washington, DC: U.S. Department of Justice, Office of Juvenile Justice and Delinquency Prevention.

Monod, Jean. 1967. Juvenile gangs in Paris: Toward a structural analysis. *Journal of Research in Crime and Delinquency* 4: 142–165.

Moore, Joan W. 1978. *Homeboys: Gangs, drugs, and prison in the barrios of Los Angeles.* Philadelphia: Temple University Press.

Moore, Joan W. 1991. *Going down to the barrio: Homeboys and homegirls in change.* Philadelphia: Temple University Press.

Moore, Joan W. 2002. Foreword. In James D. Vigil, *A rainbow of gangs: Street cultures in the mega-city*. Austin: University of Texas Press.

Moore, Joan, and John Hagedorn. 2001. *Female gangs: A focus on research.* Washington, DC: Office of Juvenile Justice and Delinquency Prevention.

Moore, Joan, and James D. Vigil. 1989. Chicano gangs: Group norms and individual factors related to adult criminality. *Aztlan* 18: 31–42.

National Youth Gang Center. 1998. *1996 National Youth Gang Survey Program Summary*. Washington, DC: Office of Juvenile Justice and Delinquency Prevention.

National Youth Gang Center. 1999. *1997 National Youth Gang Survey: OJJDP Summary*. Washington, DC: Office of Juvenile Justice and Delinquency Prevention.

National Youth Gang Center. 2000a. *1998 National Youth Gang Survey: OJJDP Summary*. Washington, DC: Office of Juvenile Justice and Delinquency Prevention.

National Youth Gang Center. 2000b. *Special survey preliminary results* (unpublished). Tallahassee, FL: National Youth Gang Center.

National Youth Gang Center. N.d. *1998 National Youth Gang Survey*. Tallahassee, FL: Institute for Intergovernmental Research.

Needle, Jerome A., and William Vaughan Stapleton. 1983. *Report of the National Juvenile Justice assessment centers: Police handling of youth gangs*. Washington, DC: U.S. Department of Justice.

New York City Youth Board. 1960. *Reaching the fighting gang*. New York: New York City Youth Board.

Oberwittler, Dietrich. 2004. A multilevel analysis of neighbourhood contextual effects on serious juvenile offending: The role of subcultural values and social disorganization. *European Journal of Criminology* 1(2): 201–235.

Office of Juvenile Justice and Delinquency Prevention. 1999. *1997 National Youth Gang Survey: Summary*. Washington, DC: U.S. Department of Justice, Office of Juvenile Justice and Delinquency Prevention.

Osgood, D. Wayne, and Amy L. Anderson. 2004. Unstructured socializing and rates of delinquency. *Criminology* 42(3): 519–549.

Padilla, Felix M. 1992. *The gang as an American enterprise*. New Brunswick, NJ: Rutgers University Press.

Parker, Robert Nash. 2002. *Project Bridge local evaluation, 1994 to 1999*. Riverside, CA: Presley Center for Crime and Justice Studies, University of California, Riverside.

Patrick, James. 1973. *A Glasgow gang observed*. London: Eyre Methuen.

Pattillo, Mary E. 1998. Sweet mothers and gangbangers: Managing crime in a black middle-class neighborhood. *Social Forces* 76(3): 747–774.

Pawloski, Randy, and Bryan Brown. 1998. Gang expert testimony for S.T.E.P. act, penal code sections 186.22. *Prosecutor's Brief* 20(3): 4–47.

Peterson, Dana, Jody Miller, and Finn-Aage Esbensen. 2001. The impact of sex compositions in gangs and gang member delinquency. *Criminology* 39(2): 411–439.

Peterson, Dana, Terrance J. Taylor, and Finn-Aage Esbensen. 2004. Gang membership and violent victimization. *Justice Quarterly* 21(4): 793–815.

Pyle, Amy. 1995. County takes first step to prohibiting gangs from parks. In *The modern gang reader*, ed. Malcolm W. Klein, Cheryl L. Maxson, and Jody Miller, 332. Los Angeles: Roxbury.

Reiner, Ira. 1992. *Gangs, crime and violence in Los Angeles*. Los Angeles: Office of the District Attorney, County of Los Angeles.

Ripston, Ramona. 1997. In conversation with Fr. Greg Boyle. (*Los Angeles ACLU*) *Open Forum* Fall: 4–5.

Rosenbaum, D. P., and J. A. Grant. 1983. *Gangs and youth problems in Evanston*.

Evanston, IL: Northwestern University, Center for Urban Affairs and Policy Research.

Rosenbaum, Dennis P., and Gordon S. Hanson. 1998. Assessing the effects of school-based drug education: A six-year multi-level analysis of Project D.A.R.E. *Journal of Research in Crime and Delinquency* 35(4): 381–412.

Rosenfeld, Richard, Timothy M. Bray, and Arlen Egley. 1999. Facilitating violence: A comparison of gang-motivated, gang affiliated and nongang youth homicides. *Journal of Quantitative Criminology* 15(4): 495–516.

Sahagun, Louis, 1999. The new college gang. *Los Angeles Times*, January 13.

Salagaev, Alexander. 2001. Evolution of delinquent gangs in Russia. In *The Eurogang paradox: Street gangs and youth groups in the U.S. and Europe*, ed. Malcolm W. Klein, Hans-Juergen Kerner, Cheryl L. Maxson, and Elmar G. M. Weitekamp, 195–202. Dordrecht: Kluwer Academic.

Sampson, Robert J., and Byron Groves. 1989. Community structure and crime: Testing social-disorganization theory. *American Journal of Sociology* 94: 774–802.

Sampson, Robert J., Jeffrey D. Morenoff, and Thomas Gannon-Rowley. 2002. Assessing "neighborhood effects": Social processes and new directions in research. *Annual Review of Sociology* 28: 443–78.

Sampson, Robert J., S. W. Raudenbush, and Felton Earls. 1997. Neighborhoods and violent crime: A multilevel study of collective efficacy. *Science* 277: 918–924.

Sanchez-Jankowski, Martin. 1991. *Islands in the street: Gangs and American urban society.* Berkeley: University of California Press.

Sanders, William B. 1994. *Gangbangs and drive-bys: Grounded culture and juvenile gang violence.* New York: de Gruyter.

Scott, Greg. 2000. *Illinois law enforcement responses to street gangs: Interim report.* Chicago: Gang Crime Prevention Center, Office of the Illinois Attorney General.

Sheley, Joseph F., and James D. Wright. 1995. *In the line of fire: Youth, guns and violence in urban America.* New York: de Gruyter.

Sherif, Muzafer, and Carolyn W. Sherif. 1967. Group process and collective interaction in delinquent activities. *Journal of Research in Crime and Delinquency* 4(1): 43–62.

Short, James F., Jr. 1996. *Gangs and adolescent violence.* Boulder: University of Colorado, Center for the Study and Prevention of Violence.

Short, James F., Jr., and Fred L. Strodtbeck. 1965. *Group process and gang delinquency.* Chicago: University of Chicago Press.

Skolnick, Jerome. 1990. Gangs and crime old as time: But drugs change gang culture. In *Crime and delinquency in California, 1980–1989*, 171–179. Sacramento: Bureau of Criminal Statistics and Special Services, Office of the Attorney General, Department of Justice, State of California.

Slater, Eric. 1999. Cicero says new gangs personae non gratae. *Los Angeles Times*, April 29.

Snyder, Howard N., and Melissa Sickmund. 1999. *Juvenile offenders and victims: 1999 national report.* Washington, DC: U.S. Department of Justice, Office of Juvenile Justice and Delinquency Prevention.

Spergel, Irving. 1964. *Racketville, Slumtown, Haulburg: An exploratory study of delinquent subcultures.* Chicago: University of Chicago Press.

Spergel, Irving. 1966. *Street gang work: Theory and practice.* Reading, MA: Addison-Wesley.

Spergel, Irving A. 1995. *The youth gang problem: A community approach.* New York: Oxford University Press.

Spergel, Irving A. 2001. *Executive summary: Evaluation of the Bloomington-Normal comprehensive gang program.* Chicago: University of Chicago, School of Social Service.

Spergel, Irving A., and G. David Curry. 1990. Strategies and perceived agency effectiveness in dealing with the youth gang problem. In *Gangs in America*, ed. C. Ronald Huff, 288–309. Thousand Oaks, CA: Sage.

Spergel, Irving A., and G. David Curry. 1993. The National Youth Gang Survey: A research and development process. In *The gang intervention handbook*, ed. Arnold P. Goldstein and C. Ronald Huff, 359–392. Champaign, IL: Research Press.

Starbuck, David, James C. Howell, and Donna J. Lindquist. 2001. *Hybrid and other modern gangs.* Washington, DC: Office of Juvenile Justice and Delinquency Prevention.

Taylor, Carl S. 1990. *Dangerous society.* East Lansing: Michigan Sate University Press.

Thereux, Peter. 1995. Off the wall: Experts agree: Ganging up on graffiti is beginning to pay off. (*Automobile Club of Southern California*) *Avenues* (September–October): 22–27.

Thompson, Kevin M., David Brownfield, and Ann Marie Sorenson. 1996. Specialization patterns of gang and nongang offending: A latent structure analysis. *Journal of Gang Research* 3(3): 25–35.

Thornberry, Terence. 1998. Membership in youth gangs and involvement in serious and violent offending. In *Serious and violent offenders: Risk factors and successful interventions*, ed. Rolf Loeber and David P. Farrington, 147–166. Newbury Park, CA: Sage.

Thornberry, Terence P., David Huizinga, and Rolf Loeber. 2004. The causes and correlates studies: Findings and policy implications. *Juvenile Justice* 9(1): 3–19.

Thornberry, Terence, Marvin D. Krohn, Alan J. Lizotte, and Deborah Chard-Wierschem. 1993. The role of juvenile gangs in facilitating delinquent behavior. *Journal of Research in Crime and Delinquency* 30(1): 55–87.

Thornberry, Terence P., Marvin D. Krohn, Alan J. Lizotte, Carolyn A. Smith, and

Kimberly Tobin. 2003. *Gangs and delinquency in developmental perspective.* Cambridge: Cambridge University Press.

Thornberry, Terence P., and Pamela K. Porter. 2001. Advantages of longitudinal research designs in studying gang behavior. In *The Eurogang paradox: Street gangs and youth groups in the U.S. and Europe*, ed. Malcolm W. Klein, Hans-Juergen Kerner, Cheryl L. Maxson, and Elmar G. M. Weitekamp, 59–78. Dordrecht: Kluwer Academic.

Thrasher, Frederic M. 1927. *The gang: A study of 1313 gangs in Chicago*. Chicago: University of Chicago Press.

Tita, George, and Allan Abrahamse. 2004. *Gang homicide in LA, 1981–2001.* Sacramento: California Attorney General's Office.

Tita, George E., Jacqueline Cohen, and John Engberg. 2005. An ecological study of the location of gang "set space." *Social Problems* 52(2): 272–299.

Tita, George, K. Jack Riley, and Peter Greenwood. 2003. From Boston to Boyle Heights: The process and prospects of a "pulling levers" strategy in a Los Angeles barrio. In *Policing gangs and youth violence*, ed. Scott H. Decker, 102–130. Belmont, CA: Wadsworth/Thomas Learning.

Tyson, Gail. 2004. Redemption that works. *Mission* (Fall): 14–21.

Valdez, Al. 2000. *Gangs: A guide to understanding street gangs.* San Clemente, CA: Law Tech Publishing.

Valdez, Avelardo, and Stephen Sifaneck. 2004. "Getting high and getting by": Dimensions of drug selling behavior among American Mexican gang members in south Texas. *Journal of Research in Crime and Delinquency* 41(1): 82–105.

Van den Haag, Ernest. 1975. *Punishing criminals: Concerning a very old and painful question.* New York: Basic.

Vaz, Edmond W. 1962. Juvenile gang delinquency in Paris. *Social Problems* 10(1): 23–31.

Venkatesh, Sudhir. 1999a. Community-based interventions into street gang activity. *Journal of Community Psychology* 27: 1–17.

Venkatesh, Sudhir. 1999b. The financial activity of a modern American street gang. *NIJ Research Forum* (November): 1–11.

Vigil, James D. 1988. *Barrio gangs: Street life and identity in southern California.* Austin: University of Texas Press.

Vigil, James D. 2002. *A rainbow of gangs: Street cultures in the mega-city.* Austin: University of Texas Press.

Waldorf, Dan. 1993. When the Crips invaded San Francisco. *Gang Journal* 4(1): 11–16.

Walker-Barnes, Chanequa J., and Craig A. Mason. 2001. Ethnic differences in the effect of parenting on gang involvement and delinquency: A longitudinal, hierarchical linear modeling perspective. *Child Development* 72(6): 1814–1831.

Washington Crime News Services. 1997. Violent gangs spread largely through migration of families. *Crime Control Digest* 31(17): 1.

Webb, Vincent J., and Charles M. Katz. 2003. Policing gangs in an era of community policing. In *Policing gangs and youth violence*, ed. Scott H. Decker, 17–50. Belmont, CA: Wadsworth.

Weisel, Deborah Lamm. 2002. The evolution of street gangs: An examination of form and variation. In *Responding to gangs: Evaluation and research*, ed. Winnie L. Reed and Scott H. Decker, 25–65. Washington, DC: National Institute of Justice.

Weisel, Deborah Lamm, Scott H. Decker, and Timothy S. Bynum. 1997. *Gangs and organized crime groups: Connections and similarities*. Washington, DC: Police Executive Research Forum.

Weisheit, Ralph A., and L. Edward Wells. 2004. Youth gangs in rural America. *NIJ Journal* 251: 1–6 (NCJ204515).

Weitekamp, Elmar G. M. 2001. Gangs in Europe: Assessments at the millennium. In *The Eurogang paradox: Street gangs and youth groups in the U.S. and Europe*, ed. Malcolm W. Klein, Hans-Juergen Kerner, Cheryl L. Maxson, and Elmar G. M. Weitekamp, 309–322. Dordrecht: Kluwer Academic.

Wells, L. Edward, and Ralph A. Weisheit. 2001. Gang problems in nonmetropolitan areas: A longitudinal assessment. *Justice Quarterly* 18(4): 791–823.

Weston, Jim. 1993. Community policing: An approach to youth gangs in a medium sized city. *Police Chief* 60(8): 80–84.

Whitlock, Monica Lin. 2004. *Family-based risk and protective mechanisms for youth at-risk of gang joining*. Ph.D. diss. Los Angeles: University of Southern California, Department of Sociology.

Williams, Terry. 1989. *The cocaine kids: The inside story of a teenage drug ring*. Reading, MA: Addison-Wesley.

Willworth, James. 1996. Lessons learned on death row. *Time*, September 23.

Wilson, James Q. 1975. *Thinking about crime*. New York: Vintage.

Wilson, William Julius. 1987. *The truly disadvantaged: The inner city, the underclass, and public policy*. Chicago: University of Chicago Press.

Winfree, L. Thomas, Jr., Teresa Vigil Backstrom, and G. Larry Mays. 1994. Social learning theory, self-reported delinquency, and youth gangs. *Youth and Society* 26(2): 147–177.

Winfree, L. Thomas, Jr., Kathy Fuller, Teresa Vigil, and G. Larry Mays. 1992. The definition and measurement of "gang status": Policy implications for juvenile justice. *Juvenile and Family Court Journal* 43(1): 29–37.

Winfree, L. Thomas, Jr., Dana Peterson Lynskey, and James R. Maupin. 1999. Developing local police and federal law enforcement partnerships: G.R.E.A.T. as a case study of policy implementation. *Criminal Justice Review* 24: 145–168.

Wyrick, Phelan A., and James C. Howell. 2004. Strategic risk-based response to youth gangs. *Juvenile Justice* 9(September): 20–29.

Yablonsky, Lewis. 1963. *The violent gang*. New York: Macmillan.

Zatz, Marjorie S., and Edwardo L. Portillos. 2000. Voices from the barrio: Chicano/a gangs, families, and communities. *Criminology* 38(2): 369–401.

Zevitz, Richard G., and Susan R. Takata. 1992. Metropolitan gang influence and the emergence of group delinquency in a regional community. *Journal of Criminal Justice* 20(2): 93–106.

Zimring, Frank E., and George J. Hawkins. 1973. *Deterrence: The legal threat in crime control.* Chicago: University of Chicago Press.

Index

Italicized page numbers refer to figures and tables.